SCALAWAG

SCALAWAG

A WHITE
SOUTHERNER'S JOURNEY
THROUGH SEGREGATION
TO HUMAN RIGHTS
ACTIVISM

EDWARD H. PEEPLES

With Nancy MacLean

Afterword by James H. Hershman Jr.

University of Virginia Press ✳ Charlottesville and London

University of Virginia Press
© 2014 by the Rector and Visitors of the University of Virginia
All rights reserved
Printed in the United States of America on acid-free paper

First published 2014
1 3 5 7 9 8 6 4 2

Library of Congress Cataloging-in-Publication Data
Peeples, Edward H. (Edward Harden), 1935–
Scalawag : a white southerner's journey through segregation
to human rights activism / Edward H. Peeples ; with Nancy
MacLean ; afterword by James H. Hershman Jr.
pages cm
Includes bibliographical references and index.
ISBN 978-0-8139-3539-3 (cloth : alk. paper)
ISBN 978-0-8139-3540-9 (e-book)
1. Peeples, Edward H. (Edward Harden), 1935– 2. Civil rights
movements — Southern States — History — 20th century.
3. Civil rights workers — Southern States — Biography. 4. African
Americans — Segregation — Southern States — History —
20th century. 5. African Americans — Civil rights — Southern
States — History — 20th century. 6. Southern States — Race
relations — History — 20th century. I. MacLean, Nancy. II. Title.
E185.98.P44A3 2014
323.092 — dc23
[B]   2013026576

To the victims of injustice everywhere
and those who dare to join in their struggle

✳

Therefore all things whatsoever ye would that men should do to you, do ye even so to them; for this is the Law and the prophets.
— The King James Bible, as given to Edward H. Peeples at age twelve by the Woodland Heights Baptist Church, Richmond, Virginia, 1947

Scalawag—n. Origin, U.S.
A disreputable person, a rascal, a good-for-nothing, a shirker, a scamp.
2a. A Southern White who supported Reconstruction.
— *The New Shorter Oxford English Dictionary*

CONTENTS

Illustrations follow page 67.

PREFACE

IT WAS A blistering hot summer day in 2011 at a Richmond suburban strip mall. Reading in our dentist's waiting room while my daughter was being treated, I happened to look out the full-length window. On the covered walkway was a plump grandmotherly white woman with bleached-blond hair walking hand in hand with a lean and handsome African American youth of perhaps ten years. They stepped off the curb and began to make their way together toward their car, the boy skipping all the way. I saw them turn toward each other and exchange words with loving smiles, suggesting that they were somehow family.

Witnessing this in Virginia was exhilarating. It made my eyes well up with joy over how far we have come—even as I so often feel frustration and anger over how far we still have to go. When I was growing up, such a relationship was strictly forbidden. Seeing this older white woman and her seeming black grandson so comfortable in their connection brought to mind a long struggle, the struggle that has enabled such simple joyfulness in a strip mall in the hinterlands of the old capitol of the Confederacy.

Watching them put me in touch with how grateful I feel to have been part of the long human rights movement that so changed my own life as well as the prospects for countless others. Here follows the story of how, inspired by Martin Luther King Jr., I came to join hundreds of grassroots heroes on a journey to change America.

Peeples's History as Social Movement History

Nancy MacLean

THIS IS THE STORY of a lifetime of human rights activism outside the spotlight. For the half century since he was a college student, Ed Peeples has been trying to make a difference in the world. But unlike the social movement leaders seen on the evening news and featured in weighty biographies, his have been efforts of the kind that ordinary mortals can manage: squeezed in between classes and deadlines when in school, improvised on the job, and juggled with parenting and work obligations. He has volunteered, written letters, organized petitions, attended meetings, picketed, marched, sat in, recruited others—and researched, produced reports, and changed institutions from within.

His story confounds the widespread assumption that the activists of the sixties were all students. When Peeples was engaging in sit-ins to desegregate Richmond, he was a veteran of the Navy and a city social worker; alongside him were other young adults with jobs and older African American businesspeople and professionals. This activism was not a fulltime occupation but a vocation. A marathon rather than a sprint, it required pacing, and it altered in nature over his lifecycle and along with the times. Ed Peeples's life reveals how everyday people, those who rarely appear in history books, can advance justice through individual acts and in collective efforts with others.

His life is also a story of boundary-crossing: of how a working-class boy near the bottom of his junior high and high school classes managed to become a professor in adult life; and, even more surprisingly, of how a white man raised to be a racist managed to climb off that conveyer belt and join the black freedom struggle. Black civil rights activists' determined stand for human dignity resonated with his personal pain; their example redirected his life. His telling of how that happened and what followed illuminates what one writer has called the soul of a citizen.[1] It shows how civic engagement can become a way of life, a habit-forming practice that imbues life with meaning, hope, and connection unobtainable to the isolated and disengaged.

Peeples's experience reveals how activism can enhance the lives of activists. In trying to make his life count, he transformed it. As scholars of social movements have paid more attention to the cultural dimensions of social movements and to the identities and motives of participants, they have become more aware of how an initial commitment can become a gateway to a new world of ideas, relationships, and concerns and to skills that are transferrable to other efforts. Contrary to the cynical axiom that people give up their ideals as they age, studies of sixties activists have found that those who became deeply involved in the movement tended to continue their pursuit of justice in other ways.[2]

Peeples's narrative brings to life how this happens. The same values of fairness and human dignity that led him into civil rights then drew him to seek justice for others he saw being treated unjustly: poor people, black, white, and Latino; women; disaster victims; gays and lesbians; and the prisoners whose numbers so multiplied as declining employment in agriculture and manufacturing was compounded by the war on drugs.

I first met Ed Peeples in 2006 when I was embarking on research involving the contest over equal education in Virginia in the wake of the Supreme Court's *Brown v. Board of Education* decision. Everyone I consulted said, "You must talk to Ed Peeples." I wrote to him with some trepidation; he seemed so revered that I feared he might be aloof. Yet he replied immediately and generously. He and his family welcomed me to stay in the attic guest room of their row house in Richmond's Fan District for easy access to the overstuffed shelves and filing cabinets in the office down the hall (a research collection since transferred to Virginia Commonwealth University's archives). He volunteered to be my tour guide in Richmond and sent me home with cupcakes from his favorite lunch spot.

In our conversations, Peeples shared his deep knowledge of Virginia social movement history and acute analysis of the dynamics of racism and social change. Not the austere veteran I imagined, he looked a bit like Santa Claus (with a baseball hat in place of the stocking cap) and loved to get a laugh. A born storyteller, he is also an incorrigible punster.

As we got to know one another, he shared with me a collection of "vignettes" he'd written about his childhood and activism. I realized as I read the stories that they held the seed of something bigger, something precious. In all the vast and rich literature on the civil rights movement and the other struggles it inspired, it is rare to find first-person histories of rank-and-file activists, rarer still to find memoirs written in the author's own voice rather than mediated by a ghost writer and covering a whole life rather than just the peak era of activism.

Peeples's personal history was even more uncommon in its point of view: a working-class white boy who became a civil rights activist. In the eyes of most whites of all classes in his world, that made him a "traitor" to his race. A term that once stung, it eventually became a badge of pride. He embraces that identity in his title, taking on the term of abuse which former Confederates used to defame southern whites who cooperated with black voters and officeholders in the Reconstruction era: scalawag. Virginia conservatives of the 1950s and 1960s continued to enlist the term to equate white pursuit of racial justice with treason. Richmond's resident spokesman for the conservative cause, James Jackson Kilpatrick, thus announced in 1963 that to segregationists who "scarcely can abide the carpetbagger, the native scalawag is worse."[3]

Peeples did not know it back when he felt so lonely and embattled, but he was part of a long lineage of southern white rebels against racism. That lineage runs back at least to the antebellum era, when the South Carolina sisters Angelina and Sarah Grimké fled their planter family and became abolitionists, and it reached forward through the era of his own awakening, as Anne and Carl Braden of Kentucky, Clifford and Virginia Durr of Alabama, and many other southern whites joined the civil rights struggle. Several such southerners produced memoirs that offer deep insight into the workings of white supremacy and the struggle to escape its grasp and end racial privilege.

Yet most of the white civil rights memoir writers have come from middle-class or wealthy families. By contrast, Ed grew up "common," in a working-class family and a troubled one at that. His father worked as a store clerk, losing job after job due to his drinking and belligerence. His mother, who prided herself on her Florida "cracker" roots, supported the family as a hairdresser from the time Ed was about seven. Until Ed was in his early twenties, it looked like he would become a manual worker. Like nearly ten million other white and black southerners between World War II and 1960, Peeples left the region in search of better employment opportunities. Had he been able to find a factory job in Cleveland as he'd hoped, he would likely have remained working class the rest of his life.

Ironically, the prejudice against "hillbillies" he met in the North sent him back to the South—and, by a circuitous route, to college. Fearing for her unemployed son, his mother found a commuter college that would admit a kid with lousy grades: Richmond Professional Institute, part of a tier of new state-funded colleges that promoted social mobility among non-elite students in the baby-boom era. Peeples came to call it "Cinderella U.," because he was "re-born" there. Indeed, his life shows the volatility of class standing. His father hailed from a line of South Carolina Low Country slaveholders who lost their standing after the Civil War, while Ed's position improved thanks to public investment in affordable higher education after World War II. ~ for whites?

Peeples's revealing account of how racism is learned deepens our understanding of how white racial privilege varied with power and status. He painstakingly recounts how elders instilled the "rules of race" in children in so many ways that those rules came to seem commonsensical. He himself never encountered anyone who questioned white supremacy until he was eighteen; at the same time, he often experienced humiliation for coming from a "poor white trash" family. Acutely aware of their lack of status in white society and proximity to blacks in elite eyes, some of the boys in his neighborhood—and Ed, too, for a time—performed their power as white males with aggression toward blacks. Police who were otherwise gruff with working-class kids treated their abuse of African Americans as innocent antics, conveying the kind of permission for cruelty that was once granted to slave patrols to boys they might hound and humiliate another day.

 Yet Peeples's story also reveals how class disadvantage and personal pain can sometimes open space to question oppression. In his early life, the injuries of class combined with family trouble to complicate the inculcation of racism. His lived experience of class prejudice from teachers, principals, a Boy Scout troop leader, and other whites exposed the falsity of the rhetoric of white solidarity, while his family's private pains put distance between him and even his working-class peers. These combined experiences stranded him "outside the magic circle," in Virginia Durr's apt phrase, in a liminal realm open to skepticism of the claims of the white mainstream.[4]

Peeples's evolution also points to how education can open the mind and free the spirit, for this questioning did not arise automatically. Rather, when a lone college teacher pushed him to think critically about race and other social distinctions, her challenge set off a process of discovery that led him to identify with the developing civil rights movement. The anger at abusive authority induced by his hard-drinking father and condescending middle-class teachers turned out to be transferrable to white supremacy.

At the moment when he was realigning his loyalties, Peeples won admission to the Encampment for Citizenship, a youth leadership training program set up by an earlier generation of progressives. His transformative experience there shows what a difference welcoming institutions can make by offering inspiring vision and practical support to young people as they face the choice between conforming or standing up for their values in spite of the real costs of doing so. By showing Peeples that he would not be alone, the Encampment helped him to choose the initially harder but ultimately more satisfying path.

Not only institutions but also individual adult activists made the harder choice more inviting with their validation and support. In 1957 when Peeples wrote to an emerging leader of the black freedom movement to express admiration and solidarity, the Reverend Martin Luther King Jr. (just twenty-seven then himself) took the time from his demanding schedule to convey "deepest gratitude" to this young white ally for his "great moral support and Christian generosity." "Such encouraging words from friends sympathetic with our struggle are of inestimable value" to the morale of the movement, King wrote.[5] King's affirmation that Peeples was a valued "friend" helped the young letter writer to cross the Rubicon. Guidance from the Reverend Eugene Pickett, a Richmond minister who made his church a haven for social-justice seekers, then helped Peeples to develop as an organizer, tempering his brash energy with wise counsel about how to approach the African American community in a way that respected its internal leadership and traditions and contributed something of genuine value.

Conscription into the Cold War military, ironically, completed the conversion. Many scholars have noted how participation in the armed services broadened the horizons of black soldiers. Some whites experienced the same effect.

In the navy, Peeples had his first sustained experience of living and working side by side with African Americans, a few of whom became close friends and comrades in ingenious "hand-to-hand combat" against racism.

Peeples's memoir stands out not only for its distinctive content and point of view, but also for its setting: Virginia. The Deep South has generated the lion's share of books on the southern civil rights movement. As the place where whites were most prone to violence in defense of racial privilege, the Lower South attracted more focus from contemporary journalists, drawn to it by their trade's maxim that "if it bleeds, it leads." Their coverage, in turn, became the rough draft of the civil rights movement story for scholars, fixing their attention on the Mississippi Delta, Montgomery, Selma, and other sites heavily covered by the press. There is no question that activists waged titanic struggles in the Deep South that richly deserve and reward examination. Yet attention to these dramas need not lead to neglect of places where less violent conflicts took place that also have much to teach. Their stories are not duller versions of the same story, but different stories—more predictive, sometimes, of outcomes nationally.

Virginia was the site of one of the first mass direct action struggles of the modern era, which involved teenagers still in high school. Four years before the Montgomery bus boycott and nine years before the Greensboro sit-ins, a Prince Edward County high school student named Barbara Rose Johns led her classmates, with 100 percent participation, in a two-week strike to demand a school equal to that of their white peers. After the students appealed to the NAACP for assistance, their case became one of the five folded into the landmark *Brown v. Board of Education* litigation. The student strike was an early Virginia innovation; a later one was the election of the first black governor in the United States, L. Douglas "Doug" Wilder, in 1989. Both events figure in Peeples's story. The first drew him into a leadership role in activism for the first time, as he organized the Richmond Committee of Volunteers to Prince Edward, which conducted baseball, children's games, and a variety of other recreational and learning activities for the black children whose schools were padlocked for five years as their white peers went to subsidized private schools.

Virginia's segregationists also pioneered in the merger of white southerners with the northern-based modern conservative movement. James Jackson Kilpatrick, the *Richmond News Leader* editor who became nationally known for his advocacy of massive resistance, went on to help craft conservatives' subsequent strategy to limit civil rights reforms. He used the language of civil rights against the movement in a kind of political jujitsu, with calls for "color-blind" policies based on formal equality to supplant remedies designed to create substantive fairness.[6] Peeples's narrative gives readers a ground-level view of the tactics employed by the state's civil rights opponents, which by the 1970s also included the cultivation of black political and intellectual surrogates.

Peeples's story bears out the historian Jacquelyn Hall's generative concept of the "long civil rights movement." Seeking to unsettle popular misremembering of the struggle as an exclusively southern, primarily legal battle confined to the period 1955 to 1965, Hall advances a quite different view. Synthesizing a wide range of recent scholarship, she depicts, instead, a national movement that reaches back to the radical civil rights unionism of the New Deal and wartime era, that has had an ambitious economic and urban agenda as well as a legal and rural one, that was hemmed in by a conservative backlash long before the 1960s, that incubated movements of other oppressed groups, and that continued long after the mid-1960s, "undefeated but unfinished."[7]

Indeed, although Peeples was unaware of it at the time, Virginia civil rights and labor radicals in the 1930s and 1940s had laid the groundwork for the upheaval that came a generation later. Even the teacher who challenged him to see with new eyes, Dr. Alice Davis, had cut her teeth as a community organizer in West Virginia during the Great Depression. While he was in high school, a Richmond FBI agent was keeping tabs on her and her companion, Nadia Danilevsky, another teacher. Like other progressive activists, they were suspected of communism because they questioned racism and advocated social justice.

This memoir shows, too, that the movement was wider than what textbooks capture, involving under-studied organizations such as the American Friends Service Committee and the Virginia Council on Human Relations, an affiliate of the Atlanta-based Southern Regional Council. The civil rights movement motivated President Lyndon Johnson to launch a national War on Poverty in which the federal government and community activists partnered to create programs to improve the life chances of millions of disadvantaged Americans and enable them to wield their fair share of political power. Peeples participated in some of these community action initiatives, first leading a group of volunteers in a coal-mining area of eastern Kentucky and later helping with community health centers in rural Tennessee and Texas. His firsthand account suggests how polarized Appalachian communities became when young activists, backed by the federal government, sought to help the region's poor people achieve some political power in the region. Partnering with local activists, they met a furious, sometimes violent, resistance.

The movement extended long after the sixties as well as long before them. Like other places, Virginia experienced a wide-ranging progressive upsurge set off by the civil rights struggle, including feminism, gay rights activism, antiwar organizing, and more. Although scholars tend to study these causes in isolation, grassroots activists like Peeples often participated in multiple efforts. Their organizations sometimes joined together in alliances such as the Richmond Human Rights Coalition, which Peeples cofounded in 1975.

In sharing his reflections, Peeples hopes to inspire others to embrace the marathon quest for social justice. He also wants to encourage young people to learn more about the historic struggles waged in Virginia. Those who want to carry out their own research will find voluminous original documentation and elaboration of various elements of the story told here in his papers, located at Virginia Commonwealth University. Peeples collected correspondence, clippings, minutes, and brochures and tracts almost compulsively for nearly sixty years.

His papers are a treasure trove of records on Virginia social movement history from the late fifties to the present: efforts to aid the victims of the Prince Edward County school closures from 1959–64; the Virginia Council on Human Relations and the college student affiliate he helped launch; the youth-led direct action sit-in movement in Richmond; the national Encampment for Citizenship and its young activists' work in Appalachia and elsewhere; the American Friends Service Committee's decades-long work for justice in the South; the desegregation of higher education and the development of African American Studies; discrimination against gays and lesbians in Richmond; coalition building between civil rights organizers and feminists, peace activists, and gay and lesbian activists; organizing against environmental racism; public health work; prisoners' rights projects; and more. Peeples also collected material on the opposition to such causes, making his papers a source as well for the study of segregationists, both mainstream and militant, and conservatism more generally in Virginia over the last fifty years. He has also helped the VCU library secure the papers of other Virginia activists.

With an eye toward inspiring further research, and so as not to burden the text with numerous notes, we have included at the end of this book a beginning bibliography on Virginia civil rights history. We have also compiled a listing of other underreported Virginia activists in Peeples's acquaintance, along with some information on each, so that their stories, too, may be told. That listing, along with a fuller bibliography, can be found with the finding aid to Peeples's papers at VCU. One of Ed Peeples's favorite sayings comes from the theologian and philosopher Albert Schweitzer, who wrote, "It is not always granted for the sower to see the harvest. All work that is worth anything is done in faith." Nothing would gratify Ed, born in 1935 and now nearing eighty, more than for his story to inspire the making and remembrance of other activist lives.

NOTES

1. Paul Rogat Loeb, *The Soul of a Citizen: Living with Conviction in a Cynical Time* (New York: St. Martin's Griffin, 1999).

2. See, for example, Doug McAdam, *Freedom Summer* (New York: Oxford University Press, 1988); Annelise Orleck, *Storming Caesar's Palace: How Black Mothers Fought Their Own War on Poverty* (Boston: Beacon Press, 2005).

3. James Jackson Kilpatrick, "The South is Up for Grabs," *National Review,* December 17, 1963, 523. On the origin of the term, see Ted Tunnell, "Creating 'The Propaganda of History': Southern Editors and the Origins of 'Carpetbagger and Scalawag,'" *Journal of Southern History* 72 (Nov. 2006): 789–822.

4. Virginia Foster Durr, *Outside the Magic Circle: The Autobiography of Virginia Foster Durr* (Tuscaloosa: University of Alabama Press, 1985).

5. Martin Luther King Jr. to Edward H. Peeples Jr., May 10, 1957, copy in Edward H. Peeples Jr. manuscript collection, VCU.

6. For Kilpatrick's pivotal role, see Nancy MacLean, *Freedom Is Not Enough: The Opening of the American Workplace* (Cambridge: Harvard University Press, 2006), especially chapters 2 and 7.

7. Jacquelyn Dowd Hall, "The Long Civil Rights Movement and the Political Uses of the Past," *Journal of American History* 91 (March 2005): 1263.

PART ONE

Learning Whiteness

The Arrival of Another
Birthright Segregationist

M Y MOTHER PICKED a helluva day for me to arrive on this earth: April 20, 1935, the same birthday as Adolf Hitler, who at that very moment was engaged in the violent creation of his Aryan empire. This proved to be a strange coincidence, because I contended all my adult life with some of the ideas that Hitler and the German Nazi regime had borrowed from America's white supremacist ideology, especially as it was applied in my native Virginia.

One such dose of poison came to the Old Dominion from the eugenics movement. In 1922 Dr. H. H. Laughlin, a preacher's son from Iowa, published a model sterilization law known as the Eugenical Sterilization Act, which he promulgated all across the country as a standard for maintaining "racial integrity" to keep America's white population "pure." In 1924 Laughlin was asked by the Virginia General Assembly to help them draft their own Racial Integrity Act, which defined who was "white," made it illegal for whites to marry outside their race, and declared it a felony to fail to report one's "correct" officially designated race on state documents. An accompanying law, the Virginia Eugenical Sterilization Act, unleashed state-imposed sterilization on thousands of poor whites, blacks, and others presumed to be mentally or physically defective by the Commonwealth's ruling whites. In a troubling similarity, after gaining power in Germany in 1933, the Nazi Party used Harry Laughlin's model act to draft its own "Law for Protection against Genetically Defective Offspring." The Nazis also looked with interest on my state's racial laws and the eugenics program initiated by Dr. Walter Ashby Plecker, Virginia's first vital statistics registrar.*

So white supremacists had already convinced Virginia's voting public of their ideological justification for segregation—it was just "what everybody knew"—when I let out my very first screech. No one who heard it that day could have predicted that the evils promoted by racial supremacists like Dr. Plecker and Adolf Hitler would become the central preoccupation in the life of this white boy delivered at the segregated St. Luke's Hospital in Richmond.

AT THE TIME of my birth my father, Edward Harden Peeples IV, was the grocery clerk and butcher in a one-clerk store on Hull Street owned by the Norfolk-based Pender Grocery Company.

My father got the job because a relative was in management there. While Pender was a large grocery chain covering much of Virginia, its stores were all very small, as supermarkets had not yet been introduced in our part of the country. In this store around the corner from my first home on Bainbridge Street, my father stood behind the counter and fetched each item a shopper requested from the floor-to-ceiling shelves behind him.

In the late thirties, about the time I was three, my father got a promotion and we moved to Charlottesville. In the middle of the Great Depression, we were very lucky that my father had landed a coveted job as a supervisor of several one- and two-clerk Pender stores scattered up and down the Valley of Virginia. Shortly thereafter, we welcomed my only sibling, Stephen Hill Peeples, into the world. Things looked bright for us, even as many others were struggling mightily to keep food on their tables and shelter above their heads.

But the bliss for us was short-lived. Owing to my father's inability to work with people, he began to be progressively demoted. Before long he was fired altogether. With World War II beginning, we found ourselves back in Richmond experiencing our belated share of the Great Depression. Soon my father began to drink heavily and lose jobs. Turning sullen, he socially isolated himself and became psychologically abusive to my mother and occasionally physically abusive to me. I still have vivid early childhood memories of occa-

*See Gregory Michael Dorr, *Segregation's Science: Eugenics and Society in Virginia* (Charlottesville, University of Virginia Press, 2008), 168–69, for similarities and differences between the Nazis and the Virginia eugenicists; and 181, 188, for Dr. Plecker and the Nazis.

sions when he humiliated me in front of other adults, apparently attempting to impress them with his paternal authority. Looking back, he appeared to have an inordinate need to dominate my will. Living under his rule no doubt sowed the seeds of my future contempt for immoral or abusive authority. I stopped thinking of him as a father and started seeing him only as an authority figure.

AT FIRST GLANCE one might have assumed that Richmond was relatively cosmopolitan for a southern city. On U.S. Route 1, then the nation's main north-south highway, it was the capital of Virginia, the site of one of the regional Federal Reserve Banks, a significant financial trading center with a respectable industrial base, and the home for a number of international tobacco interests. Yet, even with these features of modern urbanity, our town was a showcase of regional provincialism, filled with monuments to its Confederate past. Richmond was really a sleepy southern town of overwhelmingly native-born people, still steeped in the nostalgia of the "War Between the States"—as so many white Virginians liked to remember it. So in my generation the city groomed more than its share of ethnocentric and creed-bound whites. Few could escape the ubiquitous white supremacy and cultural insularity. It was in the natural order of things to be satisfied with knowing little of other worlds.

For example, the way that white people in Richmond thought of Washington, DC, only 110 miles north, was a good measure of our social isolation at the time. Most folks I knew would never think to travel to DC because they considered it "up north" and presumed that they would not feel comfortable there because "Yankees" did not understand "our way of life." Never mind that the nation's capital was nearly as segregated as the old capital of the Confederacy. Richmond was an apt locale for learning the malevolent etiquette of white supremacy.

BUT THE SOURCES of my socialization were not confined to mandates from the living; my ancestors also imparted a legacy. My grandfather, Edward Harden Peeples III, was eleven years old at the end of the Civil War. Like his father before him, he grew up in Barnwell and Hampton Counties in South Carolina, witnessing the master-slave relationship and enjoying the privileges afforded the family by the many slaves on his grandfather's plantation at Peeplesville. His own father, a Confederate Army officer who later held the positions of postmaster and sheriff in Barnwell County, appears to have owned no more than a few slaves—but quite enough to provide my grandfather with many advantages as a child.

As a young adult my grandfather poured his anger and humiliation from the South's loss of the war into the Redeemer movement, which aimed to restore white power and run all the "aliens" out of South Carolina. He became a lieutenant in the Hampton Redshirts during the post-Reconstruction era. Along with hundreds of other local whites, at election time he stormed on horseback through local polling places in order to intimidate and turn away black and pro-Union voters. He was later much taken by the populist racism of "Pitchfork" Ben Tillman. Living well into the twentieth century, my grandfather remained active in white supremacist politics until his health failed.

My grandfather and his worldview had an enormous impact on my father's perceptions of race, class, and gender issues, which he, in turn, brought into my early life. After all, in 1905 when my father was born there was little or no access to national news through radio or television, there were no telephones for common use, and there were no motor vehicles, no airplanes, and virtually no paved roads in his corner of the world. The South Carolina Low Country set the boundaries of the world my father knew growing up.

Much later, he revealed how that upbringing had also shrunk his emotional universe. In the early eighties he told me that his father had taken him to witness the lynching of Walter Best, a black man, in the nearby town of Fairfax.* My father showed not a scintilla of feeling as he described it. That drove home to me that his capacity to identify with the plight of black people was severely obstructed. The lifelong subjugation of his mental and emotional development by his father and the cultural remnants of antebellum South Carolina arrested his growth as an empathetic person. Much of what my father brought to my young life arose out of this internal barrenness and the Lost Cause cult of indignation and melancholy.

As my father entered his twenties, having been nurtured in the promise of being a lord of a manor, he was faced with becoming a serf. By the twenties agriculture began to wane as the primary focus of southern life. Rural areas and

*See Ralph Ginzburg, *100 Years of Lynchings* (New York: Lancer Books, 1962), 267, for an account of what I believe is the same lynching.

small towns in the South began to slip into economic decline and cities became attractive to young men looking for employment alternatives. So to find jobs my father had to make his way to Charleston, Jacksonville, and other southern cities where he discovered that he had to work alongside and in competition with people he had been led to believe were below him. He was bewildered by these conditions so unfamiliar to his youth of guaranteed class and race privileges. By the late thirties when he began drinking heavily and losing one job after another, he had hit rock bottom and plunged my mother, me, and my brother into what could have been a dismal future.

Fortunately, our mother, Lula Jane Stephens, stepped up as the breadwinner and our only real parent. She was a capable, decisive, hardworking, and resourceful woman, who at about age fourteen had to leave school and her family's isolated and hardscrabble farm for the promise of a better future in the small town of Bradenton, Florida. She went there to work as a live-in servant to a prosperous family. Yet after seeing her potential, they began to introduce her to the tastes and ambitions of the comfortable classes and then helped her become a hairdresser. Our mother never let poverty, a lack of formal education, or her marital problems stand in her way. She was a good and steady parent and a proud model for survival in hard times to both my brother and me. It was our mother's strong and loving hand and her income as a hairdresser that saved us. The fact that my brother and I became the first generation on either side of our family to grow up mostly in a city, an environment of more alternatives, may also have helped.

Like my father, my mother was a racist who tutored me in "our way of life." But she was a gentle and affectionate woman whose attitudes toward blacks were less filled with hubris. Blacks to her were just different from us because God made us both this way. Her brand of racism did not countenance deliberate cruelty toward black people, though she lacked the confidence to challenge those who perpetrated it. She came from a different southern tradition, one where there was little pretense or affectation. She was born in 1908 in what today would be called a shack at Myakka Head in sparsely populated backcountry Florida. In fact, there was nothing much for her to be superior about. So, although the sense of racial and elitist entitlement of Virginia's and South Carolina's landed gentry may have been in our background from my father's side, it was not the prevailing influence in our upbringing. My mother's humility told her that when there were "racial troubles" we must trust the sheriff and God to sort them out.

In my early years, the shrinking capabilities of my father did not diminish his influence on me. I had far too little experience with the outside world to compare him to others or see him critically. "Normality" was whatever was up close. And it was my father who was up close: the first and foremost authority I knew on how we were to regard blacks under Jim Crow. One might imagine that I am describing one of those blustering bigots from the Deep South once commonly seen on television and in movies. But, no, my father did not brandish that kind of hate. His racism was the more common version practiced by the guarded types who later were mislabeled "moderates."

In keeping with his accustomed class protocol, my father did not often engage in the obstreperous racial taunts his people associated with "white trash" or "po' whites." Like many white southerners he maintained a softer edge in his use of such words as *nigra* and *nigger*. It was as if he was trying to make the words acceptable in polite company without losing any of their white supremacist punch, all the while hoping to differentiate himself from the "common" people.

OF COURSE, my grounding in how to become a "good" white person went beyond my father, my mother, and the Richmond milieu. There was also instruction coming from other people and places in my southern experience. My father's mother commanded her own whiteness training camp in South Carolina. Martha "Mattie" Wood Peeples had a large presence in my growing up. She lived in a propped-up dream of the nineteenth-century landed gentry and petty aristocracy of the Old South. My grandmother's home and town were museum exhibits of that time and place, imparting a contorted memory of slavery and Reconstruction fused with Jim Crow. When we went to visit her in the small black-belt town of Allendale, in the upper reaches of the South Carolina Low Country, she always portrayed herself and the Peeples family as part of the community's upper class, even as her only remaining possessions were her modest house and its quaint furnishings. Her cash flow might not have been impressive, but her membership in the United Daughters of the Confederacy and the Daughters of the American Revolution assured her high standing in the town. My father apparently feared awakening her from her dream. Defying the reckoning promised in Proverbs 16:18 ("Pride goeth before destruction, and haughty spirit before a fall"), he ordered my mother to never reveal to my grandmother that she was a hairdresser, even as that job provided his children with the sustenance he could not give us.

Since more than 80 percent of folks in Allendale County were black, racial segregation entered the warp and woof of everything we did. Visits to my grandmother in Allendale provided prime examples of this. Our daily and weekly rituals appeared innocent enough but somehow always became celebrations of "our way of life." Sundays we spent all day at church, a white Southern Baptist church. We were back at church every Wednesday evening and on many other occasions, especially for funerals—lots of funerals. Then there was the ladies bridge game and luncheon. My grandmother's friends came "calling" at least once each day. And there was a weekly visit by an old black gentleman, somehow linked to past servants or farmhands for the Peepleses, who brought beautiful fresh vegetables from his garden. She gave him a dollar and thanked him, addressing him by his first name, while he replied, "Thank you, Miz Mattie" or "Thank you, Miz Peeples." Later my grandmother would seize the stage to remind us all of how the "negra people of Allendale loved Mr. Peeples," my grandfather, and "would do anything for us."

But the premier rituals on Memorial Avenue were the repasts served in the dining room on a long table laid out with an heirloom linen-and-lace tablecloth with matching napkins, set with the treasured family china and silverware dating back to the mid-nineteenth century. Two of our meals each day were treated as grand productions, breakfast about seven or eight in the morning and "dinnah" around two in the afternoon. My grandmother's daughter Vivia, a school teacher, provided her with the miserly few dollars a week necessary to keep a black servant, Carrie. Carrie performed the bulk of the hard work of preparing meals and maintaining the household. My grandmother spoke often of how we all "loved" Carrie and, in return, how steadfast was her loyalty to the Peeples family. My grandmother frequently boasted in her distinctive Low Country accent, "We have had Cay-ree for more than foh-ty ye-ahs."

Carrie was very sweet to me and my brother when we were young. Even through the tainted prism of racism, I could see a strong and lovely person in her. Her family and most of the Allendale blacks endured a harsh life. I, like most white children, was sealed off from full knowledge of the conditions they faced. But for some unknown reason I was sometimes allowed to ride with my father to drive Carrie home. I recall so well the first of those visits when I saw the house and neighborhood where she and her family were condemned to live. I can still remember the gnawing horror I felt when I witnessed that scene.

The dwelling in which this family of some nine people lived was an unpainted wooden shotgun shack, gray from age. It was little more than one long room stretching from the front door to the back. It had no windows, just rectangular holes in the walls with wooden shutters. It sat on several flimsy looking pilings about three feet or more above the ground. I thought how cold it must have been in the winter when a chilly wind whipped up through those floor boards and the countless cracks in the buckled plank walls. I remember asking Carrie why her was house set up so high on stilts. Without a pause, she said, "To keep the snakes off the children." That memory has replenished my commitment on many occasions.

Carrie was expected to be at my grandmother's six days a week from early morning to dark—cooking, cleaning, and serving her every wish, all for about $12 a week. Whatever might have been her thoughts about the injustice in her situation, they never lessened how scrumptious were the meals she made for us.

My grandmother charged me with helping Carrie set the table and serve the food. She insisted that I favor my father with the best silverware and china and the first or largest choice of the entrees and desserts. It galled me to do this because my father was not the adult in my house who was worthy of being honored. It was my mother who deserved this tribute, as she was the one who put the bread on our table and she was our only genuine parent. But in the interest of staying out of trouble, I bit my tongue and played my allotted role.

While the social circumstances of these meals did nothing good for your digestion, the epicurean pleasure for me was as sublime as it was southern. Every morning for breakfast we had mouth-watering cinnamon raisin rolls baked fresh and served piping hot with the icing still trickling down the sides, usually accompanied by eggs fresh from the chicken coop and smoked bacon, country ham, or some other "side meat," and a heapin' serving of grits with gravy. As folks used to say at that table, foodwise, we were "living high on the hog."

The biggest event of the day was dinner, featuring fried chicken, baked ham, or some other pork cut. From the same batch of dough from breakfast, we had delicious hot dinner rolls with country butter. Snap beans, field peas, black-eyed peas, grits, fried or boiled okra, or collard greens cooked all day long with ham hocks, streak-o-lean, or fatback were also a mainstay. In season there were fresh vegetables straight from our garden, and there was always plenty of sweet iced tea year round. The grand finale was a home-baked pie or cake, sometimes pecan pie made with what I gathered from the colossal pecan tree in the backyard. My grandmother always got the praise for her spread, but it was Carrie who made it praiseworthy.

Despite the many treasured adventures I had visiting our grandmother's house, there was something that seemed odd to me about what took place there, even at my tender age. I came to think that my grandmother, and many of the people in her world, lived in a kind of apparition; it resembled the fanciful fiction of *Gone with the Wind*. My grandmother played out this dream, and she expected the rest of us to do the same.

I think that what kept the image of southern glory culturally viable for so many folks like my father and his mother was the fact that they still knew or recalled Civil War– and Reconstruction-era survivors who endlessly recounted their perceptions of those days. On one occasion, several of us youngsters and a couple of adults, including my father, sat on the front porch listening to a very old man regale us with tales about the "War Between the States" and the turmoil of Reconstruction. I remember being impressed with how horrible were the "Yankees" and how uncivilized the "negras." He claimed to be a Confederate veteran, though he would have, at best, been a young teenager during the war. Whatever his actual past, folks in Allendale looked on his stories as the gospel truth.

My grandmother and her people possessed no evident "hate" for blacks. They even claimed to "love" those black individuals who served their interests well. But the "love" they offered to their black neighbors was strictly qualified. Whites such as my grandmother grew up with a deep sense of entitlement. They were led to believe that Mother Nature and history had provided them with a permanent supply of servants, a circumstance that they were certain was sanctioned by God himself. They imagined their dominance as beneficial for the "child-like" black people who they insisted lacked "our kind of ambition." They saw themselves as providers and protectors for the "good Negroes" and saw blacks' apparent compliance as a confirmation of contentment with their situation. Mattie Wood Peeples insisted that she "loved her Negroes." All she asked of life was to have a few obedient servants around to shore up her grandiose reveries of the Old South.

✳ 2 ✳

Learning God's Primary Colors

WHILE WE OFTEN visited South Carolina, the preponderance of my whiteness education took place in Richmond, and the basic message was the same. I can recall sensing as early as about age five how much race mattered to adults. They impressed upon me that there were two kinds of God's creatures that mattered most in life: "white people" and "the coloreds." In those days, a white child was expected to learn several essential lessons about race: (1) what racial category each person you encountered should be put in; (2) the diction, tones of voice, body language, and facial expressions necessary to make your words work the way you intended with each; and (3) the required social distance and ranking of each racial group.

The first lesson in white race consciousness was how to classify people on the street by their "color." The job was much messier than the Virginia Constitution made out. Criteria like facial features and hair texture proved to be equivocal predictors of race. It was not easy for a young child. We could make a lot of errors and as a consequence do forbidden things like hug a black person for whom we had some affection. But with careful instruction from our elders, we eventually got better at it.

Adults sought to prepare us well, because they knew that every child at some time or another was going to have to determine a stranger's race based on appearance in order to gauge how to behave toward that person. Of course, when a person had distinctly dark or light skin, the determination seemed straightforward. But I was perplexed by those many individuals who appeared somewhere in between. Finally, I got an explanation for all the "coffee and cream people you see around here." They were in fact, "negras from nearby

Charles City County where the white people, the Indians, and the coloreds got all mixed up a long time ago."

Still there were other confusing cases where dark-skinned people seemed to be enjoying the liberties that I had been told were reserved for whites. They had straight hair but darker skin than me. When I asked adults about this discrepancy in a man I sometimes saw at family gatherings, I was informed in a hushed voice that he was related to one of our kinfolks. For those people who defied classification because of their uncertain features, I was urged by my elders to just walk up to them and ask outright, "What are you?" Most white adults I knew just couldn't sit still until they could find out the race of anyone with ambiguous features. Reluctant to make the inquiry themselves, they used us youngsters to find out for them. So my eyes were the first part of me to surrender to the racist ideology; they became my first organs of selective perception.

But there was always some odd twist found in the white supremacist taxonomy of my day. Roman Catholics were a case in point. Because of widespread anti-Catholic prejudice, we "Christian" (that is, Protestant) fundamentalists saw them as somewhat less than pure white. Yet as a practical matter we found that we often needed a little wiggle room in the race classification department because someone close to us was always falling in love with the wrong kind of person. My aunt Vela, for example, married a Catholic, Bubby, and converted to his faith. I later learned that some of my people at first had been uneasy about him being unlike us, despite the fact that he had blond hair, blue eyes, and very fair skin.

WHEN SPEAKING TO blacks or about blacks in polite company with white people who were mindful of their diction, the choice was "Negro" or "colored." If with working-class or poor whites who tended to slur their words, or politicians seeking their support, then the pronunciation of "Negro" could be made to come out "negra." This was very handy if you needed to show solidarity with some agitated white racist because it sounded almost identical to "nigger." But in everyday conversation, I heard many other terms used, without challenge, to describe African American people: "darkie," "coon," "jig," "jigaboo," "sambo," "ape," "monkey," and "chocolate drop," to mention but a few. Older whites would often refer to a young black male as a "buck" or a "young buck" and a black child as a "pickaninny." My father's favorite such term was "darkie." Whether they were being used as deliberate racial slurs depended on the context and tone of voice. In many instances, when a white used the term "negra," it was meant to be emotionally neutral. Needless to say, to the blacks of that day, these utterances were anything but neutral.

But the ultimate test for me was which name to use in the widely variable circumstances in which I found myself: among "polite company," in the presence of aggressive racists, alone with a member of the other race, or with a black whose two bullnecked brothers were also present. A poor choice had consequences.

JIM CROW DID NOT segregate us whites bodily from blacks as much as it partitioned our minds from their reality. In most of our daily public associations, we moved more or less freely in close proximity with few apparent restraints. But when it came to eating, sleeping, sitting down, swimming, going to school, buying clothes, seeing a movie, getting a good job, or loving someone, that was very much another matter. For these and other activities, there were stringent legal prohibitions. And if there happened not to be a specific law on the books to keep us apart in some overlooked scenario, then there were two other measures for enforcing segregation: universally understood customs and, finally, the last resort—ad hoc disposition of the case by the most virulent white supremacist on the scene.

So blacks, except for the most isolated or those with high income, found themselves engaged in complicated daily negotiations with white dominance in nearly every arena essential to their survival. Many of these frustrating encounters took place right before our white eyes and yet most of us saw none of the injustice in it. For example, many times I witnessed white people making degrading remarks about blacks in the presence of black individuals, as if they were just potted plants. We whites were deaf, dumb, and blind to the black experience. We never dreamed that someday the compulsory separation of the races would be illegal and, in the eyes of most Americans, immoral.

RACE MAY HAVE BEEN the number one preoccupation for most people I encountered in my early years, but social class distinctions were not far behind.

Given our financial circumstances, my household would be called "working class" by any standard, notwithstanding my father's lineage. But my parents made every effort to make sure that we were not mistaken for the lowly "po' whites." Rather, we were blessed by God, while poor whites were, according to the oft-repeated phrase, "reaping the harvest of their sinful ways." Even as a young child I could see that there were white people in our community who were treated as inherently different. I gathered that the hierarchy for white people went something like this: the poor whites made up the bottom; we, the "working people," were next; then came what we called the "well-fixed" classes (white collar, business, professional, and others of comfortable status); and finally on top were "the rich," many of whom were actually not that wealthy but simply enjoyed enough income to have conspicuous upscale possessions.

The bottom end of this scheme was confusing for me since I saw so many hardships common among the poor whites befalling my own family: struggles with money, jobs, health, alcohol, violence, and familial relationships. Sometimes I could not see a clear distinction between us and them. It was more befuddling because the more advantaged people, especially at school, sometimes called me "common" or "poor white trash."

I saw no open class warfare in my hometown of Richmond, but there was a widespread sense that the upper classes, through their commerce and influence over government, ultimately controlled our lives. Low-income workers and labor unions were widely held in disdain. We knew full well that there were higher rungs on the ladder of success that could lead to living in a mansion on Richmond's posh Cary Street Road. We also understood that we had no access to that ladder. Most folks I knew either admired or envied what they saw the rich enjoy; some others bitterly resented or even hated wealthy people. But no one I knew ever revealed their true feelings in the presence of a person of means, out of uneasy respect or just plain fear of their power. Whatever the precise facts of social stratification, there was something alive out there in the community that unmistakably declared that my family and I were outside the genteel classes. In the context of the class and race relations of that era, being called "common" or "poor white trash" had a sharp cutting edge to it. Together with the troubles in my family, hearing it left me with a heavy dose of self-doubt.

AT THE FRONT OF my consciousness when I was a teenager was a first cousin
of our anti-black attitudes—an ideology which I later learned was called "anti-
Semitism." I recall being warned by my elders at school and in church that
a wave of Jews was descending upon us from New York and that they were
greedy, cunning, and from the tribe that had killed our Savior. More than
once, I heard something to the effect of, "I don't know why we are fighting
Hitler, at least he knows how to take care of the Jews." At Thomas Jefferson
High School, our basketball coaches made it clear to us that Jewish boys were
not welcome to play for the Jeffs.

Although I must have encountered Jews in my early life, I was not conscious
of it. So I mindlessly assumed that my role models in the adult world knew
what they were talking about. I stowed this stereotype down deep in the same
place where I kept my attitudes about "niggers," "wops and chinks," "cripples,"
"fags," and others I was told were less deserving than us.

But there was a trap set out for me in holding these attitudes about Jews:
I had dark hair and a long sharply defined nose. In my class in junior high
school was an Italian American kid with Mediterranean features who, like
me, had dark hair and an ample snout. Sitting next to me one day in the school
auditorium waiting for a program to begin, this boy, playing to the prevailing
prejudice, suddenly in a scornful tone declared to everyone around us that I
was a "Jew boy." Carrying a heavy load of anti-Semitism, I was stung. I felt
reviled and shrunk down into my seat, trying to disappear from my classmates.
With antipathy toward Jews so common, I became haunted by the fear that
people might think I was one. It was not until college that I began to grapple
with the lies planted inside me about the tribes of Moses—also the patriarch
of the Southern Baptist faith of my birth.

RELIGIOUS CHAUVINISM was another element in the catechism of bigotry
I was taught. For years, it never occurred to me that the whole civilized world
might not be some variety of "Bab-dist" and the kind of fundamentalists we
were. From my earliest memory, I studied the Bible and listened attentively to
elders telling me how God had declared that because of my personal acceptance of Jesus I would be saved from the fate of the unbelievers who did not
follow our faith. The fact that all the blacks we knew were fundamentalist
Christians just like us did nothing to make us think of them as brothers and

sisters or question segregated worship. The proposition that Jesus smiled only on us was very compelling, because the Jesus I knew from pictures looked like my people. He was a tall, angular, creamy-skinned man with blue eyes and very long light brown hair. So my church became a significant source of my feelings about black people and others not like us. And everyone I knew went to church—except my father.

Despite my Baptist credulity, my mother worried about me and solicited help from Jesus to keep me on the right path. As I started school, my mother, miserable in her marriage, and I, beset with a mounting antipathy for my father, submerged ourselves in a succession of fundamentalist churches, dragging my little brother along with us. After my seventh birthday I was constantly pushed by my mother and others in the church to "give my life to Christ," a process that culminated in the total immersion rite known as baptism. As any dutiful child of that age might, I "answered the call," even though I never really had any kind of "born again" experience. Believing that adults knew best, I also knew enough of the stories of the Old Testament to be certain that a little guy like me shouldn't provoke a wrathful God. So at a very tender age that my preacher called the "age of reason," I was led to the baptismal pool in our church sanctuary clad only in a sheer white cotton robe, which when wet revealed all of one's anatomical secrets. Thankfully, my young secrets were small and probably could not be detected past the first two pews.

When I was ushered into the pool by the deacon, the preacher was already standing in water up past his groin. As I approached he reached out, took my hand, and assisted me down the steps into the water. Without any warning, he clasped one of his hands over my mouth and pinched my nose closed. With the other hand he seized me in the small of my back and with a powerful thrust dunked me backwards into the water. He had moved so fast that I had not had a chance to take a deep breath. So there I was, totally submerged and gasping for air, as the preacher continued his exhortation. He detected nothing of my struggle to break free from his grip and breathe. I thought that I was done for. Luckily I survived my purification, but for a long time I was troubled about whether my panicked immersion passed metaphysical muster.

I went through most all of the other motions that the Baptists told me were steps on the path to glory and eternal salvation, because I wanted to avoid burning in hell. My mother demonstrated the horrible prospect of hell in our kitchen. After turning on a gas stove burner, she would periodically ask me, "Do you see the hot fire on that stove? Well, if you don't know Jesus and you keep on sinning, a flame like that is going to burn your skin in hell—all over your body! For eternity!" So I went with her to church five times a week, sat through my share of long and incomprehensible sermons, endured rote recitations in Sunday school, and imbibed the subtle message that Jesus loved us white true believers more than anyone else.

✳ 3 ✳

Boys Will Be Boys

UNFORTUNATELY THE Jesus of my faith proved to be no match for the malicious white kids from my Southside neighborhood who lured me into some of their racist acts of cruelty. In my time, much of the white South observed a proud tradition of hypermasculine truculence, and we had more than our share of power-lusting teenage boys roaming our streets in the so-called good old days. When the opportunity arose this aggression was directed at blacks. But African Americans were not the boys' only victims. They also took pleasure in bullying white youth who seemed different or vulnerable. Kids who were small or weak, had uncommon physical features, or looked nerdy, sad, effeminate, or arty were targeted by bullies, as were those who dared to befriend them. Whether the victims were black or white, the tormentors had what seemed an insatiable appetite for the domination of others, and they took particular delight in afflicting their prey in public spaces where they might attract an enthusiastic audience to witness their manly conquests. My side of town in the forties was no Quaker settlement.

On my third day as a seventh grader at Bainbridge Junior High School, I found myself on the playground surrounded by a pack of eighth grade wolves. I guess they had their eyes on me because I was pudgy and my lack of confidence was conspicuous even at twenty paces. These guys forced me and a couple of other boys to swipe stuff for them from stores in a nearby business district. I never got caught by the merchants and the success taught me that stealing was a good substitute for money, of which I had very little. Ironically the skill set forced upon me by these young hoodlums later provided me with the tools, bicycle parts, and sports gear that I otherwise would have had to do without.

But this miniature extortion racket only provided the bullies with material goods; it didn't satiate their lust for degrading people. One source of merriment for them could only be implemented in a school with our particular architecture. Instead of a staircase, the center of the building had a series of four inclined ramps that descended from the second floor to the basement. One day after school, without warning, I was seized by a gang of maybe half a dozen guys and hauled to the top of the incline on the second floor. There they stuffed me head first into a very large metal garbage can taken from the cafeteria. They pushed on my feet until my legs folded up into the can and my knees tucked nearly under my chin. When they had me securely trapped in the can, they laid it on its side. Somebody gave it a big shove and off I rattled and rolled down the incline spinning over and over inside. The boys chased the tumbling torture chamber down the incline, howling with laughter as it slammed against the first landing wall with a tumultuous clanking sound. My head crashed against the side of the can. I was terrified, sure that I was going mad and that my head and all of my internal organs were going to explode.

Someone turned the can around and kicked it down the second incline to the first floor where it again came to a halt—and then I was kicked down the next two inclines to the basement. There the can finally stopped and the laughter and shouting faded. Dimly, I felt someone pulling on my legs until I emerged from the can. Clearing the bits of garbage from my face, I saw that my rescuers were girls with horrified expressions. The sight of them unleashed a piercing sense of shame. I was speechless, even as I felt a rush of relief and gratitude. One of the girls asked if I was all right. I nodded yes. Everyone disappeared, and there came an eerie quiet in the building. Lifting myself up, I went to the boys' room and washed up.

I didn't tell my mother about the events of the day. I figured she had enough trouble, and I knew she always worried about me. I thought, "I will deal with this myself, and maybe I'll just skip school tomorrow." Why the school administration tolerated this practice has always been a mystery to me. They had to have witnessed or heard about at least some of the most conspicuous incidents. It seemed they just didn't care about what happened to the sons of "white trash"; they saved their attention for the middle-class kids who we were frequently reminded had more promise than us. All this got me to thinking—"Where can I turn to feel like a somebody?" I felt such a need to blow off steam about my rotten life.

Social psychologists use the phrase "moving toward the aggressor" to describe how the victimized can become victimizers. I think that's what happened with me in my adolescent years. To avoid further victimization, boys like me came to understand that we had to adopt the attitudes of those who harassed us and convince them that we were the same as them so they would lay off. The more we were able to emulate the predatory behavior of these boys, the safer we felt from their torments. Some of us did horrible things that otherwise seem inexplicable given our intrinsic natures. In short, we surrendered ourselves to them to save our own butts.

I began trying to make friends with guys who I imagined to be the only ones who would have me; that is, boys engaged in activities that would have horrified my mother had she known. I joined them in vandalizing property and more. For example, one of these "friends," who came to be known as Shady later in life, convinced me to help him set the underbrush in a vacant lot in our neighborhood on fire and then gleefully watch the firemen who were called to put it out. I was queasy about doing it, but the desperate drive to hold on to the promise of a friendship was stronger than my boyhood conscience.

MANY BOYS I KNEW "took papers" to make some money. Since delivering the *Richmond News Leader,* the afternoon paper, was considered by my peers to be only for "sissies," I took the morning paper, the *Richmond Times-Dispatch,* to show I was a real man. By this time my mother thought I was old enough to own a rifle. Early on it was an air rifle, a BB gun. But a couple of years later I received a .22 caliber rifle for Christmas. The fact that I received such an expensive gift pleasantly surprised me, because my father added little or nothing to my mother's wages of $25–30 a week as a hairdresser. But I think that my mother saw the rifle as an essential totem of my pending manhood. She also may have been thinking that I would rid our backyard chicken coop of rats, the BB gun having proved useless for protecting our small flock, from which we derived a few eggs a week and an occasional fried chicken or roasted hen dinner. I learned to shoot that .22 with considerable precision for a boy my age. I pretty much eliminated the rat population from the burrows and crevices in the back of the old shed that shared a wall with our chicken coop. My victories over the rats gave me a gratifying manly feeling and made me think I was protecting my mother and my brother from the kind of pestilence I read about in the Bible. I think my mother was grateful for any protection from the

vicissitudes of her life at that point. Her husband certainly was of no use to her;
he was her biggest problem.

But now I am ashamed to admit the other ways I used that BB gun and
.22 rifle. The most horrid was our weekly Saturday morning invasion of the
black neighborhood around Bainbridge and Pilkington Streets on the way
to a storefront building on Cowardin Avenue where our district circulation
manager collected our payments for the week's newspapers. Sometimes when
we saw one of the older paper carriers from my district on the street or at the
playground, he would tell us younger guys to bring our guns on the ride down
to pay our paper bill. He'd add, "And we can have some fun down in nigger
town." Without any warning, our marauding band of white teenagers on bicy-
cles would come roaring down the hill yelling like rebel soldiers toward a row
of attached slum houses. There were always a variety of adults and children
sitting on the steps and porches and hanging out of the open windows. We
hurled one kind of missile or another at those innocent people while mounted
on our speeding bikes, as if in some imagined cavalry raid. Some boys threw
rocks, sticks, or firecrackers at the porches while others of us would fire shots
in their direction with our .22 rifles or BB guns. The people would scream
and scatter for cover. The sense of power over the blacks and the fantasy of a
glorious Confederate cavalry charge delighted us. The rides seemed to assuage
our feelings of powerlessness.

Tormenting the "niggers" was the only deviant behavior in which we could
engage about which most white adults didn't seem to care. Passing motorists
did not stop or in any way intervene, and our newspaper manager did not consider it a problem. Word of episodes like this got around the neighborhood, so
some teachers, merchants, preachers, and others must have known of them,
yet they did nothing, leaving us to believe that it didn't matter. Some parents
I knew were even amused. I'm sure my father knew, because he got around the
neighborhood, but he said nothing to me. Most important, the cops didn't
see it as a crime. We heard that the police dismissed it with the comment that
"boys will be boys." In the South of my youth, they likely saw it as us having "a
little innocent fun."

While permissive regarding the harassment of blacks, the cops were not
so lenient with us on other occasions. They seemed to think that most of us
working-class boys were basically hooligans. So they frequently stopped us for

questioning about our "suspicious behavior" or "a crime in the area" or "a complaint by one of the residents in the neighborhood" or "something reported stolen" in a nearby store. It was always something. But our appalling behavior toward blacks seemed to be exempted because such practices made easier their job of "keeping the niggers under control," a phrase I often heard. While they may have appreciated our work as junior agents of white dominance, they kept a close eye on the rest of our lives.

IT MAY BE DIFFICULT for some folks today to understand how any of us could have engaged in such heartless cruelty, especially a boy who went on to become an activist like me. How could we not see that the black people we attacked were individuals who had feelings and suffered pain just like us? It is not an easy question to answer, because the nuances of the social-psychological reality of the forties and fifties have faded from memory and history.

The answer to this question lies in the understanding of two key factors that governed our behavior in those days: (1) the stranglehold of white supremacist ideology and (2) each boy's perceived gains from participating in these racial outrages.

White supremacist ideology was ubiquitous. Until I was about fourteen I never remember seeing a black individual depicted in a book, magazine, or newspaper unless that person was the perpetrator of a crime or was involved in some other objectionable behavior. The only exceptions were occasional stories about black major league baseball players in the late forties. In our local newspapers there were no black brides or events on the society pages and virtually no news of the black community. The segregated classified ads told me that blacks deserved only the worst jobs and housing. I never encountered in my home or school a black newspaper like the *Richmond Planet* or the *Richmond Afro-American*. All the publications I saw abounded with caricatures of African Americans that conformed to the racism I was learning. We had no television when I was growing up, and the only blacks on the radio were stereotypes, including Amos and Andy—two cartoon-like blacks portrayed by white men in blackface—and a character on *The Jack Benny Show* by the name of Rochester. I recall that when blacks first began to be seen on TV in about 1958, their appearance was angrily protested by many whites in Virginia. The only African Americans I saw in films were those in the blockbuster *Gone with the*

Wind and the character known as Stepin Fetchit, hardly portrayals that made the case for the equality of the races. No film with a black hero, such as those in which Paul Robeson appeared, was shown in a movie theater I could attend. Even when the Harlem Globetrotters came to town, blacks were assigned the worst seats in the house.

My school taught racism as Truth. Our official textbook on the history of Virginia, *Cavalier Commonwealth,* made slavery sound idyllic. The passage below gives a sense of what we were taught:

> Of course the slave was not free to change employers, to go and come as he wished, to keep what he earned, or to stand on an equal footing before the law. Yet his condition had its advantages. He usually worked the accepted work-week of the colony—from sunrise to sundown daily except Sunday. But he enjoyed long holidays, especially at Christmas. He did not work so hard as the average free laborer, since he did not have to worry about losing his job. In fact, the slave enjoyed what we might call comprehensive social security. Generally speaking, his food was plentiful, his clothing adequate, his cabin warm, his health protected, his leisure carefree. He did not have to worry about hard times, unemployment, or old age. While his master was allowed by law to punish and even under some circumstances to kill him, the slave was protected to an effective degree by his value as property.

But by far I learned the most salient portions of my white supremacy from the adults I was instructed to respect. Their words and the example of their lives taught me what would be expected in my relations with black people as I arrived at each new stage of my life. Unlike the largely cognitive racist content from books, magazines, radio, movies, and the like, their white supremacist messages added an affective dimension that had the capacity to bury these myths deep in a child's psyche.

In nearly every encounter I witnessed between these "respectable whites" and blacks, some overt act, some remark, some tone in the voice, or some telling body language instructed me how I was to treat black people. The potency of the messages of white supremacy derived from the fact that they came from people who mattered: my parents and other family members, their friends, our neighbors, my teachers, clerks in stores where we traded, delivery men we knew, customers in my mother's beauty shop, my pastor and Sunday school teachers. Add to this the segregation of white and black lives: I never met a black individual who was not poor or in other ways disadvantaged. Nor did I ever hear anything about a black teacher, doctor, or other professional, and the only black preachers I knew were uneducated men.

So what we now think of as absurd then seemed anything but absurd to us. It appeared obvious, in fact, the gospel truth. Adults would not lie to their young, right? There being no contrary egalitarian ideas in our milieu, we had no choice but to trust our elders, believe as they did, and act on it as the truth.

It was many years later before I learned that there were individuals, even white people, right in Richmond, let alone other places in the South, who did not bow to these racial myths. Historians have begun to reveal the important work that black and white radicals were starting then. But I had no way to know about that as a youth.

Our community was awash in a racial ideology so totally enveloping that it made vast numbers of white people deaf, blind, and morally numb in matters of race. For my first eighteen years I lived in a totalitarian society that made white entitlement an absolute and black inferiority its indisputable first premise. So, we white boys felt pretty comfortable tormenting black people.

As if white supremacy's sway in the South were not enough, I had other toxins stirred into this poisonous stew in my middle teens. I lived in a family in dissolution on the edge of poverty and was the special target of a troubled father. He convinced me as a youth that I was inadequate and unworthy of friends, and I was failing in school. Holding a belief that I was superior to a whole class of other human beings was not uncomplicated for me: most of the time I felt anything but superior to other people, any people. Ironically, I felt a worse failure because I could not live up to my putative superiority.

All of this, then, was a ready recipe for creating a boy who would surrender his soul to win friends and acceptance. And where was such a boy to find the most accessible friendships but among other bewildered boys who were testing their own nascent masculinity and racial identity?

✳ 4 ✳

Out of the Family Tempest

WHEN I WAS 13 we moved to Northside Richmond, much closer to the beauty shop where my mother, our breadwinner, worked. It was a more middle-class neighborhood with fewer miscreants and enticements for juvenile delinquency. I am sure my mother had this in mind when she managed to buy our little brick house on Brook Road.

At this point the conflict with my father was becoming more intense—and dangerous. He was drinking heavily, rarely had a job, and spent most of his time around the house like a zombie. My mother worked long hours, so I was trapped in the tiny house with him for countless uneasy hours every day. He rarely spoke, but when he did, it was usually an angry rebuke for not jumping to attention when he addressed me. He took unresponsiveness as disrespect for his authority as a father and as a man. I would do anything to avoid being alone in the house with him, although I had to be there when needed to look after my younger brother, Steve. So my father and I shared our own private warzone, of which my mother and my brother knew little. When they were in the house there were no live battles to be witnessed, only the hint of singed nerves.

All of this turmoil further eroded my self-confidence, snuffed out my motivation in school, and caused my grades to hit a new low. I was so preoccupied with the strife in my family that I had neither energy nor room in my thoughts for anything academic. I grew timid, painfully shy, and withdrawn.

But there was one spark of life inside me that could alleviate the distress —my growing love of sports. Under the influence of Charlie Schremp, a boy in my neighborhood, I developed a passion for baseball. Shortly thereafter, it was basketball, my lifelong most-loved game. I played football in middle school and recreational leagues, but it did not captivate me like these other two sports.

But sports in the South at this time proved confusing. Major league base-ball was finally accepting a few African Americans and other players of color, but the racial bar in Richmond held fast. As an avid New York Giants fan in the late forties and early fifties, I would sit for hours on the floor with my ear pressed against the speaker of our old floor-model radio, trying to catch every word of the play-by-play accounts of the exploits of, among others, their three black stars, Monte Irvin, Hank Thompson, and Willie Mays. But my growing emotional attachment to these black men was perplexing to me. Was I sup-posed to have feelings like this about black men? Whites might think of it as odd to admire black stars. I knew some people who would call me a "nigger lover" for such sentiments. But for the first time, I began to sense what I might be missing in my hometown.

This may have been at the back of my mind when my friend Charlie and I learned that Satchel Paige was coming to town to pitch in a Negro League exhibition game. We decided we couldn't miss it because he was a legend in baseball, even among some white boys. While he was old for a player, he was reputed to be superior to many of the white pitchers in the major leagues.

The game was at Mooers Field, the home of the Richmond Colts and the only professional baseball venue in the area. The all-white Colts team and their ballpark were owned by a local businessman named Eddie Mooers. Mooers Field was less than a thirty minute walk from our houses. The seating was strictly segregated at Colts games. In fact Mooers was such a zealous rac-ist that in 1946 he cancelled a scheduled exhibition game when he learned that the Montreal Royals had black players, including Jackie Robinson. But because black dollars were as green as white ones, Mooers leased the park to black promoters when Negro League teams came to town. On those nights it was jammed with blacks coming from miles around to see the great stars from the Negro Leagues. Since virtually no whites showed up, the seats were not segregated.

I remember walking up the ramp and suddenly catching sight of the massive crowd. The Colts never had crowds like that. I had never seen so many black people in one place in my life. Paige was on the mound and his every pitch electrified the crowd. It was truly a magic time for us. Here we were seeing live perhaps the greatest baseball pitcher of all time, amidst maybe ten thousand screaming fans who knew just like us what a remarkable moment this was. It suddenly hit me that neither Satchel Paige nor any of these fans were allowed to sit in good seats to see the Colts play. It was a sobering thought for a boy who had never thought to question the segregation of his hometown. Somehow Charlie and I, for the moment, were so awestruck by this man's majestic arm and competitive audacity that we lost cognizance of the fact that we were perhaps the only whites in the stands. When we returned home, though, that sensation of solidarity with thousands of black fans faded as we slipped back into our white world.

Obsession with baseball may have sometimes given me joy, but on other occasions it got me into trouble with my father. In moments of rapture with the play-by-play of a Giants game coming from our radio, I could hear nothing else. With some regularity while I was listening, my father would come up behind me without warning and lash out at my back, neck, or head with a long brown leather belt. In his drunken state he would shout, "I'm talking to you!" After some experience with his rages, I learned to predict the timing of his attacks, so that I could slip away before he approached or elude him by scrambling across the floor on my hands and knees and then racing off to some hiding place such as the tool shed.

Many nights I lay awake in bed for hours imagining myself finally getting the courage to take him on. I began to comprehend that my father was a small-boned man who, because of his drinking and poor diet, had become somewhat emaciated. Meanwhile, I had grown taller and larger. So I finally came to recognize that I didn't have to take it anymore: I could overpower him in a confrontation. I decided to start retaliating. The next time he came up behind me with his belt raised high, I leapt off the floor swinging at him until I was beyond his reach. He seemed stunned, even fearful. I raced out the front screen door, slamming it in his face while cursing him. I then hid, as I had done before, in Charlie Schremp's garage. I waited there until I was sure that my mother had come home from work, and then I walked back to our house. I had nothing to worry about if my mother was at home. He never confronted me when she was around. The problem for me was that she worked six ten-hour days a week.

My mother recognized I was somehow in trouble and tried in many ways to get me on track. One valiant effort was to sign me up with a Boy Scout troop at a nearby church. Somehow I took hold of the idea and began to imagine myself deeply involved in all the good things they did. But after a month of weekly meetings, the scout master took me aside and told me that I needed to buy a full uniform and the basic scout camping equipment. My mother gave me around $5–10 to shop for it. I went downtown to the clothing store where everyone made these purchases. I laid my money on the glass display case and told the clerk that I was a new scout and wished to buy all the things that Boy Scouts needed. With a scowl, he informed me that what I wanted would cost about $85. I was struck dumb. After gathering myself, I asked what I could buy with the cash I had. He replied, "A cap and a scarf." Stunned, I was still pleased with the two fine-looking icons of my membership in the Robert E. Lee Council of the Boy Scouts of America.

I proudly marched into the next meeting with my cap sitting squarely, per regulation, and the scarf tied perfectly around my neck. I felt truly a Boy Scout. Just before the meeting was to begin, however, the scout master came up to me and said, "I thought you were going to get your uniform." I explained that this was all I could get with the money I had. Irritated, he declared, "Go back and get the whole uniform. It is required in order to be in the troop." My heart sank. Over the next few days I lost my enthusiasm for the Boy Scouts. The Scouts promised to teach boys how to fly, but instead they had clipped my wings.

Another time my mother thought she had found a foolproof way to fix my life. She took me to the Fork Union Military Academy, near Dixie, Virginia, in a remote rural spot forty-five miles up the James River, to explore enrolling me. The school was known for reining in wayward boys with military discipline, instruction by immersion in one subject a month, and intensive involvement in sports. But as soon as the man in the uniform revealed what it cost, my mother stood up and without another word took me by the hand and walked out. She never again spoke of sending me to a private school.

While my mother never told me outright that she, too, had severe problems with my father, I knew that she was extremely unhappy. I could see many signs of her misery. It was not a marriage but a prison for her, as it was for me. One of the clues to my mother's feelings was how she came to avoid having visitors to our house, even relatives. We only saw her friends and people on visits to their places. I know now that she felt disgraced to have visitors see our household turmoil.

The last visitor we ever had in Richmond was our Baptist preacher, whom

I suspected my mother had invited in the hope that he could get my father back onto the path with Jesus. He came after church one Sunday for one of my mother's scrumptious crispy fried chicken dinners. When the pastor arrived, my mother, my little brother, and I were still all decked out in our Sunday finest. But when she called us to dinner my father came out of the bedroom boozed up and in his sleeveless undershirt. He sat down at the table and, ignoring the rest of us, set upon a heap of chicken and Spanish rice, even as the preacher was saying the blessing.

My mother was embarrassed almost to tears. Her husband acted as if he were alone at the table. Losing interest in the food, the rest of us went through the motions of the meal, hardly saying a word and carefully avoiding eye contact. The preacher seemed more ill at ease than us. He probably thought my father was a job too big even for Jesus. At my mother's first sign that the meal was ending, he stood up, declined her offer of dessert, and said he "had to run." That preacher couldn't get out the door fast enough. This episode marked the incontrovertible end of our family as we had known it. I was sixteen years old.

Not many weeks elapsed before my mother sat me down on our old flowered settee, tattered in the way that upholstery gets when hope in a home disintegrates. It was just the two of us. Cautiously, not knowing how I would respond, she asked if I would be willing to leave Richmond with her and my brother to live with her sister, Mamie, in Jacksonville, Florida. I was exhilarated to hear her say that she would get us out of our hellhole—until I thought of what I would have to leave behind. I was devastated that in order to get relief, we would have to pull up roots just as I was finally acquiring some friends. I was faced with making friends all over again—and in a strange place. But it was our only way out. So after I said goodbye to my basketball buddies, we packed the Dodge to the roof and drove off to the Sunshine State.

For a long time after that move, I remained alienated from my father and did not communicate with him. But in the years after we left him he began to clean up his act. He had to in order to eat and keep a roof over his head. For years I mulled over how to think of him, before concluding that he had never really been a father in a positive way. Where my mother was a warm, caring, tireless, and conscientious parent, his affect was flat. He took no genuine interest in his children, only in an unspoken agenda of revenge for how life had treated him. It was as if he wanted to stick pins into people who represented modern life, which failed to respect the racial and class entitlement of his upbringing.

As these ruminations settled I became less bitter and sought ways to acknowledge his humanity. This led to intermittent trials of rapprochement. It also stimulated me to search for explanations for why my father became the person he was, a curiosity that gave the first hint of the embryonic social psychologist growing in me.

✳ 5 ✳

Receiving My Class Assignment
in High School

HAVING LEFT MY father standing on the stoop at our Richmond house in February 1952, my mother, Steve, and I headed for Jacksonville to start a new life. We moved into my Aunt Mamie's spare room for a few months until we found a two-room apartment near our schools. My mother got a job for a little over $100 a month as a beautician in the hair salon of the city's largest department store, and my brother entered the neighborhood elementary school.

I warily entered my second high school, Robert E. Lee High. In Richmond I had attended Thomas Jefferson High School. While the two schools were 555 miles apart, their responses to me seemed identical. At Thomas Jefferson, my teachers and principal appeared to have learned early that I was the child of a beautician and a drinker who was often out of work. The plot thickened when I arrived at Lee, where my mother was known simply as a single mother who was a hairdresser. In those days, that was all the officials needed to know to place me in the social hierarchy of the school. They may have picked up more about my standing from the hand-me-downs from my cousins that I wore to school. My wardrobe was a radical departure from the khaki slacks and cotton button-down shirts worn by the school's favored boys.

Teachers branded me as a working-class boy for whom a college-bound track was unrealistic. Before long, I could see that I was being treated differently from better-off students. It was obviously due to money, appearances, language, and bearing. Once painted as a poor risk by a critical mass of adults, I felt invisible next to the favored teens from "better" families. The school seemed to belong to them. Another curious similarity between the two high schools, four states apart, was the fact that their English teachers gave me identical career advice: "You need to quit school and learn a trade." As the primary guardians of the language, apparently it was their job to guide us to our ultimate class destinations.

I had no reason at the time to doubt their assessment of me. After all, most of them went to college, and my people did not. So as I came to internalize this dim view of my prospects, I grew more and more intimidated by the teachers, the successful students, the academic challenges, and even the person who oversaw the one realm where I had been somebody, my basketball coach. It all convinced me that I was incapable of earning decent grades or obtaining a job in which I would ever need anything they taught. I became allergic to high school.

But my mother apparently saw something I didn't. When she realized how the school was sorting out my future, she went to see the principal and demanded that he put me in their college preparatory track. They had no defense when Lula Jane Stephens went to bat for her boy.

Ironically, my experience in high school whetted my appetite for learning, but not their kind of learning. I embarked on such weird adventures as reading and relishing nearly all the articles from A to Z in *Compton's Encyclopedia,* and each week I made trips to a newsstand where I could use the *World Almanac* and *Information Please* to look up and compare population figures from all around the world. But I was never able to connect this appetite for learning to what happened in high school.

Of all the consequences of the class hierarchy in high school, the most painful was the implication that I was unworthy of having friends from among the "better people" in our school. This was especially painful when I pondered dating. I kept hearing that voice inside saying, "You've got no money, you're scrawny, you don't know how to dance, and you wear hand-me-down clothes. You don't have a chance in the world to have a girlfriend!" Pretty much the only time I felt comfortable was with my one faithful companion, basketball.

In Jacksonville, I again sought friends among the also-lost: peers involved with vandalism and petty thievery, high school dropouts, and work-shy twenty-somethings hanging out on the streets looking to create trouble. On occasions I joined their marauding at such places as Riverside Park, where we harassed and took money from the "queers" who hung out there. Other times when bored we would wander about nearby streets looking for a lone, vulnerable "nigger" to hassle. I know it caused me some discomfort because of how I remember it now, with what I think of as a moral prickly heat. While I never got the fever they showed for these activities, I nevertheless participated in some way, thinking that it would earn me their acceptance. Respect was a scarce resource then, and that of my peers mattered to me. It was a miracle that involvement with these guys didn't land me in the clink. What saved me, I think, was spending the bulk of my time playing basketball on the outdoor court at a park near our little apartment.

My poor academic performance at Lee was sometimes humiliating. So I sought to escape the teachers and the other kids who seemed so smart by skipping school or sequestering myself in its remote corners. Sometimes I deliberately got into trouble for minor infractions of school rules; the punishment was spending the morning with other "delinquents" digging wide and deep holes in the outside grounds until noon and then having to fill them back up after lunch. The school set aside a specific area for this character-building opportunity.

I began to believe that I should take my teachers' advice to quit school and get a job. I could do okay as a carpenter's helper, since I was pretty good at working with wood. But my mother would have none of it, so I was stuck in a place where I felt alien, counting the days until graduation. Even playing basketball on the varsity team contributed to the downward spiral, because the coach was a cruel perfectionist and I was far from perfect. I got by on just enough school work to deceive my mother and some of the teachers. My mother did all she could for us but it wasn't easy to focus on me and my brother after a long day on her feet in the beauty shop.

I believe that my teachers, wrongheaded as their attitudes may seem today, acted without malice. The customary belief in their day, at least in the South, was that class divisions were mostly fixed in nature. While few of them would have known social Darwinism by name, most appeared to believe in it. In their view, we "poor whites" lacked the endowments to be like them; instead, not unlike black people, our task was to learn to be satisfied with a lifetime of working as laborers or in other jobs that matched our immutable limitations. I believe they thought that they were doing us a favor by saving us from inevitable and hurtful disappointment if we were to aim higher than our abilities could carry us.

With all of this upheaval in my head, I was a candidate for failure if my high school did not make up for the class differences. And it didn't. Instead of being shored up for the last leg of the journey to adulthood, I found myself in two different schools in two different states being involuntarily committed to an institution that simply sorted teenagers into their proper strata in the social hierarchy. For me, high school did not feel like it was about learning history, geography, English, foreign languages, and all the rest. It felt more like being caught in a threshing machine separating the wheat from the chaff.

PART TWO

Encountering a New World

✳ 6 ✳

The Hillbilly Blues

N 1953, A COUPLE of mornings after graduating 330 out of 424 seniors
from Robert E. Lee High School in Jacksonville, I was headed north to
Cleveland, Ohio, to look for work. I was travelling with a seventeen-year-
old named Dick who was the son of my mother's friend. Dick and I had never
gotten along very well. I only chose to go to Cleveland with him because he
had been there before and had returned with wondrous tales of big money
to be made in the city's vast manufacturing industries. We had planned this
trip for months, and he had assured me that soon we would be taking home a
hundred bucks a week. Lots of southerners were going North like us in those
years, dreaming of that pot of gold waiting at the end of the rainbow up there.

Dick and I lifted our tattered cardboard suitcases up the steep steps into
the Greyhound coach and found our seats. Some twenty dreary hours later
we pulled into the biggest bus station I had ever seen. Once on the street Dick
found us a Cleveland city bus that took us to Shaker Heights and a rooming
house that he knew from an earlier trip. I was surprised at my new neighborhood. It was such a pleasant-looking place—beautiful big trees, gentle hills,
and large, classy-looking homes. Finding this after expecting to live in a run-
down part of town, I thought, "I am going to love this place."

The landlady showed us a tiny room on the second floor. It was barely large
enough to hold what she claimed was a double bed and a small three-drawer
chest. Sleeping in that undersized bed in a cracker-box space with Dick wasn't
exactly inviting. We paid five dollars a week each, not including board. But I
discovered that by getting up before dawn, I could sneak down to the land-

lady's kitchen and confiscate some eats for breakfast and later in the day. I only had about ten bucks left and no job yet, so I couldn't lay out cash for meals.

In less than a week, Dick found a job. But despite his grandiose claims, it wasn't a hundred dollars a week. I didn't have his luck that first week, or the second week, or even the third week. I looked in the classified ads every day and applied to as many jobs as I could get to on foot, but I got no work other than a little day labor. I was scared I was going to end up on the street and starve.* But then I had the good fortune of meeting three white brothers on the basketball court in a nearby park. We became friends, and they often shared vittles and other bounty with me. Once they even took me to see my first 3–D movie. But the third dimension in the film was not the primary novelty in my experience there. It was the first time I had ever sat in a theater with a black person. I was so taken by the oddity of it that I mostly ignored the film, frequently removing my 3–D glasses to steal glances at the young black couple sitting several rows ahead of us. I thought, "How can these white folks put up with this?" But then later, as we left the movie house, I saw black and white patrons casually exiting together; they were obviously indifferent to the distinctions in my head. It made me wonder "Why do my people down south think this is such a bad thing?"

I encountered a more challenging trial of my racism on the basketball court; it was prosecuted by a black man just a few years older than me. At the park I often played pickup games in the evenings with my three friends and anyone else who showed up. Over the summer I had built a little reputation as a hoopster, and was known as "the boy from down south." One night I arrived at the court as guys were shooting around and looking to start a game. Among the players was a black fellow about my size who, after hearing me speak, focused his attention on me. I had never been on a court with a black player before.

We chose up teams and the contest began. This guy made it known that he wanted to match up with me on defense. Before long, he was challenging me both physically and verbally, sometimes with barbs about my being a white

*I later wrote a piece about just how hungry I got that became a hit with some English teachers: Edward H. Peeples Jr., " . . . Meanwhile Humans Eat Pet Food," *New York Times,* op-ed page, Dec. 16, 1975. Later reprinted in Gerald Levin, *Short Essays: Models for Composition* (New York: Harcourt Brace Jovanovich, 1977), 311–14; and Brenda D. Smith, *Breaking Through: College Reading,* 7th Edition (New York: Pearson Longman, 2005), 479–80.

southerner. It was the first time a black person had treated me with anything other than deference. I thought, "Back home, if a nigger dared to get into our game, much less hassle a white man, he'd get his ass whupped." Then I realized, "But I ain't back home now, am I? And these boys ain't gonna hep me." I thought it might be a whole lot smarter to demonstrate what kind of ballplayer I was and keep the race business to myself. This guy played what today we would call an in-your-face game, and he was good. We had a grueling battle and played about even. After a while, he backed off on the "cracker" gibes and sort of warmed up to me. The game got me pondering, "Why is it such a big deal to play ball with a black guy? And to think, he wud-ent half bad."

I still needed a real job. I spent many days looking for work along Cleveland's great industrial boulevard, Euclid Avenue, home of Picker X-ray, Fisher Body, and other huge factories. Day after day I was turned away, even when their signs said "Help Wanted." Finally one day I learned why. Responding to a big "Hiring Now" sign in front of a factory, I walked into the employment office and said, "I'm here answering your sign." As the man behind the counter heard me speak, his smile turned to a scowl. Looking irritated, he blurted out, "We don't hire hillbillies here!" I was stunned. Why would he think I was a hillbilly? I had never lived in the hills or mountains. But to him it was not a description, just an all-purpose slur for southerners. It hurt. Finding myself the target of prejudice opened my eyes for the first time to how unfair acts of discrimination against a class of people can be.

Toward the end of summer I finally got a full-time job as a package runner on a delivery truck for a department store. But it never led me to a pot of gold. My vision of making big money and achieving my version of the American dream faded. In late August, homesick and drained of hope, I wrote my mother a postcard to tell her I was coming home. In about a week, I got an upbeat letter saying, "Eddie, I got an idea. Catch the bus to Richmond. I'll meet you there." Her idea set me on a path of discovery that changed my life.

MY MOTHER MAY HAVE quit school after eighth grade, but she was strong and competent, with an uncanny ability to weather the emotional and financial storms she faced. She commanded great respect from everyone in her family and from her friends and beauty shop customers. She drove up from Jacksonville and met me at the Richmond Greyhound station. Then she took me to a neighborhood of old Victorian homes that I had never noticed when we lived in Richmond. There on the corner was a sign that read "Richmond Professional Institute." RPI, at the time, was a scruffy little institutional vassal of the prestigious College of William and Mary. My mother somehow knew to take me to see the director of the drafting certificate program, even though to my knowledge she had never before been on a college campus. Since my only prior successes in school were in art and drafting classes, she must have thought that this would be the best program for me. Despite my lousy high school record, RPI accepted my application. I later learned that many with my kind of history gained admission in those days because the school was the institutional equivalent of ourselves—a place that was building itself from the ground up with precious few resources. In the fall of 1953 I moved into a dorm room with Lester "Les" T. Simpson, with whom I shared a room for four years and a friendship for life, born of our similar stories of growing up in hardship in the South. At RPI, we finally found a community where we truly belonged. But it took me a few tumultuous jolts to settle in and realize my potential.

As a freshman I made the RPI Green Devils basketball team. It was a thrill, even though the team at the time had little to boast about. I worked hard to improve my game and was conscientious about training and avoiding alcohol and tobacco. I was rewarded by becoming the "sixth man," then an uncommon achievement for a first-year player even at a place like RPI. In the opening game of the season, I soared when I got my chance to play. But later in the game I landed with a rebound on the side of an opposing player's foot, tearing a ligament in my ankle. I was taken off to the emergency room, where they warned me that the injury was serious and might even spell the end of my new basketball career. I was devastated. I was feeling myself on the brink of becoming "somebody"—and it all fell apart in a moment. Crushed, I accepted an invitation from some older teammates to head down to Grace Street for some beers, not something that I ordinarily saw as acceptable during training. I drank to get drunk, and it became my undoing. Upon returning to the dorm, I lost it. I broke up a couple of chairs, verbally abused the dorm manager, and defied the restraints of "Dick Tracy," the name given by the students to RPI's sole campus policeman. Four days later, the dean of students and the disciplinary committee kicked me off the basketball team and in effect expelled me from my dream.

The shame was too much. I packed up and blew what money I had from my part-time job as an architect's draftsman on a train ticket to Jacksonville, certain that I would never return to this place. About three in the morning when I arrived at Union Station in Jacksonville, there was my mother greeting me with her perpetual smile. She must have been grieved by this, my costliest debacle yet, but she tried not to show it. Back home, we sat down at the kitchen table in her little second-floor flat. I was famished after many hours on the train. My mother said nothing about my wrecking this great educational opportunity and blowing her hard-earned money. Instead, she went to the refrigerator to find me something to eat.

The fridge was one of the early versions of the electric icebox with a coiled compressor mounted on the top. It was old when we bought it used, and its time with us had not improved its condition. As she swung open the door, its rusty hinges gave way and the heavy door fell to the floor with a mighty thud, missing her feet by inches. It startled us silent at first. But then my mother sat down at the table, put her face in her hands, and began to sob. I had never seen her cry before. A hot flash surged through me. "What have I done? My poor mother has always done it all for me and I screw up over and over again." I embraced her, but was at a total loss for words.

The next morning, I awoke with a semiconscious notion of the direction I must take. I leapt into the gargantuan task of finishing all of my neglected school assignments. I was vaguely aware that I was somehow a new person. I think that my mother saw it, too. It was my first understanding of what it was to be an adult, to take responsibility, and to reach down deep into one's self for the strengths and talents lying fallow there to do what had to be done.

I returned to RPI in January and pleaded with the dean to reinstate me. My remorseful posture and my portfolio of completed working drawings got me welcomed back into the fold. There in this nurturing environment of educational missionaries, over the next three and a half years as a major in physical education, I met with one success after another. My mother had miraculously found me a place where even a fallen "hillbilly" could earn respect.

Dr. Alice Recruits Another Justice Seeker

MY REINSTATEMENT AT RPI began a process of transforming a provincial, naive, and bigoted southern white boy into a young man with a budding passion for racial justice and human rights. One person who made a huge difference for me and many other students was a sociology professor named Alice Davis, whom we students affectionately called "Dr. Alice." Most students initially took her class because it didn't have required readings, homework, or tests. All you had to do was join in the class polemics over what at first seemed to us weird controversial topics, then dash off your opinions at exam time. No matter what I did in the class, I got that solid C. It was the perfect setup for a jock majoring in phys ed.

Dr. Davis was not a handsome woman. She was about five foot five, lean, and a bit time-worn. She had the dress, plain look, and countenance of an older traditional Quaker or Mennonite. But the warm and knowing smile that gleamed through the deep wrinkles on her face told us to be still and listen. We were in the presence of an oracle for our time and place.

Often seen with Dr. Alice on campus was Dr. Nadia Davilevsky. They met in Russia during the early Stalin days. Davis was there on a Quaker-sponsored program to work with the masses of people being relocated. Davilevsky was on the losing side of the Bolshevik revolution, and consequently her husband was executed and she was imprisoned. However, with help from Davis she finally was able to come to America where they became lifelong companions and then colleagues at RPI.

During the Great Depression the two of them spent time in West Virginia doing community organizing and relief work with federal New Deal programs

and the American Friends Service Committee. Davis became friends with Eleanor Roosevelt while she was there, promoting relief efforts for the president
and working on projects of her own. In 1939 Davis earned a master's degree in
social work at RPI. She then joined Davilevsky at the University of North Carolina at Chapel Hill, where they each attained a PhD in Howard W. Odum's
legendary southern regional studies program. They came to teach at RPI in
1941. Davis taught sociology courses and Danilevsky statistics. As a student at
RPI, I had no idea what you would call people like Dr. Alice and Dr. Davilevsky, the first bona fide political intellectuals I had ever encountered. It being
the era of Joseph McCarthy, we students thought they might be subversives,
yet we were drawn to them just the same.

When Dr. Alice spoke in class, it wasn't for long. She preferred to throw out
a provocative proposition like a piece of raw meat and then watch the students
leap on it like a pack of jackals. Her class was like some great morality play,
where she used the more articulate and mature students, often Korean War
veterans, as her supporting cast. I was awestruck and a bit frightened by how
people in the class spoke with such abandon on topics that, if ever brought
up in my earlier orbit, evoked only heat, never light. They talked about racial bigotry and equality; the rights of women to pursue abortions, equal pay,
and professional careers; poverty and progressive economics; labor unions and
working people; colonialism; nuclear war; environmental conservation; religious controversies; and world politics. Her classes took my breath away.

I never had a mentoring relationship with Dr. Alice like some of the students did. But getting close to her was not the only way to learn from her. Her
classes stirred critical thinking and conversations that spread like kudzu all
about our little campus; her wisdom put down roots wherever it could find a
fertile mind. It opened mine to a new vision for how I would spend my life. I
signed up for several courses with Dr. Alice. Each one, no matter the title, was
the same: a salon where, without the usual academic fanfare, we would debate
ceaselessly the great ideas that drove the second half of the twentieth century.

The one that most registered in my gut came one spring day when Dr. Alice
stunned us by announcing, "Take out a piece of paper and a pencil." I thought,
"Oh my God, a pop quiz—in Dr. Alice's class?! Oh Jesus, I haven't even bought
the textbook." Continuing, she said, "I want you to trace back your ancestors
ten generations. Just show your mother's and father's names and then each of

your ancestors from which they are descended, and so on—for ten generations back." We all began the assignment by effortlessly listing our parents and
then our four grandparents. But as we attempted to enumerate our eight great-
grandparents, recognition of the difficulty of the assignment hit us. Recogniz-
ing how complicated it was to specify our sixteen great-great-grandparents, I
heard someone mutter, "So what's the point?" Then a baffled student piped
up, "We can't know all of our ancestors back ten generations, there are way too
many." Dr. Alice stood silently at the front of the room for a couple of minutes,
allowing each of us to wrestle personally with the many lost roads down which
our southern families had come in ten generations. Then she leaned over and
in a husky whisper asked, "Are you sure that you are not a Negro?"

Her question singed my ears. I thought of all the boasting of sexual conquests of black women I had heard from men in my family and my acquaintances over the years. Her question drove a dagger into the heart of the racial
myth that governed our lives. "My God, I could, in fact, be a Negro!" After all,
we followed the "one-drop" rule for assigning race. After class, all of us white
southerners filed out of the room in dead silence. In the months to follow, I
began losing my comfort with white supremacist notions. She never knew it,
but Dr. Alice redirected my life with that dagger of truth. It was my first day
as a race traitor.

AS SUCH MIND-EXPANDING experiences at RPI took hold, so did my will
to act upon them. Little by little I became sensitized to the injustice of some
situations that I would never have noticed before. With awareness also grew
the passion to do something. Because I was an athlete and I expected to be a
phys ed teacher these moments arose mostly in the context of sports, when opportunities presented themselves for small individual acts of defiance against
racial segregation.

For example, in 1955 I had a part-time job as a coach at the very playground
where I had first been introduced to sports as a child, Fonticello Park. Since
this playground had been my sanctuary as a young teen, where I began to find
myself through baseball, football, and later basketball, the chance to work
there had profound meaning to me. Returning to the park as a college junior,
I understood how much the playground could mean to a young boy as a place
to escape demons and discover his potential. My job was coaching football in

the fall and baseball in the spring for preteen boys. Imagining a future career as a coach, I took the job very seriously and struggled to help these youngsters learn the game and become more mature in the process.

I gave little thought at first to the fact that all of these children were white, but I soon learned that white boys were not the only kids who loved to play football. Every afternoon when the team was playing, black youngsters would drift onto the edge of the field, sit down, and intently watch the boys run, pass, punt, block, and tackle. After a few days, it dawned on me that they were wishing they had an opportunity to play. The next day I made a grave error. When my supervisor, who came periodically in a city car to check on me, showed up, I told him that I was going to invite these black kids to join us. Outraged at the prospect, he gave me an angry scolding. "We don't want these niggers here," he exclaimed. "Besides, they have their own places. And my boss won't stand for this! Don't you dare." I didn't know what he was talking about when he said they had their own places. I had been to nearly all of the playgrounds in south Richmond and had never seen any facility comparable to Fonticello that was designated for blacks. "Separate," yes; "equal," no.

I never again brought up the issue with my supervisor. But I did wrangle a way to get the black kids into our games. I taught them to race off and hide behind a house at the edge of the field at the first sign of the supervisor's car. And I got the white kids to swear not to breathe a word about the integrated games in front of the supervisor. All the kids bought into the undercover plot to do right, and for the rest of the season they enjoyed "race-mixing" on the football field. We only had to activate the race evacuation plan once, and the supervisor never caught on.

AS MY SENSITIVITY TO the unfairness of segregation heightened, I struggled over how and when to intervene and what costs I was willing to pay for actions despised by most of the white people in my life. One particular episode illustrates how complicated the choices became. On December 3, 1955, two days after Rosa Parks stood up for freedom by keeping her seat on a city bus in Montgomery, Alabama, the Gallaudet College basketball team came to Richmond by bus from Washington, DC, for a game against our RPI Green Devils. They arrived in time for an early supper. The fact that the players were deaf and their speech difficult to understand did not make it any less clear that

they were anxious to chow down. My job, in return for my minuscule basketball scholarship, was to play host to all the visiting teams, so I led them to the
college cafeteria and ushered them through the serving line. This was the beginning of the era of "massive resistance," the aggressive defense of segregation
fomented by the *Richmond News Leader* editor James Jackson Kilpatrick and
Virginia's ruling "Byrd Organization" in reaction to the Supreme Court's 1954
decision in *Brown v. Board of Education*. Among other provisions, Virginia's
massive resistance statute affirmed the ban on interracial athletic competition
at state colleges like RPI.

Washington, DC, was mostly segregated, too, so Gallaudet's players were all
white. However, their bus driver was a black man, an individual whose image
became seared into my memory for a lifetime. He was short, in his forties, and
he wore a dark cloth jacket and a busman's cap. He was very quiet and unassuming in the line of basketball players filing by the steam tables. But as it was
his turn to select his silverware, the cafeteria manager caught sight of him and
leaped around the railing to bark, "You can't be served here!" The bus driver's
initial shock quickly gave way to resignation. Without a hint of anger, he set
his tray down, turned around, and made his way past the tall young white
men in the supper line. All eyes were fixed on the bus driver as he walked a
gauntlet of humiliation. I was astonished by his poise and dignity in the face of
this piercing insult; his bearing struck a nerve deep inside me. I had spent the
prior year and a half trying to wrench myself intellectually from the clutches
of a racist upbringing, and watching him debased like this brought home how
profoundly evil white supremacy was—and that I must do something to protest. Enraged, I raced up to the cafeteria manager, whom I knew well, and
growled, "He is our guest! Where else can he eat? How can you do this?" But
my reputation as a basketball ace held no sway here. I could not believe what
was happening—or the intensity of my anger over it. In the past, I would not
have risked my reputation by making a scene like this, but this day my soul
commanded me to act.

No doubt, I added grief to the Gallaudet bus driver's already heavy burden. In those days, it was often assumed that even good and civil white people
should not protest on behalf of a victim of racial abuse because—as the rea-
soning went—that might only draw further harm to the victim. The prospect

of violence hovered as the ultimate arbiter of any racial impropriety. But I was possessed. I ran to the telephone. I was sure that Mr. English, the business manager of the college, who knew me well as a basketball player and campus leader, would reverse the cafeteria manager's decision and stop this shameless treatment of our guest. But Mr. English only said, "I'm sorry, but the law is the law." "So where is he to be fed as a guest of the college?" I asked. Irritated, he snapped, "I don't care where or what he eats, he can't go through the line reserved for whites or eat in the cafeteria dining area." Hanging up the phone, it occurred to me that the linchpin of segregation was the "separate but equal" doctrine, the contention that the wall between the races entailed no inequities for blacks. Here was a classic example of the absurdity of this claim. As a twenty-year-old white southerner I finally saw the lie in utter clarity.

I also got an idea. If they would not treat our guest with the dignity he deserved, I could at least raise the price of segregation. So with great embarrassment, I asked the bus driver if he would be willing to take his meal in an adjacent building. I took him to an unoccupied classroom, filled with old-style school desks with writing arms. I invited him to sit in one and told him I'd be right back with his dinner. Returning to the cafeteria, I picked up a tray and proceeded to fill it with a salad, a serving of roast beef and mashed potatoes, rolls and butter, a dessert, and a large glass of iced tea, and then raced back to deliver the meal. As my guest turned to dig into his long-awaited meal, I said, "Wait. Don't eat yet, you haven't got all of the choices." He put his fork down as I returned to the cafeteria to assemble a second tray of selections—the choices he was denied. I again raced past the cashier, gloating over the fact that she could not stop me because I was complying with the letter of Mr. English's command. Meanwhile, the student diners and everyone else in the cafeteria began to catch on, but they were too dumbfounded to know how to respond. I hurried back to my guest with the second tray and again asked him to wait. Scurrying back once more to the cafeteria, I grabbed a third tray with all the remaining choices and rushed past the exasperated cashier, the cafeteria manager, and the vexed white onlookers, all steaming at how their racial conventions were being tweaked by one of their own.

Delivering the third tray to my guest, I informed him that he now had every selection from which the whites got to choose. A tiny smile came to his lips and then promptly disappeared. Without a word, he began to eat his lonesome feast. Groping for words that might heal some of the hurt, I said, "It's all yours, all three trays are yours. It cost them three times more to do you this way." He said nothing and went on eating. I sat in another chair watching him in silence for a good five minutes, then bid him goodbye and left for the gym to get ready for the game. We won 74–61, but it didn't feel to me like a triumph.

✳ 8 ✳

Boot Camp for Human Rights

B Y THE END OF my sophomore year at RPI, I was struggling with a torrent of questions about my upbringing. New ideas and experiences and reading were showing me that much of our precious "southern way of life" was a preposterous and cruel fabrication. I felt betrayed by my family, my preacher, my teachers, and all the other adults in my community. They had told me ugly lies about African Americans and others who they said were fundamentally different from us and therefore less deserving of life's gifts. They had used my innocence to make me complicit in their white supremacist empire.

But what I came to see as most reprehensible was their confiscation of what could have been our moral anchor—the church. They twisted it into a fortress for the defense of segregation. On the one hand they insisted that we children follow the message of Jesus Christ from the New Testament. My Sunday-school classes admonished me to practice the virtues of charity, mercy, and kindness. But on the other hand they demanded obedience to an all-powerful, all-knowing, and often harsh god from the Old Testament. And when it came to cruel human institutions like Jim Crow, my preachers found in their readings of the Bible a policy of celestial hands-off.

Mistreatment of blacks was not the only issue of injustice I was awakened to at this time. When I was coming of age at the end of World War II, almost all of the Christians I knew scorned Jews or were at least unfeeling about the news of the Holocaust. I was confused over how some seemed so indifferent to the plight of a people who had been annihilated by our own mortal enemy, Adolf Hitler. But the most bewildering thing about this anti-Semitism was how my Christian brethren could speak of Jews this way when we all knew Jesus Christ was a Jew. Witnessing such incongruities planted somewhere deep in my pre-intellectual understanding of the world the seeds of doubt about this faith. By age twenty, I found the Christianity of my youth too corrupt for the ideals I was beginning to adopt. The bigoted and provincial world of "our way of life," as they were so fond of calling it, had begun to make my blood boil.

Expressing my new views put a painful distance between me and my beloved mother, and it led to outright rejection from many of my other kin and their friends. A cold silence also set in among some of my own friends and acquaintances. I no longer felt accepted in places where heretofore I had been welcome. This ever enlarging curtain of isolation hurt. Vestiges of the loneliness I knew as a child returned with a vengeance. But at the same time RPI fortified me with new experiences and ideas. My new passion for reading about the world's religions and the anthropology of race and my successes with basketball and campus leadership opened the door to a new life.

Feeling new confidence, I began to challenge racism when I encountered it and argue with the more reasonable folks around me to abandon white supremacy. I also searched for brothers and sisters in the struggle. In that day, those who stood up for racial justice, if not charged as outright "Communist traitors," were labeled "fellow travelers" by the segregationists. It was generally presumed by many whites in the South that only Communists would favor extending human rights to blacks. I didn't care what they were called; I just wanted to meet people who were more like what I had become. My suspicion was that I would find them up north.

Yet what first lured me to the North in the summer of 1955 was not a search for allies but the pursuit of my first true love. One of my psychology professors offered me a job as athletic director at Camp Ranger, near Dover, New Jersey, where he was the summer camp director. I leaped at his offer because my girl-friend lived only an hour or so away. Alas, I lost the girl by summer's end, but at Camp Ranger I discovered one of the most significant influences in my life from then on: the Encampment for Citizenship.

The Camp Ranger campers came from a variety of families from all over the New York metro area, from the prosperous and well-educated to the poor and near-poor. The father of one of the boys in my tent belonged to a progressive "religious" organization known as the Society for Ethical Culture, and we began chatting when he visited his son. We talked at length about social justice and our shared doubts about traditional religion. I had never heard of Ethical Culture, so he told me all about it. The American Ethical Union was founded by the philosopher Felix Adler in 1876 and was headquartered in Manhattan. Each local affiliate was a fraternity of religious freethinkers and humanists dedicated to personal ethical growth and the furthering of a just and democratic society. Ethical Culture was a nondoctrinaire movement; it did not dwell on ritual or dogma, and social justice activism was central to its practice. I thought, "Wow! This sounds like my kind of religion."

In one of our chats the camper's father told me about the Encampment for Citizenship, an organization created under the sponsorship of the American Ethical Union in 1946. The Encampment was a six-week, multicultural leadership training experience for young people from all over the country and abroad. He saw my keen interest and said that he would send information about it. Upon returning home to Virginia, I received an encouraging note and several brochures about Ethical Culture and the Encampment for Citizenship.

After learning of the Encampment I fixed my sights on getting into one of the sessions at the Fieldston School in the Bronx. For the next twenty months I repeatedly wrote to the Encampment office requesting more information. They were very responsive and, after learning of my financial situation, awarded me a full scholarship for the New York Encampment in the summer of 1957.

Meanwhile, as I was finishing my senior year at RPI, I sought to connect with civil rights activists I heard about on the news. Among those I wrote to express solidarity was Dr. Martin Luther King Jr. Imagine my delight when I received a gracious reply from him, dated May 10, 1957, telling me of his gratitude for the support. Needless to say, I was greatly honored. His response let me feel that I was now part of a larger community in the struggle.

In June, I left for the New York Encampment. As I drove over the George Washington Bridge, New York City presented a dazzling sight. Its gargantuan scale was exhilarating—as was the prospect of finally being in a place where my views on race would be accepted. Arriving at Fieldston late in the afternoon, I pulled up to an imposing gray-stone building reminiscent of the entrance to a European castle, short of the moat and drawbridge. Walking inside I encountered a sloped quadrangle shaded by several old giant oak trees. I loved it instantly and later learned this was to be our outdoor lecture site.

The Fieldston School, a private high school run by the Ethical Culture

Union, relinquished its campus to the Encampment in summer. There were excellent meeting rooms, a swimming pool, an outdoor sports field, and a fine gym, where I got to play basketball, free from the segregation laws of my part of the country. But the hub of Encampment life was an enormous dining hall where I met the other campers and staff. The number of articulate, self-assured, assertive, well-informed, and progressive young people that I met in just the first few minutes was startling. And, what would be shocking to folks back home but was exciting to me, several of them were black. I had never before been in such impressive and vibrant company. I couldn't help wondering how I could have been selected for this. "I'll never measure up to these folks," I thought. "Perhaps they made a mistake."

After supper, we had our initial meeting of about 125 of us campers and a dozen and a half staff members and friends of the Encampment. Bill Shannon, the executive director, welcomed us. Then Algernon Black, the educational director, spoke. I was captivated by the wild snow-white tufts of hair rising from the sides of his mostly bald head, his pipe held steady in the side of his mouth even as he talked, and the perpetual little smile hinting that he was pleased with the commitment in our hearts. He spoke forcefully about the vast spectrum of global and domestic injustices, beautifully about the potential for genuine democracy, and persuasively about our obligation to serve justice. He was a marvel. Each time Al Black spoke during the summer, I imagined myself someday speaking with the authority he had. I later learned that he and several others had founded the Encampment in 1946. In the wake of the racial horrors of World War II, they had asked themselves, in essence: We know what democracy is not, but do we know what democracy is? What are the irreducible principles of democracy, and how do we convey those principles to upcoming generations of young leaders? One way they came up with was the Encampment for Citizenship.

After Al Black's remarks, I sat quietly nursing my sense of inadequacy as we were each asked to stand up and say a little about ourselves. Many of the other campers were so worldly and impressive. When my turn came around, I clumsily shared my aim to be a part of overturning segregation in the South, the loneliness it had led to, and the joy and relief of being among people who shared my ideals.

We then got to the task of organizing our camper government. After some edgy wrangling, which I learned was the way cerebral northerners did such things, we settled on a town meeting format calling for a president and a vice president. We then elected as president a young man named Robert D. Collier. He was an extraordinarily bright, highly animated, amiable, and thoughtful guy, very savvy about politics and human relations. He was a prominent student leader at, I believe, the University of Southern California, and he was black. The campers then turned to the vice-presidential slot. I was stupefied to be nominated but it felt great to be affirmed like that. The selection of the two of us, a black westerner and a white southerner, was a proclamation about our collective sense of purpose for the summer.

The Encampment program was a rich experience for me. I built close relationships with a number of the campers and staff. Among the campers was Eleanor Holmes (later Norton), who went on to become a law professor, chair of the U.S. Equal Employment Opportunity Commission, and later representative of the District of Columbia in the U.S. Congress. Alexander P. Tureaud Jr., the son of Louisiana's distinguished civil rights lawyer A. P. Tureaud from New Orleans, also attended. Over the summer we had guest speakers widely known for their work on peace and justice issues, such as Dr. Kenneth Clark, the social psychologist famous for his expert witness testimony in the 1954 *Brown v. Board of Education* school desegregation case. We also had a visit by Charles Abrams, a prominent leader of efforts to create antidiscrimination laws in New York. We visited the United Nations and heard presentations from Dr. Ralph Bunche, undersecretary for special political affairs, who later came to Fieldston and spent more time with us. We had a picnic lunch with Eleanor Roosevelt on the lawn at her Hyde Park home. Mrs. Roosevelt was a devoted supporter of the Encampment from its founding, enough so that J. Edgar Hoover had it noted in her FBI file that it was a haven for her alleged Communist-sympathizing friends. In one discussion I asked for her view on how we might achieve desegregation in the South and what she expected the reaction to be. She said that change in the South was inevitable and that it was crucial that we southern Encampment youth take up the leadership to shape it. That charge stayed with me.

On July 26, Al Black stood up at lunch and announced, "This afternoon we will have a guest lecturer. I am not sure how much you know about him, but I know that you will remember this day. His name is Dr. Martin Luther King

Jr., and he comes to us from the Montgomery Improvement Association where he and his colleagues led the boycott that desegregated the city buses there." Dr. King spoke to us about nonviolent direct action as their key tactic in overcoming Jim Crow. I spoke briefly with him after his talk and mentioned that we had exchanged letters. Whether or not he truly remembered, he graciously commended me for my involvement. This personal encounter with Dr. King awakened me to the fact that my involvement thus far had been individual, without organizational roots. I had no relationships with the black activist community or their handful of white supporters back home. I had to change that.

Dr. King stayed at Fieldston all afternoon. He stopped for a while at our civil rights workshop where he addressed our concerns about how nonviolent direct action might work in our various hometowns. Before leaving, he praised our commitment.

That civil rights workshop further jolted my race consciousness. Our two workshop staff leaders could not have been better. One was June Shagaloff, with the NAACP Legal Defense Fund. She was the most knowledgeable person I had ever heard on questions of racial discrimination and the tools needed to combat it nationwide. She was a tough-minded, no-nonsense individual with little patience for anyone who was poorly informed about the issues. She demanded that we get acquainted with the minutia of civil rights laws, court decisions, government agencies, and various civil rights organizations. This was second nature to her but daunting to me. It appeared that the pursuit of civil rights justice was June Shagaloff's life; listening to her was exhilarating. It made commitment to racial justice as a life's work even more appealing to me.

The other workshop leader, Dr. James A. Moss, a sociology professor at Queens College, used a more indirect, mellow approach. His knowledge of race relations was also vast, but he introduced the social-psychological nuances of change. His style was gentle, but there was no doubting his commitment. Jim was a wise teacher while June was a determined person of action. I wanted to be like both of them!

The workshop was not always peaches and cream. Although intensely engaged by then, I had almost no up-close experience with blacks who spoke honestly and forthrightly about race. I had never met anyone who in those days might be referred to as a "race man": a black person of either sex who was an avid advocate of black advancement and racial justice. One well-informed and outspoken young black woman in the civil rights workshop turned to me, the only white southerner in the group, and attacked southern bigotry in a manner that clearly implicated me as part of the problem. It felt like she saw me as just another southern white racist. My throat and chest filled with hurt and tears rolled down my cheeks. I thought, "God, I have alienated family and friends by breaking with white supremacy—and now she throws me in with these people!" I jumped up and fled the group for the empty dining hall where I could wrestle privately with my anguish. Over and over I thought, "I don't fit anywhere." That old feeling of isolation overwhelmed the optimism I had been experiencing at the Encampment.

But this was a sustaining community that knew how to make such clashes part of the learning experience. Before the day was over, Jim Moss and some of the campers in my workshop reached out to me with reassurances. I felt better, but also now realized that I was answerable for a society that had privileged me to the exclusion of others—even if I wanted to reject it. I came to understood what happens in dynamics like these—how blacks, even if they meant no personal attack, might need to use a white face to make a point lost on other whites if conveyed in the abstract. It wasn't about me personally, but about the structures that affected us all.

I crossed yet another racial frontier beyond my southern upbringing that summer. I became infatuated with a woman of color, a fellow camper named Juliette Lucille Grey, an elegant and beautiful young woman from an upscale community called Hastings-on-Hudson, north of New York City. A student at Vassar College, Juliette was at once sophisticated and cultured and genuinely caring about the oppressed. I had never known anyone like her, white or black, and I fell for her. We spent time together, even off campus, which at least I thought of as dates.

She once invited me up to her family's mansion where I met her father, a corporate lawyer, whose appearance, bearing, and speech erased any doubt about their social status. I still remember my awkwardness as he and I stood talking over the rush of water cascading down a fountain in their exquisitely appointed foyer. But, alas, it turned out that Juliette had a boyfriend, one of her own social class.

On the last night of the Encampment, we had a final banquet in the dining hall. I was nervous because Robert Collier, our camper president, had left the

Encampment early to meet some student leadership obligations at his university, so I had to replace him as the master of ceremonies and give a closing address. It was expected to be both entertaining and profound. I was terrified. To
make it worse, there would be luminaries in attendance, including Dr. Ralph
Bunche. And one of my favorite RPI professors, who was visiting New York,
was coming too.

I was so unnerved by the audience that nothing I wrote seemed adequate.
Finally, I decided to settle for whatever came naturally. What came was a
grateful testimony about the impact the Encampment had on me, an edito-
rial about our obligations as we headed home, and a comment about the rare
kind of love and idealism we had shared. It was more than a bit schmaltzy, so
I was stunned when the two hundred or so people at the banquet stood and
applauded. To hear that response to my idealism was a startlingly new and
encouraging experience.

The evening was rich with testimonials from others and with folk and social movement music, so much the lifeblood of our experience there. But the
most dramatic moment of the evening was the appearance of Encampment
cofounder Alice K. "Nanny" Pollitzer, who was in her late eighties then. As
she stood to share her message, a stone crashed through the window behind
us, accompanied by screams of "Communists! Filthy nigger-loving Communists!" The rock and shards of the shattered glass hit Pollitzer in the back and
she nearly fell. But she regained her balance and composure and resumed right
where she had left off before the hatemongers' intrusion. Her show of strength
electrified us all. When she was done, there were thunderous cheers. This elderly woman, a veteran of so many decades in human rights struggles, showed
me how to stand one's ground against white supremacy, this time of the "Deep
North" variety.

The next morning, after shedding tears and sharing hugs and kisses and
addresses, we scattered across the globe, each with a transformed soul. My plan
was to drive to my mother's in Jacksonville because I had to face up to the draft
board there. I hardly wanted to go into the military, especially when I was eager
to fight in a more immediate war—the war on Jim Crow—for which I had just
completed boot camp. Yet although there were many pacifists at the Encampment, I still felt that my country deserved service in the armed forces from
its young people. The Korean "police action" was our nation's latest military

adventure. But the model that shaped my thinking then was the fight against Hitler and the Nazis in World War II; it was the most momentous armed struggle against bigotry in my lifetime.

The drive home was long, slow, hot, and humid. I knew I was "home" in the South when I was finally able to buy a Royal Crown Cola and a Moon Pie— and hear open racist remarks during an overnight stop at my aunt and uncle's house in Richmond. The next day I drove on, my head still up at the Encampment but my body back down in Dixie. Near the South Carolina line, I picked up two young hitchhikers in U.S. Air Force uniforms who were sweltering in the tortuous August afternoon sun.

With my 1948 Chevy pushing on, we got acquainted. One was from Danville, Virginia, and the other from Montgomery, Alabama. In but a few miles one of them said, "The dumbass niggers are taking over the military!" With my fuse for racism now shorter than ever, I exploded with a rant taken straight from the dialogues at the Encampment. It was not a judicious response. Before I knew what was happening, the guy in the back seat was reaching over to strangle me while the one in the front seat turned to slug me. These guys were oblivious to the danger they posed to all three of us moving at about fifty miles per hour.

I have no idea how I got that car over to the shoulder and stopped, but once there, the guy in the front seat jumped out and raced around to my side, intending to pull me out where he could get in some freewheeling swings. Fortunately the door was already locked. Somehow I freed myself from the choke hold of the guy in the backseat and got hold of the tire iron on the floor. Blindly, I swung it backhanded. It hit pay dirt, because he let out a yell and scrambled over the folded-down front seat and out onto the ground. Pulling the door shut, I pushed down the lock button and gunned it out of there. In the rear view mirror I watched the two of them, arms flailing, fade into the ribbon of country road with an incredible sense of relief. I then realized that I still had their caps, jackets, and duffle bags. So I stopped a good bit ahead, dumped their gear on the shoulder of US 301, and thought, "Welcome home, Ed."

After I arrived, exhausted, at my mom's house in Jacksonville, it was but a few hours until my stepfather, John Gammon, began going on about "the niggers." John was a brassy working-class Irish-American widower from Boston who came to Florida later in life to find work. There he met and married my divorced mother. She didn't approve of folks using the "n-word," but she did nothing when her husband used it because aggressive males intimidated her.

Of course, my mother and I talked about the Encampment experience. I had never before had a full-blown conversation with her about racial justice. This trip home was the first real opportunity to share the truth about myself. She loathed open conflict, usually choosing silence over it, so I could see how painful it was for her to listen to me about this. I was asking her to reach across the deep chasm between our worlds. I had considered keeping my mouth shut and just pretending. But she and I had never before related in a dishonest way, and I could not imagine a future in which she did not know who I had become. So I felt that I had to be honest with her, whatever the cost. As I unburdened my soul, she listened in quiet resignation. While she was disturbed at me having these alien ideas, I think that her greater emotion was fear—fear for what was to become of me, because she knew what happened to others who "betrayed" the white race. We eventually got around to the topic of interracial dating and the fact that I no longer respected any law or custom that obstructed my marrying anyone I might love. Those words visibly crushed her. But this was 1957. A new world was in the making, and I wanted to be a part of it. After all, she was one of those adults who had uncritically passed on the lies about race. I was going off to the military, and I was determined never again to equivocate about racial justice. This was my declaration of independence from the tyranny of white supremacy with the person who mattered most to me.

She concluded this heart-wrenching exchange by saying something to the effect of, "I guess that it is time for your generation to run this world." It was very sad to hear my parent abdicate, but I heard in her words a small hint of trust in my generation to do better than her own. The saddest consequence of that visit was that for the rest of my mother's life, her devotion to me and later my children notwithstanding, she would never again stay overnight in my house. She always found an alternative place to stay, I am sure because she was fearful of the conversations we might have about race.

At the draft board, I learned that my name was coming up in just a week or two, so I went down to the naval reserve unit where I had been an inactive member for four years and activated myself in order to avoid the army. I assumed that the navy would ship me to some exotic shore offering rich new cultural experiences, while as a draftee in the army I would become an infantry grunt in some remote dust bowl.

A few days before I shipped off to boot camp, some local guys gave me a surprise send-off. North Florida at this time was a notorious hotbed of Ku Klux Klan activity. In my mother's community, you never knew who had a secret life—or what friend or client might have a husband or brother in the Klan. There were also freelance guerrillas who may not have paid dues but did their part to police race relations.

I learned this on a double date to a movie with the daughter of one of my mother's local friends. When the other couple picked my date and me up in the other guy's convertible, they seemed normal enough—except for his breakneck speeding on city streets. We bought our tickets and went inside. The two women went off to the ladies room, so we guys headed for the men's room. At first we were the only two men in the place. While doing our business at the urinals, this guy, out of the blue, began to pitch the Ku Klux Klan to me. He told me about a meeting out in Duval County and insisted that I go with him and join up. I responded with what I thought, and within minutes I found myself in a heap of trouble.

Out of nowhere came two more guys to help show what happens to people who disrespect the Klan. These two young men must have already been in the theater, lending support to my later theory that this was a planned set-up, perhaps because they'd already learned about me from my date. One of them held the door shut so no one else could get into the men's room as the other two pinned me against a wall and proceeded to hammer me with their fists. I tried to resist but was trapped between them, a sink, the wall, and a stall partition. So I doubled up and used my arms to protect myself as best I could. One of the men then kneed me in the groin several times.

Finally, someone forced the door open and came in. The three guys slithered out of the men's room in great haste, leaving me to gather my wits and tend my wounds. I grabbed a few paper towels, wetted them down, and cautiously left the restroom, mopping blood off my face as I hurried out of the theater and got a cab home. I concluded two things from that evening. Number one, that girl was not the one for me. Number two, if I wanted to be a civil rights worker for very long, I had better be a smarter one.

✹ 9 ✹

Some Shipmates Are
More Equal than Others

NCLE SAM INSISTED that my quest for democracy in America would
have to wait. He needed me in his "Power for Peace" military force to
help spread "freedom" across the world. My fantasy that the navy would
give me a billet somewhere like the South Pacific proved to be just that—a
fantasy. In September 1957 I found myself at the Great Lakes Naval Training
Center in northern Illinois for boot camp, and after that I traveled across the
road to Camp Barry for my duty station. My home for the next twenty months
of 1958 and 1959 was the Recruit Evaluation Unit in Building 172. Entering the
authoritarian world of the navy right on the heels of the liberating Encampment experience was jarring.

The REU was a cross between a psychiatric clinic and a garbage disposal.
Our job was to screen new naval recruits for boot camp and kick out those
determined to be misfits of one sort or another. Occasionally, we also had "patients" from among "ship's company"—those already trained and serving on
the base. Because Great Lakes naval base was such an enormous recruit training command, traffic at the REU was very heavy. Building 172 housed a barracks for a hundred or so recruits held over for evaluation and paper processing;
a sick bay; a dental unit; and an office for psychiatrists, psychologists, and the
hospital corpsmen who supported them. I was one of those corpsman.

Vast numbers of new recruits, sometimes as many as eight hundred, arrived
at Great Lakes every night. Many were desperately poor southerners who had
never had any dental care or much medical attention either. So once in the

navy, they had to have many of their teeth extracted. The inpatient dental unit regularly held six or seven seventeen- and eighteen-year-olds, tossing about on blood-soaked pillows and groaning with pain from swollen jaws from which half of their teeth had been pulled. Many of these teen recruits were also functionally if not totally illiterate.

From what I saw, the two largest single categories of recruits we processed for discharge from the navy were homosexuals and epileptics. The policy regarding homosexuality then was apparently, "If we find out, you're out of here." It was much the same for the epileptics.

My day job was as a research assistant for a frumpish, highly focused civilian psychologist by the name of John Plag. He was working on a gargantuan study that sought to identify the few best predictors of successful performance in recruit training by statistically distilling them from a three-hundred-item questionnaire. He had me administer the questionnaire to each night's recruit receipts, ultimately to some twenty-two thousand aspiring sailors. Plag taught me a lot about research.

My evening job was playing assistant coach to the base's varsity basketball team, the Great Lakes Naval Center Bluejackets. With the pick of over forty-five thousand sailors and marines on the base, we had an odd assortment of excellent college, high school, and playground players. In our more than seventy-five games that season, I was able to compete against top-notch multiracial talent all over the Midwest. At Fort Leonard Wood, Missouri, I went head to head with K. C. Jones, later with the Boston Celtics. Several other All-Americans from the Big Ten and a couple of guys from the Harlem Globetrotters also played in that tournament.

At the REU we corpsmen worked long hours, sometimes at a frenzied pace. Other times there was mind-numbing boredom from idleness. There were a lot of smart guys there for whom navy life was a real drag. The countless bureaucratic fetishes and orders that made no sense; the reduction of nearly all conversation to four letter words; the prevalence of drug, alcohol, and tobacco abuse; and the aggression and anger among so many sailors and marines on the base were among the things that gnawed at us.

Despite all this, there was something enriching and comforting about the REU: the comradery with my "shipmates." It was a little like the Encampment that way—except we were all male. There was Killian, a reserved and handsome black guy from Chicago; Jose, a sweet-tempered Mexican-American from El Paso; Cooley, a tall white fellow with a razor-sharp sense of humor and graduate training in psychology; and Tommy Holland, a volatile black jazz flute player. And there was T. J. Donovan, a hidebound Boston Irish-American who eventually joined in the odd little family we corpsmen created. Finally, there was Allison Cyrus, whom we called "Stick and Stache" because he was pencil-thin and had a mustache. He was a meditative and gentle man from Pittsburgh who on his lunch break would curl up on top of a row of file cabinets and fall fast asleep. When Cyrus first arrived he attained a perfect score on the navy's IQ-like test and subsequently was charged with cheating—because the navy "knew" that no black man could be that smart. Forced to take another version of the test, he again scored at the very top.

This occurred nearly a decade after President Harry Truman's order to desegregate the military. I thought at the time that much of the racism I saw in the navy resulted from the paucity of black officers and senior noncommissioned officers who could have brought minority sensibilities to bear on our lives on the base. I often witnessed racist incidents in which that could have made a world of difference.

One such episode involved Tommy Holland. Tommy was officially a third-class hospitalman. We knew him as a gifted musician and the bright light in any gathering. He had an acerbic wit and was known, like all of us short-timers, as a "malcontent." I witnessed many incidents in which white officers, especially young ones, found plainspoken African Americans like Tommy threatening. But I never saw Tommy willfully disobey an order or disrespect any person of higher rank in any manner that was not tolerated from white sailors. There was a small margin of grumbling allowed among the troops to keep us ventilated. But when African Americans bellyached, the tolerance would wane. One morning I arrived for work at the REU at the usual 0700 and learned that Tommy had disappeared. Speculation soared: "Holland has gone AWOL," "He's taken off to go home to St. Louis," or, "Maybe he went out to the strip in North Chicago and is just late coming back from his liberty." But he never showed up, all day long. I worried because he was looking forward to getting out of the navy in but a few months, and an AWOL charge would wreck his plan.

Since we had so little liberty, only one weekend a month, and my home was so far away, I had once gone home with Tommy to St. Louis. It was close enough to get there and back over a weekend. I spent much of my time there in the company of his mother, Gladys Brown, and we became friends. She might have believed that as a college grad I would be a good influence on her son. As the days of Holland's absence stretched into a couple of weeks, his mother contacted us at the REU. She told us that his usual and frequent contact with her had stopped. This sent panic though our unit. Discussion among the corpsmen led to a joint decision to ask Lt. Commander Flaherty to try to locate Tommy for us. If he was still alive, and our calls to local police suggested that he was, then there was only one other place he could be: the Great Lakes brig.

Flaherty confirmed for us that Holland was indeed locked up and told us how he got there. Years later I heard the story confirmed by Tommy: when he and two of his friends returned to the barracks early in the morning from liberty, the shore patrol suddenly showed up, arrested the three men, and hauled them off to the brig. The pretense was that they had in the past possessed marijuana, although they did not have any on them or in their lockers this particular night. All three were sequestered in the brig without formal charges and without informing any of their loved ones. Flaherty hinted that Holland's irreverent demeanor was a habitual irritant to a couple of white chief petty officers and a junior officer or two who cooked up this charge to get Tommy put away for a while.

As two months passed, Tommy had not even been given a trial; that is, a military court martial. So I got back to Mrs. Brown with what we had learned and recommended, as did several of her friends, that she contact the St. Louis NAACP or her congressman for help. I felt a responsibility to do more, but what could a swab at the bottom of the navy heap do to help? I decided to call the NAACP and the ACLU in Chicago myself to see what pressure they would bring to bear on the base command to get Tommy out of the brig. Then it occurred to me that creating pressure on the inside of the base might also help. I got the idea of staging the calls on the hall payphone and speaking loudly enough to be overheard by our officers. But then what if the phone conversations didn't yield the message I wanted our officers, especially Flaherty and Commander Schwenker, head of the REU, to hear? I couldn't afford to allow the people on the other end of the phone to dictate the script, so I prepared my own. After all, our officers already saw me as a nautical version of a "jailhouse lawyer." My reputation as a troublemaker had grown a few months before, thanks to a letter to the editor I wrote criticizing the navy, which was published in *Look* magazine right under a similar one from Adlai Stevenson. Maybe one of the officers might intervene with the base commander for Tommy to avoid embarrassing publicity for the navy.

So on the appointed day when I knew that all the key people were in hearing distance, I went to the pay phone and made my faux call to the Chicago NAACP. After telling the phantom NAACP lawyer the full story about Tommy Holland, I asked what the NAACP intended to do. I thanked him loudly for the "plan to start an investigation of the treatment of blacks at the Great Lakes naval base," and then pretended to hang up before placing another "call" to the ACLU. Again I repeated loudly a sham promise to "look into the racial practices at Great Lakes." I even added a little caveat, repeating out loud their "warning" that "members of the military were not governed by the same laws as civilians." I thought that would make it sound more realistic.

After "hanging up," I walked around the corner to the main office and acted startled to see several of the doctors, Lt. Commander Flaherty, and most of my corpsmen pals staring at me. Commander Schwenker's door was partially open, and I could see his feet under his desk. "Oops," I said. The message had reached everyone it needed to.

Within a week or so, after six months in the brig, Tommy finally got a court martial that exonerated him. He was released back to our unit. Who knows what really caused the navy's change of course. Did the NAACP in St. Louis or a congressman get to the base commander? Did word about my "calls" have the desired effect? Or was his release just a coincidence? I don't know the answer, but Mrs. Brown seemed to think I had helped and that was enough for me. Tommy and I don't write or call nearly enough, but Gladys Brown sends me a Christmas card almost every year—for more than fifty years now.

I had entered the navy in the fall of 1957 as a progressive on most issues of the time. However, I was still something of a hawk when it came to military matters, believing force necessary to deal with the bad guys in the world. As a patriot with a capital *P*, I felt obliged to serve. But witnessing so much waste, corruption, substance abuse, racism, and wanton disregard for the needs of the enlisted ranks eroded my naive faith in the military. I learned that we had damn well better keep it under civilian control and use it sparingly, only when there are direct threats to our shores. My tour of duty in the navy didn't make me a full-fledged pacifist, but it came close. The day I was finally discharged I put my uniforms in a pile in the street as my pals looked on, doused them with alcohol, and set a match to them. I waved to my friends with a big grin and my fist flung high, jumped into my old Pontiac and headed for the main gate, honking my horn until my shipmates and the flames disappeared from my rearview mirror.

The Peeples family about 1945, including younger brother Stephen (*far left*) and dog Skeeter.

Peeples's father ran a grocery store in the mid-forties on the first floor of this Southside Richmond building. As he drank more, he stayed in back and slept while in front Ed served customers, mostly tobacco workers from a nearby factory.

Playing for the RPI Green Devils in 1956, Peeples (number 32) lands a left-handed hook shot. As co-captain the next year, he helped lead the team to the school's first winning season, earning a basketball reputation that helped in "hand-to-hand combat" with Jim Crow. (Special Collections and Archives, James Branch Cabell Library, VCU Libraries)

Dr. Alice Davis, a professor of sociology at Richmond Professional Institute, who challenged her students to think critically about white supremacy and other social injustices. She was viewed as "subversive" by the FBI, which monitored her activities. (Special Collections and Archives, James Branch Cabell Library, VCU Libraries)

Rev. Edward Meeks "Pope" Gregory, vicar of St. Peter's Episcopal Church and an outspoken human rights activist for over thirty years. In 1978, the year of this photo, Reverend Gregory conducted a "celebration of union" for two of his gay parishioners at St. Peter's and called for a city human rights ordinance to bar sexual orientation discrimination. (Special Collections and Archives, James Branch Cabell Library, VCU Libraries. Photo by Bob Swisher)

Acting out the state's official policy of massive resistance, officials in Prince Edward County, Virginia, completely shut down the public school system for five years, beginning in September of 1959, to prevent desegregation. This sign went up on the padlocked black high school. (Special Collections and Archives, James Branch Cabell Library, VCU Libraries. Photo by Edward H. Peeples)

This photo, taken by Peeples in about 1961, shows the conditions that prevailed in about three-quarters of Prince Edward's Jim Crow black schools at the time of the shutdowns. Moved by solidarity with the students and their families, Peeples and his friends became more committed civil rights activists. (Special Collections and Archives, James Branch Cabell Library, VCU Libraries. Photo by Edward H. Peeples)

The Kentucky Encampment for Citizenship staff jokingly threatened to drive a stake through Peeples, the project director, to punish him for the harassment, bomb threats, and beatings they and student participants suffered while trying to bring interracial, participatory democracy to a community in southeastern Kentucky in 1966. (Special Collections and Archives, James Branch Cabell Library, VCU Libraries)

Vincent Wright, ca. 1969, when Peeples recruited him to become assistant dean of students at Virginia Commonwealth University. The two desegregated several Richmond apartment complexes, launched the school's Afro-American Studies program with some other faculty, and became lifelong close friends. (Photo by Duncan Brogan)

Hasib and Emma Muqsit, participants in the Family Life Program that Peeples helped create with a group of Black Muslim inmates in Virginia State Penitentiary in the 1970s. The program was designed to keep families together while members were incarcerated. A leader in the group, Hasib now runs an adult care facility for seniors. Another participant, Evans D. Hopkins, later wrote a memoir, *Life after Life: A Story of Rage and Redemption,* and founded a program to keep other young African Americans from prison.

A typical Thanksgiving gathering of family and friends at the Peepleses' Richmond home, this one in 1975. *From top left:* Vincent Wright, Shelly Habeck, Ernest Moore, Mary Adamson, Ed Peeples, Neisha Wright, Suzy Peeples, Randall Wright, Toby Wright, Cecily Peeples, Katy Peeples, and James Elam. The annual get-togethers, which persisted for over twenty years, maintained a special open invitation to divorced fathers, their children, and unattached friends, often attracting much larger numbers than seen here.

When someone abandoned a television set on the sidewalk across from the Peeples home in the Fan District in the mid-1980s, Ed seized the opportunity for a visual pun and persuaded his teenage daughter, Cecily, to get the shot.

Virginia Commonwealth University
Professor Appears on Local TV

Ruby Clayton Walker and Peeples at the Moton Museum in Farmville on September 1, 1996, for a celebration of the reissuing of R. C. Smith's book *They Closed Their Schools*. Having become friends on the job as social workers in the late fifties, Walker and Peeples participated in many human rights efforts together over the years. (Special Collections and Archives, James Branch Cabell Library, VCU Libraries)

In 1987, Peeples remarried to Karen Wawrzyn, an occupational therapist. Nine years later, they adopted a daughter, Camille, from Vietnam, and shared their joy with readers of the *Richmond Times-Dispatch,* which ran this photo. (Courtesy *Richmond Times-Dispatch*)

Peeples's three adult daughters enjoying a gathering at Katy's home in 1993. *Left to right:* Katy, Suzy, and Cecily.

In his later years, Peeples discovered that another person in his family tree had been branded a "traitor to the race" by white supremacists. Dr. William Henry Brisbane renounced slavery in the 1830s, gave up his South Carolina plantation, and became an abolitionist agitator. Brisbane (*center,* pictured with abolitionist leaders Edward Harwood and Levi Coffin) wrote pamphlets and traveled the country speaking against slavery. He urged that abolitionist strategy should include driving a wedge between poor whites and planters. (Courtesy Wisconsin Historical Society)

Ed credits his children, friends, and comrades with sustaining his spirit over more than fifty years of activism for social justice. Many of those supporters gathered to celebrate his seventieth birthday in 2005, when this photo was taken.

PART THREE

Battling the Hydra

✳ IO ✳

Reconnecting with the Struggle
on the Home Front

BACK IN RICHMOND after my discharge in September of 1959, I longed
to meet other committed people and get into the justice struggle. My un-
willingness to hide my liberal racial and religious views made it difficult
to find work as a teacher and coach. But I finally landed a job as a caseworker
with the city Social Service Bureau, an agency desperate for anyone with a
college degree. This was the unit of the Department of Welfare responsible
for investigating eligibility and administering public assistance grants for the
elderly, the disabled, families with dependent children, and those who qualified for emergency financial assistance. Because the agency was so hard up for
caseworkers, it became one of the few decent opportunities open to college-
trained blacks in our segregated commonwealth. There were some fifty-five
or so caseworkers in the agency and close to half of them were black. This was
my good fortune because I got to meet people who became comrades in the
struggle and lifelong friends.

While there had been a few breakthroughs, old racial ways continued to
grip the city of Richmond. Most whites still held fierce pride in the city's Civil
War shrines like the White House of the Confederacy and rituals like the
Civil War commemorative parades held on Monument Avenue, which was
lined with statues of Virginia's Confederate generals. Much of that old Virginia thinking persisted even in the SSB. I realized how psychologically close
we still were to the Civil War every time I had to go out to conduct a financial
review at the nursing home of Virginia's United Daughters of the Confederacy.

I was expected to confirm that each elderly lady there continued to receive her $14 Confederate pension and then deduct it from the federal old-age assistance grant she received through the city.

More revealing of the absurd world we lived in was the telephone line conduit running along the floor across the large office I shared with some twenty other caseworkers. It was commandeered by the managers to serve as a racial "fence." The desks for the black social workers sat largely on one side, those for whites on the other. While it was less than three-quarters of an inch off the floor, its social-psychological height reached to the ceiling. Without ever referencing it, most of our white supervisors made it clear that permission to cross it required something akin to a passport.

The egalitarian ideals associated with the profession of social work notwithstanding, white supremacy abounded in our daily tasks. White clients were required to have only white caseworkers, but black clients could have either white or black caseworkers. There were only a couple of black supervisors, so most black caseworkers had white supervisors, but no white caseworker could have a black supervisor. Many other equally twisted Jim Crow laws and customs governed us. Until about 1960 a Whites Only sign hung on the door of the staff women's restroom. Only after my spirited friend Hilda Warden led some of the caseworkers in a month of open defiance of the rule did the agency officials open the restroom to everyone.

Some of the blacks had master of social work degrees or other related professional training, yet only one of the white caseworkers had any prior social work training or experience. I had a degree in physical education, which wasn't much help. Most of the white caseworkers were young women with degrees in subjects like home economics and art history. For many this was their first full-time job, as it was for me and one of the other two white men. Several of the white supervisors were older "southern ladies." Mine in particular was a vivid example of the classic Virginia matron.

It took only a few weeks on the job to see that I had less in common with the whites than I did with the black caseworkers, especially with a new graduate from Virginia Union University, Ruby Clayton. She was idealistic, committed to the freedom struggle, and resolute in her convictions. Often we "scaled" the imaginary fence to talk to each other, especially as we got involved in civil rights actions together. My friendships with Ruby and other blacks in the agency did not escape the attention of my supervisor. She claimed that I was spending too much time speaking with black women and insisted that I spend equal time with the young white women. It was like she was running a dating service rather than a social service agency.

ANOTHER PLACE TO MEET activists and forge alliances at the end of the fifties and the opening of the sixties was Richmond's Village Cafe. Located on a busy commercial street near RPI and the residential area known as the Fan District, it attracted a lively circle of artists, writers, intellectuals, progressive politicos, and white civil rights activists like me.

One of the regulars, a commercial art professor at RPI, was alleged by the FBI to be a member of the local Communist Party (which had perhaps a half-dozen members at most). Two agents came to see me at work and grilled me about him; they even asked me to spy on him. I declined, but with some concern that I might become their target. For a good year thereafter, FBI agents parked in front of the professor's house and strolled about the street. They were easy to recognize in their uniform of black suits, fedoras, and white socks.

I dropped in at the Village a couple of times a week. Among others who frequented the Village was the future novelist Tom Robbins, once a student at RPI but by then working for the *Richmond Times-Dispatch*. Whenever he, I, and our friends sat together to eat or have a beer, the conversation was filled with the sardonic wit for which he soon became nationally famous. I suspect that some of the imagery of his books was inspired by the zany crowd at the Village.

Notwithstanding the cluster of progressives at the Village, racist attitudes held sway in the neighborhood. Segregationists ran the local and state government and protected their own. More importantly, racists could count on the police to enforce their will. The Village also drew a number of college-educated white-supremacist ideologues who came to argue their case for segregation and strut their imagined intellectual superiority before us. They sported the official University of Virginia uniform: blue blazer, khaki slacks, cotton button-down shirts, narrow striped ties, and penny loafers. Promoting pseudoscientific racist ideas, they especially honored James Jackson Kilpatrick, the editor of the *Richmond News Leader* who had incited massive resistance to *Brown*, as their mentor and inspiration.

They were quick to advertise themselves as learned and literary in the mold of conservatives like Kilpatrick, Russell Kirk, William F. Buckley, and other elitist writers who were building the "new" conservative movement. They made a big fuss over IQ scores; the incomparable virtue of classical literature; the nobility of Virginia aristocrats; the genius of Ayn Rand; social Darwinism and eugenics; the righteousness of the War between the States; and the threat to Western civilization if we were to allow "racial amalgamation."

Two guys who epitomized this archetype at the Village, William Stephenson and Lacy Jeffreys, apparently mistook my pink skin, local accent, and Southside Virginia surname as a sign that I was one of them. They were particularly taken and friendly with the internationally connected white supremacist Earnest Sevier Cox, who also lived in our neighborhood. So on a couple of occasions they invited me to their homes for "discussions" about the "noble work" of Cox and Kilpatrick. I readily accepted because I wanted to learn what they were up to. I posed as a passive sponge for their message and asked lots of questions; they were so smug and self-absorbed that they never got my purpose for being there. Spending that time with them was good training for getting into the heads of racist ideologues in my later work.

THE DAWN OF THE SIXTIES in Richmond was another turning point for me. I had a college degree, was done with my military service obligation, and could count on a full-time, year-round civilian job. But trying to make a living and also remain true to my convictions was getting harder. I was moving more and more into the civil rights activist orbit and becoming better attuned to the aspirations of blacks, yet I still inhabited a white world where many had not a clue. It was an awkward fit, to say the least.

I felt an obligation to challenge even the smallest racist remark or stunt. I hated feeling complicit in that honor-among-thieves culture in which whites assumed that because you were white you must be racist like them. But my conspicuous antics annoyed a good share of whites around me, including a few who held pieces of my future in their hands. Their responses varied from low-level social control like ignoring or shunning me; to mid-level tactics like threatening my job, my credit, or my housing; to more menacing ones like intimidating gestures or violent assault. The worst thing, though, was the uncertainty: encounters where you couldn't always tell who was a racist time bomb and who wasn't—like that Florida blind date from hell. It was clear that if I was going to take on the cherished institution of segregation, then I should expect some kind of retaliation from those devoted to it.

My rising militancy also affected my relations with my family and their friends. Steeped in a lifetime of segregation, they found it hard to see my actions as anything but traitorous—to our race, to our country, to God and nature. But most importantly, I "betrayed" their good name in the community. Thus estranged from my family, I felt a terrible sense of loss—even as I would have felt worse if I were untrue to myself. We became separated in such a profound way that there was no longer a connection between my new life and the world of "my people," as southerners like to say. The wall between our two contending perceptions of racial reality was impenetrable.

But the alienation came as much from me as from them. When I sensed uneasiness, I usually responded by pulling away so as not to hurt them, especially with my mother and her sisters. I saw but two choices: keep quiet and deny my true self or engage in unending and deeply hurtful verbal battles. I eventually learned to make my convictions clear whenever racial matters came up while trying hard to keep my comments short, to the point, and containing as little emotive content as I could manage. The result was an emotional standoff, an inclination to avoid the subject—or each other. The estrangement felt all the weirder because our family on my mother's side was big and warm-hearted. They and their friends had always smothered my brother and me with affection and caring when we were young. The lessening of their tenderness and trust in me felt like punishment, the harshest betrayal of love I could imagine. The only good thing, in retrospect, was that they didn't know the half of my involvement in the radicalism they feared.

We still occasionally spoke on the phone when necessary, exchanged customary greeting cards, and continued the core family rituals, but with a stiffness I had never known. Family visits and holidays together became rare. It was mainly "mandatory attendance" events like funerals that brought us together. The greatest heartache of all came after I had children and my mother still avoided staying overnight with us for fear of the race issue arising.

I later learned that I was not the only one who experienced conflict with family over civil rights involvement in this era. Even some of my black peers in the movement felt disapproval for their activism, in their cases because their parents and other elders feared that challenging segregation could back-fire and further harm them and the entire black community. But at least the blacks—young or old, conservative or rebellious—shared a common unifying experience from which a dialogue could begin: they all faced racial discrimina-tion. White activists had no such firm ground on which to begin conversation with family or other whites who mattered to them. The distance between us was vast.

✳ II ✳

Sit-ins Come to the Old Capitol
of the Confederacy

WHEN I WENT to work at the city welfare department, I had only undertaken small personal acts against segregation. But by 1960 many of my new Richmond friends and I were looking to widen our involvement in the fight for civil rights. Our generation of activists was determined to take the battle for equality beyond the courts to direct action. In Richmond segregated restaurants and the racist practices of retail stores became our targets. The civil rights movement in other parts of the South had fueled our confidence; segregation finally seemed vulnerable.

Having followed the news of the sit-ins in Greensboro, North Carolina, that began two weeks earlier, I awoke on Saturday, February 20, 1960, with a sense that something very big was about to unfold. I called three of my white friends who lived nearby and learned that they shared my inkling that we must go downtown. The four of us scurried to the Broad Street retail district. Virginia Union University students had already conducted sit-ins at the lunch counters at three variety stores: Murphy's, F. W. Woolworth's, and Grant's, which by the time we arrived had all been closed. So the Union students had moved on to Thalhimers, one of Richmond's two preeminent department stores. Here they attempted to sit-in at each of the store's four eateries. My friends and I caught up with the students at noon at the entrance to the Richmond Room on the fourth floor. There were about thirty-five of them, all well dressed, standing silently alongside an aisle leading to an escalator and then on to the dining room. The restaurant entrance was blocked off with a rope. Beyond the rope in the restaurant anteroom stood several white male store officials, one of whom had attended college with me. The officials moved about nervously, sometimes sharing whispers behind their cupped hands. One tall man in a dark suit paced back and forth, up and down, the wrinkles growing deeper on his forehead by the minute. His curly, perfectly parted gray-streaked hair made clear that he was the executive there to represent the Thalhimers "policy." Years later I learned that this man was Newman B. Hamblett, the vice president and operating manager of Thalhimers.

At first, my three friends and I watched from amidst the gathering crowd of antagonistic, disbelieving white onlookers stretching out nearby on the fourth floor. As these tense moments wore on, each of us wrestled with what we would face were we to join the students. The consequences for the other three would have been so serious that they eventually decided they must leave the store. Two were in the army and might have faced double jeopardy, time in both city and military jails. Despite the anxiety, I decided that I had no choice. I left the white crowd and took my place with the black protestors along the aisle. I knew none of them personally and none of them knew me. Yet I felt an intense familiarity, as if we were all part of some great collective consciousness beyond ourselves.

The young people stood silent, their faces expressionless, many holding books. I could sense their longing for an end to Jim Crow on this day and in this place and their determination to see it through. Their inner quietude swept over me. Never had I seen in black people the kind of radiance I saw this day. While intellectually I had known for years that the system was terribly wrong, only now did I feel the full power of the black desire for freedom. I yearned to show my solidarity with their struggle.

It felt like a new day in Virginia: these young people believed they could win and were committed to peaceful means to overthrow this monster of segregation. Not one made a move that could have been interpreted as aggression. They just stood, prayerfully still. The only sound was an occasional "clear the aisles, please," spoken softly by the two student leaders as they periodically patrolled up and down the line of protestors. This struck me as remarkable. In the midst of a pitched battle against those who imposed a cruel and irrational system of racial segregation, still they maintained respect for the fire code.

One of the leaders was a handsome young man with a warm smile, Charles

Sherrod from Petersburg. A divinity student at Virginia Union at the time, he later was a leading light in the Albany, Georgia, civil rights movement. The other was a shorter fellow with a stern face but a gentle voice. I was to learn that he was Frank Pinkston, also a Union divinity student. He later became a heroic civil rights leader in his hometown of Ocala, Florida.

As the white crowd increased it grew restive. I saw a couple of familiar faces, and I heard two male voices call out racist epithets. But most of the crowd appeared to be frozen in amazement at the nerve of these unwelcome black people coming in and disrupting the good order of "their" department store. Once or twice individuals caught my eye with the visual daggers reserved for traitors to their race. My gaze was then drawn to an old woman whom I recalled from my childhood in south Richmond in the forties. Her face was taut, and I could see curses forming on her lips as she peered straight into my eyes. With no warning, she marched up the aisle and spat in my face. Startled, the heat of humiliation sweeping over me, I pulled out a handkerchief and mopped my cheeks. My heart cried out, "Don't you people understand?" But my mind answered, "No, they are slaves to 'our way of life.'"

Every so often one of the student leaders would ceremoniously approach the rope barrier with a request to be admitted to the restaurant. In each instance, Hamblett would scowl and shake his head no. After some time, he unhooked the rope and started down the walkway formed by the students. I couldn't tell where he was going, but one young woman was standing less than a foot out from the group in his path. As he walked by, he bumped her slightly. Upon feeling her impact, he swung around and glared into her face, perhaps thinking she had struck him on purpose. He leaned forward as if about to retaliate, with fists clenched at his sides and lips tensely pressed together. Her lower lip curled down and I could see that she was about to explode, but Sherrod stepped up and took her hand. The indignant look on her face changed into a tiny smile as she and Sherrod stepped back together into the group of students and the face-off melted away.

Before long two Fire Bureau officers arrived. They walked around quietly for the most part, but occasionally they stopped in front of demonstrators and belted out, "Clear the aisle!," in the haughty tone often used by white authority figures when they addressed blacks. To me it felt more like harassment than an effort to maintain public safety.

Captivated by the peaceful imperative of the protestors, I stood fast with them in silent revolt. But I wondered: "Is this worth it? What are we accomplishing? What if we are arrested? Will I lose my job and have to leave Richmond? What about my family? They'll be so hurt. Such a simple act: to stand quietly in behalf of the fundamental American principle of equality. Why should that act, so obviously justified, bring hatred and not praise?" For what seemed like hours, I remained bearing moral witness with the students, all the while burning with the rebuke from "my people."

Then I noticed Hamblett pointing at me and saying something to a police captain. The officer, Hamblett, another policeman, and several other men walked the few steps over to me.

The captain demanded, "Where are you from, New York?" (New York was then shorthand for all the places "Yankees" came from.)

"No," I said.

"Then where are you from?" he demanded again.

"Richmond."

"Where do you live?"

"The West End."

"Are you a student?"

"No, I am a city employee."

Surprised, he asked, "In what department?"

"Welfare," I responded.

He paused, seemingly baffled. I assumed it was because he couldn't imagine a white Richmonder doing such an outrageous thing. Recovering, he asked my name. I told him. He said, "You are going to be escorted from the store."

Hamblett then commanded, "Leave the store!" With that, two large men in plain clothes each took one of my arms and half lifted, half dragged me onto the escalator as the contemptuous white onlookers starred. As we reached the floor below, the two men gave me a shove and I stumbled to my knees. They grasped my arms again and herded me to the next escalator, and then the next, until we reached the first floor, where they jostled me out onto the sidewalk. One of the men shouted, "Don't you ever come back here."

I walked hastily home to my apartment, keenly aware that I had crossed a threshold of no return. I was twenty-four years old, and it was the greatest number of hostile whites I had ever faced at one time. Because of my choice to stand shoulder-to-shoulder with my black peers in open defiance of white supremacy, I was now forever what such whites thought of as a traitor to the race.

No arrests occurred at the Saturday demonstration, but the next Monday the Virginia Union students returned for a second lunch counter sit-in and several dozen were arrested. There followed months of picketing organized by the local NAACP. Ruby Clayton and I were among the many who spent some lunch breaks on the picket line as Thalhimers held fast to its racist policies. We were demonstrating not only against the segregation at Thalhimers's restaurants, but also against the store's employment discrimination and practice of prohibiting black customers from trying on shoes, hats, and clothes before purchasing them, as whites could. At one of these demonstrations *Life* magazine snapped the famous photo of the petite and elderly Mrs. Ruth Tinsley, an NAACP stalwart, being dragged across Broad Street by two Richmond policemen with a German shepherd. Civil rights advocates got a lot of national moral leverage for the Richmond movement from that image.

AFTER THE FEBRUARY SIT-INS, the local NAACP chapter and the biracial Virginia Council on Human Relations attracted some new popular support. Publicity about the sit-ins also stiffened the segregationists' opposition. Many of us who had been working for racial justice only on our little personal battlefields were now finding homes in these organizations. At this point I began to invest my energy in our local chapter of the VCHR, the Richmond Council on Human Relations. But what attracted me scared some elders. As the picket lines and restaurant sit-ins became more frequent in Virginia, some of the older white male leaders in the VCHR expressed disapproval of direct action in the name of the organization. They were stuck back in the mid-fifties when public demonstrations would have been certain suicide for the VCHR.

Now there was an emerging generation of twenty-somethings, black and white, who saw a need for head-on confrontation. But we were too new to the organization to successfully press this agenda on the older leadership. We had no money and no standing and were still a bit naive about the raw power of the segregationist decision makers. We did have one thing going for us though. We were young enough not to have been paralyzed by the fatalism born from a long lifetime of witnessing seemingly intractable segregation.

The young people felt that these older leaders failed to see that times had already changed: direct action had achieved a legitimacy and moral gravitas that commanded deployment. The leaders resisted, countering that the most desirable change would be accomplished through education and persuasion. We thought that was inadequate, that education and persuasion alone meant capitulation.

This led to a modest generational rift in the VCHR. One heated debate took place at an annual board meeting of the statewide council. Several of us had attended with the purpose of petitioning the board to add a direct action provision to our charter. The dialogue was not particularly pretty, and the elders won. The youth caucus came out of the meetings saying that it was time to do what Martin Luther King had done in Alabama and the students had done in Greensboro. If the VCHR wouldn't authorize such action, we would just do it on our own. And so we did.

We joined NAACP public demonstrations and organized our own. From this activity grew an informal cadre that attempted to systematically desegregate the more than six hundred white eating establishments in the Richmond area, one by one. Two to three nights a week for over a year, I joined a biracial band of five to ten foot soldiers to try to get into one restaurant or another. Often we were refused. Sometimes we pushed our way in and the restaurateur called the police to drag us out. Some folks were arrested at some sites; I never was. A few restaurants conceded to us, and we encouraged all in our network to reward them with our patronage.

The financial burden of this restaurant desegregation campaign was not easy for young people to bear. My meager salary as a city caseworker didn't allow for much eating out. So more often than not, on occasions when we were served, I just ordered a bowl of soup or a cup of coffee. The composition of the various sit-in teams fascinated me. There were several prominent black leaders such as Jay Nickens, president of the black Consolidated Bank; Doug Wilder, a promising young lawyer who in 1990 would become the first black elected governor of a U.S. state; and several highly respected older black clergy. Occasionally older white clergyman such as the Reverend Edward Meeks Gregory joined us. We all referred affectionately to him as "Pope Gregory." Pope was a scion of the First Families of Virginia, a loosely applied tag given to Virginia's prominent families of the seventeenth century. He had a distinct upper-class east Virginia accent and at first was the curate at St. Mark's Episcopal Church.

But because of his perpetual witness in behalf of justice, he eventually lost his position at St. Marks and the usual privileges accorded to Episcopalian priests by the Virginia plutocracy. Pope was there for us on many occasions, as a flesh and blood exemplar of the Christ I had never found in my churches.

One of the first places where I joined a sit-in team was the Joy Garden Restaurant on Broad Street, Richmond's main east-west thoroughfare. It was the most popular of the few local Chinese restaurants at the time and was frequented by elites in the city, with whom the owner had personal relationships. On this occasion, we stood around the front door waiting for all of our sit-in team to arrive. You could see that our mixed-race gathering was alarming the owner and his staff. He must have called the cops, because before we even entered several officers showed up and asked us what we were up to. We said we were about to go to dinner. The police ordered us to clear the sidewalk and then attempted to herd us away from the door. But as a pack we managed to elude their corralling motion with a lateral move right through the door into the restaurant. The owner was apparently stunned to suddenly be surrounded by about eight men, three of us white and the others black, all dressed with ties. The cops, too, must have been bamboozled because it took them a moment to recover and come inside. Someone in our group asked for a table.

At that, the owner, his face twisted in frustration, turned to the police and asked them to get us out of there. The cops wasted little time in moving us, this time successfully. They began pushing us together toward the door, grabbing us by the collars if our pace was too slow. My mind darted back to a film I had recently seen of Nazi soldiers herding Jews toward a cattle car. Back out on the sidewalk the police commanded us to disperse, and we did. We had learned that the Joy Garden owner, despite the fact that his people had also experienced racial scorn from whites, had laid his bets with them.

On a few of our restaurant visits, we were confronted with a "welcoming committee" composed of a few bulging white men with baseball bats. Some of our teams had been assailed by such gangs. But no one ever personally attacked me other than to push, shove, or swing at me. While the threat of violence was often on our minds on these forays, the hardest part for me was to face people who were once schoolmates, neighbors, or friends of my family. In a couple of instances, individuals I knew taunted me by name and threatened to "settle the score" later.

At the time I could not figure out why we were not arrested. But later I heard talk that police authorities were under order to keep the reports of protests out of the public eye, so they refrained from making arrests whenever they could. The genteel image of Virginia should never be besmirched by news of blacks' dissatisfaction with their inequitable treatment in the commonwealth.

MY SMALL CIRCLE OF activist friends also organized impromptu political education, collaring people for debates and challenges on street corners and in Monroe Park, confronting authority figures at public events, and doing whatever else we could when there was an opportunity. We papered the RPI campus and selected neighborhoods with progressive posters, handbills, and literature. One of the guys I worked closely with was an edgy New Yorker named Dick Kollin who was in Richmond serving in the U.S. Army on an intelligence assignment. Dick was one of the most savvy social change organizers we had, but he was always walking a fine line between his off-duty life and the army.

For about a year or more Dick and I put out an "underground" news sheet we called the *Ghost.* Like most such ephemera then, it was mimeographed and hand-circulated, with copies left in dozens of key locations in the RPI neighborhood and beyond. It got attention and even stimulated a couple of competitors. We included critical pieces on such issues as the suffocating rules applied only to women students at RPI, the Sunday blue laws, and the outrages of racial discrimination in public accommodations. Some issues hammered at the local police for their use of dogs against black demonstrators. We called them "brownshirts," because of their brown uniforms and brutal tactics. We also printed a sprinkling of reviews of films, books, and classical music; a cultural calendar; and announcements of progressive meetings. Tom Robbins wrote a couple of pieces of satire about Richmond traditions for us. He was relatively uninterested in the struggle, but his take on the absurdities of southern culture put him in our camp.

THE POWER BROKERS in Richmond, both ardent segregationists and moderates, seemed hell-bent on suppressing news of racial conflict in the city and state. We learned from our contacts in the local newspapers that the white media was complicit in this effort to keep the noise down about discontent among our "happy Negroes." Along with the minimalist arrest policy of the police, this led us to believe there was a conscious elite strategy to "manage" what the public and wider world would know about the struggle and the reasons for it. Needless to say in such a regime as this, activists were dismissed by the majority of whites as either Communists or crackpots or both.

One example of our outlier position was a rally we organized for our candidate in the 1960 Democratic presidential primary, Adlai Stevenson. We thought he would do more to support civil rights and peace efforts than John Kennedy. But true to our status as shakers but not movers, we attracted only about a dozen and a half people and a couple of dogs to Monroe Park for Stevenson's lone campaign rally in Richmond. Even Mr. Stevenson failed to show.

Deeply immersed in the Richmond battle, we also followed justice issues elsewhere in the state. I began to think that court orders, street demonstrations, radical tracts, and the like were not enough to take down segregation. It struck me that we also needed to get the goods on the segregationists for our push-back, and inevitably the mainstream media did a slapdash job at this. We needed something of an intelligence, surveillance, and reconnaissance operation in behalf of social justice. I thought I could help do this, but only if I went back to school and prepared myself for a whole new level of justice seeking. I just had to figure out how, where, and when I could do it. As I mulled the options, a tragedy arose that came to occupy me for a lifetime: the shutdown of the public school system in Prince Edward County to avoid desegregation.

✳ 12 ✳

"They Closed Our Schools"

N THE FALL OF 1959, as I was leaving the navy, I learned that officials in Prince Edward County, Virginia, were closing the public schools to circumvent court-ordered desegregation. I was outraged and ashamed of my home state. I pledged to myself to get involved. In my first months at the welfare department this oath gnawed at me. Finally in December I drove over to Prince Edward to check it out.

The shutdowns, I learned, followed decades of struggle for equal education waged by a determined black community. But this rural, Southside Virginia county got a big jolt in April of 1951, when sixteen-year-old Barbara Johns led her 450 schoolmates at Farmville's Robert Russa Moton High School in a walkout to protest the inferior conditions there. That walkout led to *Dorothy E. Davis, et al. v. County School Board of Prince Edward County, Virginia,* one of the five cases folded into the 1954 U.S. Supreme Court decision *Brown v. Board of Education* that declared racial segregation in U.S. public schools unconstitutional. Virginia's Byrd Organization and other pro-segregation interests responded with white supremacist propaganda and a variety of legal, legislative, and administrative devices designed to thwart school desegregation, which taken together were known as massive resistance. The state defied the U.S. Supreme Court until January of 1959, when the courts ruled massive resistance unconstitutional.

Then, after eight years of legal wrangling, the all-white Prince Edward County board of supervisors was faced with a final order to desegregate in September of 1959 with no more delays. Their response: a refusal to appropriate funds for their county's public schools and an order to the school board to shut them down. The schools remained closed for five years. As the county oligar-chy choked off the funds for public schools, they immediately provided private schools for the vast majority of white students. That won generous help from the commonwealth and, as it became a racist cause célèbre, gifts came from all over the South and even the North. There had been a long history of anti–public school sentiment in Virginia, and here was the perfect opportunity for its advocates to have their way. About 2,200 black Prince Edward youngsters were left with little or no formal education, as were some 300 poor whites, over the five years of closed schools. This malicious act toward children demon-strated to me that the democracy I was said to be defending in the military was an export commodity only.

I knew pretty much what to expect from the white majority in Virginia. The courts may have outlawed the legislated version of massive resistance, but the politics, economics, and social psychology behind it were not going away so eas-ily. Obviously there was not much a twenty-four-year-old without significant political connections could do, but the fire in my belly kept me returning to the county to discover how I might be useful. After a couple of visits to Prince Edward, I went to see Rev. Gene Pickett, the minister of Richmond's First Unitarian Church and someone for whom I had enormous respect.

Gene and his church, which was adjacent to the RPI campus, provided safe harbor for all who suffered from the stifling racial humidity of Richmond. I had known him since my student days, and his intellectualism and quiet sense of justice had made a deep impression on me. I especially admired his unsung and courageous leadership in the besieged Virginia Committee for Public Schools, which spared Richmond and other Virginia school districts the fate of Prince Edward County. For this he and his family were for a long time under a storm of constant threats from a variety of angry segregationists. Gene Pickett was to me a genuine hero, so I wanted his counsel on how to help in Prince Edward.

Although he applauded my concern, he warned against just descending on the county without some invitation from the local black community. While I left his study a little disappointed, I appreciated his argument that you cannot just show up and expect to be automatically accepted, let alone achieve very much.

But I thought, "How can I get an invitation to the county if no one there knows what we might bring to the situation?" So I continued visiting and met a number of people in the black community. Among them was Rev. L. Francis Griffin, the local NAACP leader and an inspiration to everyone involved in the struggle. Witnessing the forsaken black school children and the disruption of black family and community life, even as the majority of whites went merrily along with nary a sacrifice, kept me in a state of rage. But anger did nothing to help the situation. Knowing the children were likely to be out of school for a long time, I began thinking about what might be organized for them. But we still had not heard the community say, "Come in and help us."

The Prince Edward public schools remained closed during the 1960–61 school year. Fortuitously, the January 1961 meeting of the Richmond Council on Human Relations featured a presentation by Helen Baker of the American Friends Service Committee, who worked in Prince Edward County. The AFSC, a nonprofit organization, was founded in 1917 by Quakers dedicated to relief services, community development, social justice, and peace programs throughout the world in partnerships with people of all races, religions, and cultures. The AFSC received the Nobel Peace Prize in 1947 for its postwar relief and resettlement work with interned Japanese Americans and displaced Europeans in the United States. Mrs. Baker gave a heart-wrenching account of what was happening to the school-less black children and their families. During the discussion that followed, I asked, "What can we do to help?" She replied, "Come to the county, visit with us and bring whatever skills and activities you are able to." This was the invitation I was looking for.

I began discussing with my friends specific things we might do, even small or symbolic things to show solidarity with the shut-out students and their families. I was convinced that we could find people—our friends, work colleagues, folks from the RCHR, and sundry acquaintances—to volunteer one day a week in the county. While Reverend Griffin and Helen Baker encouraged us, they asked that we do nothing to jeopardize the black plaintiffs' position, which held that the black children were receiving no formal education. We knew too that we should start small, so we began with organizing a baseball club for the teenage boys.

The first volunteer recruit was my younger brother, Steve, who was a recreational leadership major at RPI. He was twenty years old and becoming a progressive. He was also a starter on the RPI baseball and basketball teams, and he worked as a part-time gang-worker in a tough section of south Richmond. Years later he received a master's degree in social work from Temple University and went on to spend a lifetime initiating and running groundbreaking programs for children and others in need. My second partner was Mich Wilkinson, a young man who grew up on Richmond's Oregon Hill, then a notorious poor white neighborhood feared by blacks and middle-class whites alike. Mich and I had become good friends while playing together on an industrial league basketball team. He later received a PhD from the University of Virginia and served for many years as the executive director of the Virginia State Commission on Local Government.

Helen Baker, a peerless community organizer, arranged for the ball field and enlisted some local men to help launch the club. She introduced us all around and spread the word of our aims. Above all, she obtained support for us from the Prince Edward County Christian Association, which led the local struggle in behalf of the idle black children. Her mimeographed posters publicizing our effort could be found tacked up all around Farmville and sundry crossroads around the county.

Mich, Steve, and I landed in Farmville on a chilly March afternoon, carrying a bag of scrounged-up baseball equipment. We knew little about the specifics of the situation, but we were determined to fill some empty space in the lives of these boys and demonstrate to them and their families that they were not alone in their struggle. According to our sign-up list, twenty boys, ages ten to sixteen, turned out. Leading the list was fifteen-year-old James Ghee, later placed by the AFSC in a home in Iowa so that he could attend school. James Ghee ultimately became a prominent lawyer and the president of the Virginia NAACP. Three men joined us to get the club started, among them Lenrod Blowe, a man who was always in the front of the line to help his community. They helped us build trust with the teens.

The weather was bone-chilling that day. While lips turned purple and fingertips numb, the boys seemed not to mind the cold. They had baseball on their minds, so we organized a practice session, learning the positions each youngster wished to play and giving every boy plenty of turns at bat. With the help of the three Prince Edward men, we then divided the talent into two teams, with the six of us adults sharing the coaching and umpire duties. The rest of the afternoon seemed to disappear as we became lost in the intensity of the game.

But the weather wasn't the only icy wind blowing our way. Shortly after we arrived, two police cars pulled up and parked on the bluff above the playing field. Two white policemen emerged and assumed a posture to intimidate: resting the heels of their hands on their service revolvers as they swaggered back and forth, leering at our every move. Occasionally one would leave in his car and appear on the other side of the field. We tried to ignore them and to convey to the boys that we had no intention of letting them interfere with our fun. This was not easy, for all of us harbored some anxiety about what the policemen might do. After all, in this segregated society they were the law, and we were the outlaws.

With the light fading we ended the game. Despite the fact that only three hours earlier we had been total strangers, the boys seemed delighted to be together and doing something they loved. It was clear they were hungry for more, much more engagement. At dusk the boys scattered in all directions while we spoke with our three adult hosts about the future. They expressed their gratitude, and they committed to recruiting more boys and adult leaders and assuming the major coaching and umpiring responsibilities if we would continue to assist. It looked like a winner.

We bid our new friends goodbye and agreed on a game the next Saturday. Then as we pulled out onto Main Street to head home, both of the patrol cars that had shadowed our game sped over to catch up with us. They tailed us closely all the way through town as if looking for an offense for which to stop us. As we crossed the Appomattox River bridge and entered Cumberland County, where they had no jurisdiction, our worry over them faded. We moved on to talk of the baseball talent we witnessed, how welcome we had been made to feel by the men and boys, how tragic was the deprivation of these children because of the school closing, and how exciting it was to contemplate coming back again.

That evening, my thoughts turned to what we might do for the girls, the younger children, and boys who were not interested in athletics. While we continued to return to Farmville each Saturday for the baseball club, I also began working on this wider vision with others, including Ruby Clayton, my friend at the Department of Welfare. Ruby soon joined in organizing new activities for the children, recruiting more volunteers, and soliciting drivers, money, and materials to be used in the activities. Helen Baker put us in touch with Harriet Allen in Farmville. Mrs. Allen, a woman of unparalleled amiability, energy, and devotion to her community, particularly the youth, had assumed leadership of recreational activities for the black community. We all grew to love her. She prompted the Farmville Recreation Association's effort to buy and rehabilitate an old house to serve as a recreation center for the black community. It was sorely needed, because whites rarely shared the county's facilities with blacks. Harriet set up the recreation center for our program every Saturday and did everything she could to get folks to come out and join us.

The plight of the Prince Edward County children touched a tender nerve among our small progressive community in central Virginia, and many people volunteered with enthusiasm. Funds were provided by individuals, the Virginia Council on Human Relations, and Gene Pickett and his First Unitarian Church of Richmond. We also reached into our own pockets. Sam Troy, a white merchant in Jackson Ward, a lustrous black Richmond neighborhood, gave us a whole bolt of fabric and a carton full of spools of thread for our sewing circle. These donations provided essential materials for our various activities for the youth: sports, games, sewing, dramatics, industrial arts, reading, storytelling, writing, homemaking skills, music, films, arts and crafts, and African American history.

On April 29, we launched the second stage of our venture with activities for the girls and young children at the freshly painted recreation center. The turnout exceeded everyone's expectations, even Harriet Allen's. A good time was had by all, but we needed more volunteers. So we called a recruitment meeting for the next Wednesday at the First Unitarian Church and got two highly respected local civil rights advocates as speakers: Rev. Irvin Elligan, the black pastor of All Souls Presbyterian Church, and Rev. Gene Pickett, the white minister of the First Unitarian Church. Bob Tingle, a student at the University of Richmond who was persecuted for his commitment to racial progress by the school's president, George Modlin, worked tirelessly to get the word out about the meeting. (Modlin, an ardent white supremacist, had recruited Dr. Henry

Garrett, a racist social psychologist, to serve as the key expert witness for the defense of segregation in *Brown v. Board of Education*). Our meeting was a success, and we signed up a dozen new volunteers.

We called ourselves the Richmond Committee of Volunteers to Prince Edward. But we should have been the "Central Virginia Committee of Volunteers to Prince Edward," because as word traveled about our efforts, we picked up volunteers from Petersburg, Hopewell, the Richmond suburbs, and a couple of towns across Southside Virginia. By August, we had a roster of some sixty volunteers: men, women, and children of all ages and from a multitude of different racial, ethnic, religious, political, and income backgrounds. Emerging from our cars in this place so fraught with white-black discord, we must have looked like a diorama of the future of America. But the icy stares, refusals of service in stores, and occasional threats of violence showed us that inclusive democracy was a disturbing vision to some Prince Edward County whites.

Ignoring them, we continued our activities with the children and teenagers, who were craving social contact and learning opportunities. One can only imagine the hunger for meaningful stimuli in a child out of school for months then years on end, especially in a remote rural area. We witnessed revolting examples of how these young minds had been deprived, simply because a white oligarchy valued the preservation of its own privileges more highly than the lives of these children.

One lovely Saturday afternoon in Farmville, I turned to see a little white girl, perhaps eight or nine years old, hanging on her fence across the road from the recreation center, a look of yearning on her face. Her eyes were fixed on all the fun-filled activity: gleeful children running back and forth during their games, a black teenager making yard furniture with a white man on the porch, other very young children sitting quietly on benches with a woman reading a book to them. I invited our young neighbor to come over, having long hoped that some indigenous whites might, eventually, join our activities. But this hope was dashed as the child's mother roared out of her house screaming at me to "stop accosting" her child. She scooped up her daughter, shouted that she was "calling the sheriff," and ran inside, slamming the door behind her.

In about fifteen minutes, a deputy sheriff drove up to the recreation center. He got out slowly, swaggered past me with his right hand resting on his revolver, and with a scowl disappeared into the house of our accuser. In about five minutes, the deputy came out and began to march up and down the property line of the recreation center, carefully scrutinizing all the children and adults in the yard. His appetite for snooping finally satiated, he returned to his patrol car and left.

I left for graduate school in September of 1961, but the project continued into the next year under the able leadership of Ruby Clayton, with the assistance of other volunteers, especially Blanche Hope Smith. By that time larger organizations with greater resources, such as the Virginia Teachers Association, the black state teachers group, began doing similar work on a much larger scale.

Our project had shortcomings, but some good things resulted from it. It probably served over its lifetime some 400–450 children. A lot of very good people met and came to know a lot of other very good people. Many of us made good friends and contacts for our later work. Several of the local people assumed leadership of some of the activities, such as the men who continued the baseball club, and grafted them onto programs carried forward by the Farmville Recreation Association. The Prince Edward experience also made me aware of the vast potential of Virginia youth for biracial civil rights activism. In 1963 that prospect led me to propose and then organize the College Council on Human Relations under the aegis of the VCHR. But perhaps the most important effects of our presence in Prince Edward were the least visible: the message our presence conveyed, the enriching events experienced, the inspiring and enduring memories planted, and most of all the heartwarming encounters among those our society had so long unjustly kept apart. Where isolation had dwelt before, we created bridges of community. These treasured lessons shaped the rest of my life, as Prince Edward pulled me back, again and again.

✳ 13 ✳

The Bridge over the
Mason-Dixon Line

URING THE SUMMER OF 1961 I finally figured out the career I wanted
and how to train for it. I applied to graduate programs in human relations, an interdisciplinary social science field that centered on the study
of racial, ethnic, and religious intergroup encounters. With a fellowship from
the University of Pennsylvania in Philadelphia, I began work in September
on a master's degree. At the time of the move from Richmond, I was married
to my first wife. (She was a woman of rare creative and intellectual gifts and a
devoted mother to our daughters. But we later divorced, and out of respect for
her privacy I will not be saying more about our time together.)

The move to Philadelphia was not easy for me. I could never get Prince Edward or the Virginia struggle for equality out of my head. But I knew I needed to
concentrate on attaining credentials for a job in which I could both pursue my
passion for racial justice and get paid, while maybe somehow also making a contribution in Prince Edward. Making money was vital because we were blessed
with the birth of our first child, Suzannah Ruth Peeples, on November 25.

Philadelphia was a whole new world. The neighborhood in which we lived,
Powelton Village, bustled with the activism of a myriad of progressive people;
it was unlike any place I had ever known. Since my fellowship only covered
my whopping Ivy League tuition bill, I had to get a night job for our living
expenses. But my friends Bob and Emily Young, who were community leaders
in Powelton, got us settled in. I met Bob at the Encampment for Citizenship
in 1957; we had immediately hit it off thanks to our mutual passions for bas-

ketball and racial justice. Bob and Emily found us our apartment, and Emily led me to a job as a street-based gang worker out of a settlement house, United Neighbors. From six to midnight five nights a week I worked at trying to keep the peace on the streets of South Philadelphia, where Italian, African American, and Polish youth were all too frequently at each other's throats.

In those early months I learned things I never suspected about being a southerner. Philadelphia was only about 260 miles north of Richmond, and yet despite how radical I appeared to white Virginians, I saw that I was fundamentally different from the people in this giant urban polyglot. While in a way it was a relief to escape the daily trials of Jim Crow, I found that living outside the South made me ache for home. I missed the comforting familiarity of the accents, the landmarks, the food and lifestyle, and—believe it or not— confrontations with segregationists. I realized that I belonged in Virginia, and I was eager to complete the MA and get back home.

My dread of competing with Ivy League PhD students proved to be unjustified. But apparently having a southerner in their midst took them by surprise. A few of them would sometimes just stare at me in silence when I spoke in class. Some appeared to be fixed on my accent and not what I was saying, while others just seemed amused.

But it was soon obvious that a white boy with a southern accent was not going to be a success as a gang worker in a big northeastern city. Though it was not a good fit, it did help me understand more of the racial, ethnic, and class issues of big inner-city life. Despite my deficits as a gang worker, the agency director appointed me for two summers as the director of the financially strapped Camp Linden, located in a beautiful remote country setting on Brandywine Creek in nearby Chester County. Every two weeks during the summer United Neighbors sent us about fifty poor South Philly kids. Despite our meager budget, our sometimes failing pool filter system, our make-do kitchen, and a plethora of other shabby essentials, our idealistic staff somehow managed to rid the campers' heads of lice, introduce them to nature, teach them to swim, and have them experience at least once in their lives a friend of another race or ethnicity.

In the summers of 1962 and 1963 I had great experiences with our dedicated, socially conscious staff at Camp Linden. Among the things I learned was that nepotism is good when you do it right. I recruited my brother Steve who had just graduated from RPI, and his gift for working with these youths bailed me out more than once. We also learned about the potential of representative democracy. In the summer of 1963 all of us wanted to participate in the big March on Washington for Jobs and Freedom, now best known for Martin Luther King's "I Have a Dream" speech. This being impossible, we decided to send one of our number to DC to represent us all. Everyone pooled their money for the trip expenses and then did their bit to cover the responsibilities of the absent staffer, so all of us felt like we were accompanying him on the March.

IN THE FALL OF 1962, Dr. Martin P. Chworowsky, my major professor and patron saint at Penn, called me into his office to discuss my master's thesis. "I know that you have no intention of writing on anything other than Prince Edward County," he began. Of course, I said yes. He continued, "And when you go down there to interview respondents, what are you going to use for money?" When I admitted I didn't know, he said, "Get a proposal in here by the middle of next week, and I will see what I can do." I labored over that proposal, written in long hand because I had no typewriter, and turned it in by his deadline. A month passed before he called me in to announce, "I have some good news: I have found a small grant for your field work." I felt the impulse to rush around his desk and give him a big kiss, but somehow I managed to contain myself. I could not believe my good fortune. With that money and the loan of my father-in-law's Volkswagen Beetle, off I went to Prince Edward.

Martin Chworowsky was a respected scholar and trusted academic advisor, but what really drew me to him was his commitment to the struggle for racial and ethnic justice. He tried to help anyone he could prepare to join that struggle. Despite my spotty undergraduate record, Martin had seen something in me that led him to work hard to get me admission and financial support. He did everything he could to assure my success. It seemed like I was a son he never had and he was the father I never had. Though he was not the kind of person to wear his sentiments on his sleeve, he made clear his confidence in my future. He was a rare and generous soul, a great gift in my life whom I grew to truly love.

BEGINNING WITH MY first trips to Prince Edward in late 1959, I tried to converse with any folks willing to talk to me, including black victims of school closing, a variety of local whites, and state and local officials. As I began more formal research, I conducted more structured interviews until August 1963, bringing the total number of informants over time to more than 250 individuals: blacks and whites of all socioeconomic classes, individuals who agreed with and opposed school closing, and white community powerbrokers who participated in the decisions to close the schools and keep them closed. Because of the sensitivity of the situation, I did not have the luxury of taking notes on the spot for most of these interviews, but I recorded my key findings afterwards as soon as it was practical.

Conducting interviews in Prince Edward was no picnic, especially with the segregationist leaders. In the early days, my views were unknown and so it was easy to obtain appointments with members of the white oligarchy who had ordered the schools closed. Among others, I got a lengthy and very revealing interview with Barrye Wall, the editor of the *Farmville Herald,* who agitated for school closure much as James Jackson Kilpatrick of the *Richmond News Leader* had done for massive resistance. I also did an extensive interview with Robert Crawford, a local small businessman and a cofounder of the Defenders of State Sovereignty and Individual Liberties, which rallied local and state diehards and aligned itself with the White Citizens' Council in the Deep South.

Everything went well at first, in part because my Southside Virginia surname tied me to the family who owned Peebles Department Stores, a popular chain in that part of the state. (Peebles was an earlier spelling of my name.) Many whites assumed that I was, like most of the Peebleses in Virginia, a segregationist. Whatever inference they wanted to make was fine with me, if it led to candor from the white segregationist power brokers.

But as time passed some of my prospective interviewees refused to speak with me: my purpose had become suspect. I finally learned why. As old-timers might remember, when you made a local phone call in small towns in those days, you told the operator the number you wanted and she (it was always a she then) physically connected you with the other party's line. The Farmville operator was eavesdropping on calls from my room in the Weyanoke Hotel. On two separate occasions I overheard her alerting my white interview prospects.

Thanks to her spying, I never had an opportunity to talk with Charles W. "Rat" Glenn, perhaps the single most powerful man in the county. Glenn was a kingpin in the school issue because his construction and logging businesses—and some of his more burly employees—provided significant resources to the oligarchy for the enforcement of white solidarity and the surveillance of those who dared to dissent. Also thanks to the operator's tip off, Blanton Hanbury, the president of the white private school foundation, became evasive and finally refused to talk to me altogether.

Despite my promises of confidentiality, some white and black opponents of school closing refused to talk with me. A few told me outright that they had been threatened to keep quiet. Among those who offered no explanation, their demeanors conveyed that they believed they might be subjected to retribution at work, at places where they sought credit, on the street, or in other venues in the community. This was to be expected, because intimidation was the stock in trade for the Defenders of State Sovereignty in Virginia and the White Citizens' Council in other states. A few black individuals from the county have told me that even today they remain fearful of speaking critically of the white elites who engineered the school closing.

Despite widespread foreboding among dissenters about possible retaliation during the Jim Crow era, the white segregationists I interviewed at the time insisted that relations between the races in their community couldn't have been better. This was the culture of idyllic illusion encouraged by Virginia's Senator Harry Byrd and his minions, who dominated the commonwealth for so many years. One of my clients when I was at the Richmond Department of Welfare, an out-of-work truck driver, had it right. Invoking the fact of Byrd's vast apple orchards and the language of the Cold War, he quipped, "We are living behind the Apple Curtain." By late 1962, I was getting hostile responses from whites in Farmville. More than once a lawman's cruiser tailed my car. Once, several young white men shadowed me on foot downtown, apparently to send the message that I had worn out my welcome in Farmville.

But my views on the school closing were no problem for Robert Taylor. He apparently just wanted to use our interview to boast about his influence and status in the community. As I got out of my car in his parking lot, three large ominous-looking men met me and escorted me to his office as if I were a prisoner in their custody. Taylor, seated behind a desk, greeted me with a broad smile as his men retreated to lean on the wall behind him with their arms folded across their chests. The interview itself went well, because Taylor relished trumpeting his part in closing the schools and creating the private segregated school foundation. He also made much of how he was the only one in town capable of thwarting Reverend Griffin's will and congratulated himself on how he had bankrupted the NAACP. I left concluding that he was more puff than magic dragon.

In nearly every interview with segregationists, each would inevitably insist that the building of the new Moton High School for black students in 1953 forever eliminated racial inequality in the schools. They argued that the NAACP and the federal courts should therefore stop pushing for desegregation and accept that separate-but-equal schools would be "best for everybody."

This contention was repeated so frequently and with such certainty by whites that I decided to see for myself whether the schools had indeed been made equal. I visited all twenty-six public schools that state records showed were in use in the county in 1959 and took photos of the facilities. All but four of the schools were in rural areas, where over two-thirds of Prince Edward children were enrolled. Images of these rural schools had not been part of the original *Brown* petition in the early fifties. The Supreme Court case had instead centered on the inferiority of Moton High School when compared with the white high school, both in the town of Farmville. My photos and thesis confirmed what the NAACP lawyers and the black community had insisted all along: even with the addition of the new Moton High School for blacks in 1953, the white schools were dramatically superior. The new black high school represented but a few feet of the many miles the county would have had to travel to create equality. (No white Virginia officials or any other whites in a position to influence the situation were willing to examine those photographs. Nor were the *Richmond Times-Dispatch,* the *News Leader,* the *Farmville Herald,* or any mainstream newspaper willing to publish them. Only forty years later did these 130 images get publicly shown, as part of an online exhibit hosted by Special Collections and Archives at the James Branch Cabell Library of Virginia Commonwealth University.)

Taking the photographs was not easy. One day I was out in a remote area of the county shooting pictures of one of the closed two-room public school buildings used by black children prior to 1959. I was not the only one in the neighborhood with shooting on his mind. Suddenly in the distance I heard and then saw a white man loping across a field toward me with a long gun. He was yelling something unintelligible. At first I thought he was warning me of something, but then he lowered the rifle and blasted away that assumption. Hightailing it to my VW Beetle, I jumped in and took off. But I did get shots of that school. I later asked around about why people living near these old schools might care if someone took photos. Some of my well-placed contacts reported that selected members of the county's school closing oligarchy had arranged for vigilante help to scare people off of the properties and keep images of the schools out of the media. I was never able to confirm this, but the aggression I saw in that gun-toting farmer made the claim believable.

These disquieting conditions made me a bit paranoiac about what to expect around each new corner, especially after learning of what happened to Harry Boyte, a community organizer for the American Friends Service Committee. When he returned to the AFSC Farmville headquarters late one night after a civil rights meeting, waiting for him were three young white men. At knife-point they forced him to remove his clothes and threatened to castrate him if he didn't leave town.

But it was not just the fear of violence that made me uncomfortable. It was also the gnawing incongruity between what was necessary to get the job done and the kind of person I really was. Here I was in Prince Edward to dig out from the victims, the oppressors, and the indifferent the most volatile story in their community since the Civil War. At the same time, as an interviewer, I had to suppress my own passionate convictions so the respondents would speak freely. I entered each interview of a white supremacist with these war-ring impulses: I wanted to get the best possible information and I wanted to scream when I heard their racist comments. But getting out the Prince Edward story was most important, so I accepted the discomfort of self-restraint and left many interview sessions with a chest pounding from dammed-up anger.

The stress of packing down emotions like this, compounded by my loss of anonymity among the pro–school closing whites, caused constant anxiety. Finally, I decided that I should escape the county to seek renewal when needed. At those times, I would drive back to Richmond and stay on supportive turf with friends or just be alone for a day or two. When I recovered my equilib-rium, I returned to the Southside pressure cooker. I learned that year about the need to pay attention to what the body was saying if one wanted to last in the struggle. Yet I stuck with the Prince Edward story, because as early as 1959 it felt to me like a critical part of American history with many potent lessons for the future. And nothing had been written to date with the perspective and detail I envisioned, so I wanted to see it through.

I completed the eighty-four-page final version of my thesis in early May of 1963. It began with an introduction to some of the social, demographic, and economic background data about the county and an account of the legal and school closure history. Next was an analysis of how the leading white supremacist ideologues of the time, above all James Jackson Kilpatrick, sought to ensure white support for continued segregation by transforming the plain-spoken racism of the day into a new version of "respectable conservatism" aimed at preserving white privilege under a new name and vocabulary. The thesis then described many of the damaging social, health, educational, and economic consequences suffered by the black community and a number of poor white families due to the school closures. It examined the reign of intimidation experienced by blacks and well-meaning whites at the hands of the white oligarchy in the county. And it documented how most of the 2,100 children of white families escaped the majority of the harmful effects of school closing because they moved immediately into the all-white private schools that had already been in the making since the earliest signs of impending court desegregation orders—whereas the affected 2,700 black children had to either leave the county or receive no education at all. Finally, I explored some factors likely to affect the long-term aftermath of the closures.

One of the highlights of the Prince Edward research experience for me was the opportunity to share my findings with two of Virginia's most distinguished civil rights attorneys, Oliver Hill and Samuel Tucker. Hill was among those, including Thurgood Marshall and Jack Greenberg, who brought about the civil rights legal revolution and whose story Greenberg recounts in his book *Crusaders in the Courts*. I also got to interview another member of that team of legal titans, Spottswood Robinson III, who by then was the dean of Howard University Law School. Nothing in my life until then compared with the thrill of doing work that was helpful to these leading movement lawyers.

I FINISHED THE THESIS two months before my job started at Camp Linden. I don't know how people discovered it, but I was stunned to learn that by August the University of Pennsylvania library had answered about three dozen requests for copies, several from the Department of Justice and the Office of Education in Washington. Since the thesis was the first systematic look at a wide spectrum of the issues in the Prince Edward story, it became something of a "briefing paper" for federal government officials—though to my knowledge no Virginia decision-maker or media source ever took a look at it.

The thesis and contacts with the AFSC did, however, result in several invitations to Washington to attend strategy meetings on opening the schools and once to brief a deputy commissioner of education. From what I saw and heard, Washington's driving interest in the school closing at this point was not so much the fate of the black children but rather the embarrassment being heaped upon the Kennedy administration from foreign sources. Worldwide press coverage of the Prince Edward story made all too plain U.S. hypocrisy in scolding the Soviets about the oppression of their people.

In the late spring of 1963, I was asked to join a joint project of the Virginia Advisory Committee to the U.S. Commission on Civil Rights, the Virginia Council on Human Relations, and the American Friends Service Committee. The leaders asked me to expand on my thesis interviews and provide further data for a final report on the Prince Edward schools crisis to be prepared by Dr. J. Kenneth Morland. Dr. Morland was a highly respected professor of sociology and anthropology at Randolph-Macon Women's College and one of the original social science expert witnesses in *Brown v. Board of Education*. He had been recruited to prepare the report by the U.S. Commission on Civil Rights. They had assured everyone involved that the report would be immediately published in the hope that it would create enough public pressure to finally reopen the public schools of Prince Edward County. It felt good to see that my research mattered.

With the field interviews done in June, I prepared and turned over to Dr. Morland a draft report entitled "Prince Edward County: The Story without an End." Ken combined it with survey research data collected by himself and Dr. Robert Green of Michigan State University from a sample of Prince Edward black residents. He submitted the combined report, titled "The Tragedy of Closed Public Schools: Prince Edward County, Virginia," in mid-January of 1964 in the belief that it would be distributed widely within weeks.

The report arrived just as the 1964 Civil Rights Act and the future status of the U.S. Civil Rights Commission had become red-hot issues, but its publication was mysteriously put on hold. Ken and I made separate trips to the commission in Washington seeking an explanation. We were both told by staff off the record that Senator Harry Byrd and his southern allies were leaning on the commission and the new Lyndon Johnson administration, threatening to kill both the Civil Rights Act and the commission itself if this Prince Edward report went forward. Ken explained in a letter dated January 31, 1964:

The Civil Rights Commission fears that publication of the PEC study before the Supreme Court has its hearing beginning March 30th might jeopardize the commission's future. They think that southern congressmen are just looking for things to criticize the commission for, especially since the forthcoming battle over the civil rights bill involves the provision of making the commission a permanent agency. The chief comment on the report during my three hour session with legal counsel and others was that it was too "strong." I had assumed that the commission would take the position that closing the schools has been a tragic event (some at the conference thought that the title, "The Tragedy of Closed Public Schools" was "loaded"). If it were not for the pending legislation—and if Peter Sussman [the commission staffer assigned to the Prince Edward County project] were still there—I doubt that these problems would have arisen.

Much time passed with no further news. In all likelihood, the commission discarded the report by May of 1964 in a backroom deal with southern congressmen.* While the Kennedy administration initiated a make-shift school for the black children still living in the county for the 1963–64 school year, the public schools of Prince Edward County did not re-open until the fall of 1964—with less than a half-dozen whites among the 1,700 students. Traces of the effects of the five-year school shutdown can still be seen today in the black and poor white children and their families. The tragedy in Prince Edward County was indeed a story without an end.

*It is likely that President Johnson at that very time was reluctant to offend Virginia's powerful Harry Byrd, who as chairman of the Senate Finance Committee could have blocked key elements of Johnson's legislative agenda. See Robert Caro, *The Passage of Power: The Years of Lyndon Johnson* (New York: Knopf, 2012), 466–83, 552–57.

✳ 14 ✳

A New Career and
Maybe a New Virginia?

THE SUMMER OF 1963 had me scrambling: traveling back and forth between Washington for consultations on the Prince Edward issue, Pennsylvania for the camp job, and Richmond to look for a place to live before I began my new job at the Medical College of Virginia. It was my first college teaching position, as an instructor in their nursing school. My initial job was teaching introductory sociology, but before long I was teaching and very much enjoying courses in anthropology, a survey of the world's major religions, and other social science–related courses. I became one of only two full-time non–health professional faculty in the MCV School of Nursing and the only person with an office in Cabaniss Hall qualified to use the men's room. That first academic year at MCV proved very special, because on May 6, 1964, my class lecture was interrupted by an obstetric nurse with the news that at that very moment my wife was delivering our second daughter, Kathryn Dana Peeples, in the hospital just a few floors above us. In those days, men were not welcome at childbirth, so I stuck with my class. But given how excited I was, the lesson for that hour quickly shifted and became a case study of the dad side of the delivery of a baby.

Coming back to Richmond's segregation after two years in Philadelphia presented some significant reentry problems. At first I was clumsier than I had been in dealing with the absurdities of racist behavior. Though Richmond was still segregated, there had been a few concessions in some public accommodations, such as seating on city buses, and some modest progress achieved by the lunch-counter sit-ins. But local and state government and white business owners still found ways to keep whites and blacks apart.

It might be difficult for people born later to imagine what racial segregation was really like. Discrimination in the realm of medical care is an illuminating example. The MCV main hospital, the larger and more modern facility, was reserved exclusively for white patients. The two hospitals for black patients, North Hospital and St. Philip, were old, bleak, and poorly equipped buildings. Their rooms were packed beyond capacity, and the halls were often lined end to end with gurneys filled with black patients. There were two racially separate outpatient clinics and two emergency rooms in which no matter how hard the staff might have tried to overcome it, unequal conditions often resulted in worse medical outcomes for blacks. Of course, nearly all of the other hospital beds in town were reserved for whites. The exception was Richmond Community Hospital, a twenty-five-bed facility that served blacks of means who sought to avoid the humiliation and poorer prognoses awaiting them at MCV. Even the newer Richmond Memorial Hospital, built with private, state, and federal funds and initially promising nondiscrimination, for some time discouraged black admissions, even in emergencies.

Sometimes segregation in Virginia was less tragic, so nonsensical that it was amusing. I shot a photograph of the front of a diner in downtown Richmond in the sixties. There were two front doors into the establishment, separated by two wide windows. The glass panel adjacent to the door on the left side bore the words "Johnson's Grill, Home Cooking"; on the right side were the words "Johnson's Grill, Soul Kitchen." Whites were to enter the door on the left while black patrons went through the door on the right. Upon entering either door, one discovered that the diner was a single room with two parallel counters in the center where black and white customers ate facing each other. Between the two counters was the area for the grill and steam tables holding scrumptious southern vittles from which the two divided races drew identical sustenance.

AFTER I HAD BEEN AT MCV for about a month or so, students began to drop by my office just to talk. Some wanted information about my classes. Others expressed boredom with nursing and were looking for stimulation from other fields of endeavor. Still others just wanted to blow off steam about such things as the gender discrimination they saw in the health professions. But I think the main reason that students connected with me was because they were bright and would have been in other professions had those been open to women at the time. My courses exposed them to alternative ideas and career possibilities outside of nursing that they had never before considered. Beyond that, it was novel to have a male faculty member in the nursing program who was not much older than them and who cared about their concerns.

I made the most of living with three females at home—my wife and two daughters—and some 450 more at work by seizing the opportunity to learn about life in women's world. With all this traffic through my office it did not take long to encounter several dozen students who were exceptionally intelligent, curious, and open-minded and who were seeking life experience outside of the nursing school in an era of social upheaval. So I organized extracurricular experiences like screenings of educational films, guest lectures, panels, and discussion groups on timely topics such as questions of racial justice, war and peace, poverty, women's rights and male supremacy, contraception, abortion, dying and euthanasia, and the right to universal medical care. Many then considered open discussion of some of these topics taboo, especially among young women. But before long a circle of nursing students became regulars at these activities. And the majority were actually the daughters of southern families. I don't know if any of them would have been described as liberal, but they were eager to rise above the white-, male-, and elite-dominated culture of Old Virginny.

RACIAL AND CLASS-BASED inequities were ubiquitous at MCV but were officially ignored—even though they were significant factors in nursing care and medical outcomes. That made nurses and students complicit in a system of unequal treatment of patients. As a former navy hospital corpsman, I knew that this did not jibe with the noble underlying values of nursing. I therefore took pre-clinical students on guided tours of the MCV patient facilities as a requirement for my sociology course. When they learned that black patients were stuck with dramatically inferior facilities and treatment and yet were assessed hospital room rates that were sometimes 20 percent higher than those for whites in superior accommodations, many of the students became deeply troubled. And when they saw the impact these hospital conditions had on mortality, morbidity, and disability rates for blacks and other poor patients, many expanded their sense of responsibility as healthcare providers. To enhance this learning, I initiated a four-hour rolling seminar on a bus where we traversed and compared various city neighborhoods. I provided students with a demographic data handbook so they could match the census tract statistics with the actual conditions they witnessed firsthand, conditions the implications of which they would see in the clinics and hospital. We also had health professionals on board to add their observations about clinical correlations. We made several pre-planned stops where we examined how poor and elderly people coped with finding shelter, food, and other essentials. I was delighted with the changes I saw in many of my students after these experiences.

SEEING THE INTEREST some nursing students showed in the civil rights movement, I began to take some of them to community activities. Before long maybe a dozen of them got involved in local civil rights work. One of our projects was organizing a statewide College Council on Human Relations under the umbrella of the Virginia Council on Human Relations, which by now had more than two dozen adult chapters around the commonwealth. Involvement in the College Council became a hot issue when our dean, Dr. Doris Yingling, got word that such involvement was responsible for a couple of the girls dating black students from Virginia Union University. The "offending" students ended up being confined to their dorm rooms for exercising their First Amendment right to freedom of association, and I received Dean Yingling's first veiled threat to fire me. I persisted in involving students in the wider community, but thereafter only undercover.

Another of our projects involved several nursing-student volunteers working as tutors for rural poor black children in Amelia County, about thirty-five miles away. We tried, as we did with the College Council on Human Relations, to keep this quiet around school, and we were successful until we had a big scare. One weekend four students drove down to the country black church in Amelia where the tutors met with their young pupils. No sooner had they sat down with the children in the fellowship hall than a big racket went up outside. A couple of students and the pastor ran upstairs and peeped out the front door, and what they saw struck terror in each of them. Out in front was a carload of young white men with a couple of rifles sticking out of the windows of their car, aimed in the church's direction. They were yelling something about getting those "damn white girls" out of that "nigger church before we shoot it up and set it on fire." The preacher wasted no time. He bolted the front door and ushered the children, the nursing students, and the two church women helpers out a side door, and then everyone jumped in their cars and took off. The students raced down the country dirt road toward U.S. Route 360.

When the white men caught sight of the girls' car escaping, they chased after it. Fortunately, the students outdistanced their pursuers. When they arrived at a gas station where there was a phone, they thought they had ditched their pursuers. Since I had given them my home phone number, one of them called and conveyed their story. I urged them get back in the car, get onto 360, and come straight back toward Richmond and I would head toward them on that same road. The student on the phone cut me off, squealing that the other girls had seen the boys' car headed their way.

As I hung up the phone, the realization of how I had exposed these girls to danger hit me like an NFL linebacker. I rushed to find them. Gathering my wits before leaving town, I called Reverend Edward Meeks "Pope" Gregory, the Episcopal priest every activist in town knew and loved, to ask him to come with me, urging him to put on his clerical collar as we might need it for protection.

I picked Pope up and we raced out of town onto U.S. 360 West, where we both scrutinized the passengers of every car coming toward us. My heart was pounding for fear that the girls might have been caught by those white guys. I told Pope, "I will never forgive myself for dragging these girls down there, should something happen to them." Pope mumbled some kind of prayer that, surprisingly, provided some comfort. Agnostics can't be choosy at times like that. We kept driving and looking, driving and looking, until we finally arrived at the church in Amelia just before dark. We never saw the students on the highway, and now we found the church locked up tight and no one around.

Panic had me thinking the worst. Pope and I discussed what to do next. Having had bad experiences with the Amelia sheriff's office in the past, I didn't trust what side they would be on. So we decided to return to Richmond where I dropped Pope off and went straight to MCV to check on the students. I was so relieved to learn that they were back in the dorm, safe and sound. One of them told me that they outran the boys on 360 and arrived back at school without incident, but still trembling. Most of the tutors did not let this scare them off. Their courage was inspiring: they returned to Amelia for all of the remaining planned tutoring sessions with no further threats.

Several of the nursing students turned out to be among the most committed advocates for racial justice I have known. One of these was rarer still. I regret that despite an exhaustive search, I cannot find her name among my grade books or from any other source, but I remember her so well. She was a trim and attractive young woman with black hair and sharp features, perhaps no taller than five foot four. She was a soft-spoken, pensive, and unassuming person. I think she was a sophomore at the time and about twenty years old. She sometimes came to my office just to chat about justice issues but did little of the talking herself. At first it was difficult for me to appreciate how deep this young woman's intellect was, because she seemed so reluctant to reveal herself. But in time I learned that she just wanted to have her own independent thoughts somehow confirmed, and when I discovered what was on her mind I was delighted to comply.

One day in early 1965 she and some of the students were talking about the voting rights march being planned for Selma, Alabama. Despite their demanding school schedule, several remarked how they would like to join the other marchers coming from all over the country. I told them about how the staff of Camp Linden "sponsored" a volunteer to represent us at the March on Washington. This apparently inspired the group, and the sophomore student said that she wanted to be our representative in Selma. So we collected cash for her travel and sustenance and some of the students saw her off to Alabama. She was part of the attempt on March 7 to cross the Edmund Pettus Bridge, the march led by John Lewis and Hosea Williams. She was brutally beaten by the police on the approach to the bridge and after being arrested was again beaten in the Selma jail. Tears came to my eyes when I saw her in my office for the first time after her return. Both of her eyes were swollen nearly shut, her lips were striped with small lacerations, and her cheeks were swollen and blackened beyond all recognition. It was heart-wrenching to see her and hear her struggle to tell the story through her pain and disfigurement. Her heroism was an inspiration to us all—with the exception of Dean Yingling. In her view, nice girls didn't belong in civil rights marches.

The student's story quickly circulated on campus, and some of the MCV faculty, staff, and students were enraged at her for "disgracing" the nursing profession and the institution. MCV's president, Blackwell Smith, hardly friendly to the token desegregation being slowly imposed on his institution, got wind of it as well. I had already had a couple of indirect conflicts with the president over racial issues through encounters with his right-hand man, retired army colonel John Heil, whose rigid authoritarianism had led some of us to nickname him "Sieg Heil."

This was a time when the preponderance of white politicians, civic leaders, newspaper editors, and other officials were hypersensitive about any racial events that might besmirch the image of the commonwealth as the paragon of gentility in race relations. Any noise coming from either civil rights advocates or the bellowing bigots was anathema to them. I sometimes heard white Virginians of status bemoan the news of racial atrocities coming out of the Deep South, saying, "Those rubes down in Mississippi and Alabama give segregation a bad name!" The fear of racial controversy likewise plagued college administrators, compelling even moderates to act like their ardent segregationist counterparts. Indeed, these were precisely the dynamics operating when the news of our student's involvement in Selma got out. Several parents had written letters of outrage to the president and the dean over how Doris Yingling had "lost control of her girls." So she told the returned wounded civil rights warrior to pack up and get out.

Fortunately, one of the half-dozen physicians and scientists on campus who was attuned to racial injustice came to talk to me about what he might do to save the young woman's career. Dr. Sami Said was a tall, elegant, handsome Egyptian who was a kind and engaging man. I briefed him on what took place and encouraged him to go see Dean Yingling and persuade her not to send the student home. Dr. Said and I agreed that perhaps she could be convinced to administer some lesser penalty that would still satiate the jackals in the president's suite. What I did not mention to Dr. Said was my thought that Dean Yingling was single and that he was regarded as the school's most eligible bachelor among many women on campus. He did pay her a visit and the student was not kicked out. Instead, for her offense of being on the side of morality, justice, democracy, and history, she was confined to her room for more than a month—but she got to stay in school.

WHILE ALL OF THE STUDENTS showed me respect, there were a number, especially from Southside, Virginia's black belt counties, who were determined to hold on to white supremacy. They sometimes enjoyed distracting the class from serious consideration of social science findings on racial matters by arguing with me, citing the distorted negative statistics and myths about black people that abounded in the local newspapers, radio, and TV and in white southern popular culture at the time. But they were always civil, if for no other reason than that I held power over their grades.

One day I arrived a couple of moments late to class; as usual the students were sitting quietly in their desks. I went to the front of the room, put my lecture notes down, and looked up to survey the class of fifty-five students. Suddenly my gaze fixed on a large figure sitting in the back row wearing a white robe with a St. Andrew's cross over the heart, eyes peeking out at me through a tall white pointed hood. When the students saw that I had finally discovered the individual in a Klan outfit, they exploded with laughter. I was dumbfounded. But the sustained guffaws gave me several moments to think about how to seize back the stage from our visitor for a teaching moment.

I set aside my notes for the day and in a calm voice welcomed the white-clad interloper by saying, "Your visit today is opportune. We are going to review social control techniques deployed by hate groups in the South and how they parallel those of the Nazi terrorists in Europe, our mortal enemies in World War II." I then recited a list of atrocities attributed to the Klan and explained some of the reasons for its members' fear of revealing their identities. I went on to discuss the nature of prejudice, the authoritarian personality, the social-psychological inadequacies that lead individuals to need scapegoats, and the ignorance of white supremacists about genetics and physical and cultural anthropology—all the while intermittently gesturing toward my silent Exhibit A.

There was no discussion from the class. You could have heard a pin drop—this was no longer a joke. I intended to have the students do their post mortem on this session at the next class meeting when we would be without the "visual aid." The bell rang and everyone filed out without a word. I could see that the costumed figure was larger than any of the students. My inquiries among individual students turned up nothing about who was in that get-up and whether it was a joke or an act of intimidation. There was talk that a student's older brother, an actual member of the Klan, was the one "dressed to kill." But others claimed it was one of our own students. I never found out who the intruder was, but in 1965–66 the North Carolina KKK was holding rallies across southern Virginia on which the state press reported. Perhaps he was from across the border, or inspired by what he read.

IN THE FALL OF 1965, the School of Nursing was to admit its "first" two black students. They were not exactly the first, but it was the first time admission would carry a presumption of equal treatment. There had been one other black student officially enrolled in the School of Nursing, Charlotte Pollard, but she experienced what I called the "cattle pen" version of integration. This was the passive-aggressive scheme used by white institutions in response to court desegregation orders in the forties and fifties. One famous example was the 1950 Supreme Court case in which George W. McLaurin sued the School of Education of the University of Oklahoma. Mr. McLaurin won his case for admission, but the school retaliated by, among other indignities, confining him to a desk outside the classroom. While that treatment gradually disappeared, the later version applied to Charlotte still involved barbaric practices. Charlotte was not treated quite as McLaurin was, but she was required to live in separate quarters from her white classmates, was driven out of the cafeteria, and was banned from MCV-sponsored off-campus student activities, among other things.

But most important was how the majority of the students distanced themselves from her, depriving her of the usual learning opportunities arising from peer interaction. Isolation imposed countless hurdles for Charlotte in classes, laboratories, clinics, and study groups. A couple of nursing students stepped forward to befriend her for a while, but over time they pulled back in the face of intimidation from the more racist students. The uninhibited bigots targeted her with all of the standard racist taunts. One was the claim that she "smelled bad."

Charlotte as a statistic was "integrated" into the MCV School of Nursing, but as a person she was condemned to obtain her nursing education in a cold and hostile environment. Despite confinement in this Jim Crow cocoon, she emerged to soar in a career in psychiatric nursing, which is how my faculty colleagues in psychiatric nursing, Gloria Francis and Barbara Munjas, and I came to know her. We three were worried that the new black students to be admitted in 1965 might be treated no better than Charlotte, because many of the nursing faculty members were southerners without experience in settings where blacks were treated equally. So Gloria, Barbara, and I campaigned for some preparatory intergroup-relations training for our faculty. We designed a lengthy afternoon workshop during which Charlotte agreed to tell of her experience and then answer questions from Gloria. Charlotte was perfect for this: she had a heart-wrenching personal story to tell, was a wise and experienced psychiatric nurse, and was responsible for the training of the black psychiatric nursing aides in the MCV Department of Psychiatry.

We proposed the plan to Dean Yingling. She appeared edgy but reluctantly agreed to go along with it, I guess as a nod to the inevitable future. But because she thought of it as risky, she sought to clear it with President Smith. That started a firestorm. In no time Seig Heil came roaring over to jump on us. He insisted that it could not take place because "when you start talking about race, nothing but trouble follows." Never mind that race was always a burning preoccupation of nearly every Richmonder. We argued with him: if a little of that bigoted talk could be eclipsed by some thoughtful conversation about accommodating desegregation, MCV and nursing education would be much better off. Still, he left telling us to kill the project. In a day or so, to our surprise, Dean Yingling informed us that the session was back on, but it would have to be audio-recorded and if anything went wrong, Gloria, Barbara, and I were dead ducks.

On the day of the session the four of us gathered in the lecture hall with the recording equipment. Dean Yingling, the faculty, and some guests arrived and took their seats. Moments later Colonel Heil walked in and sat down. His furrowed brow and stern look made us nervous. Charlotte sat on a tall stool at the front of the room and in response to Gloria's questions proceeded to describe in vivid detail the inconvenience, insults, humiliation, and isolation she endured to receive her bachelor of science in nursing. She had graduated only three or four years earlier, so several in the audience were parties to what she experienced. I scanned the audience from time to time and saw that even two of the faculty members who objected to desegregating the school were visibly moved. When the questions ended, Gloria led a discussion of some of the proven principles and practices for successful intergroup work, such as analyzing cultural assumptions in course materials and making time for constructive

debriefing sessions after a racially sensitive situation. It was all civil and professional. The racists in the room bit their tongues in the face of the emergence
of a new cultural standard for race relations in our school, in a way that gave
me chills. At the end Colonel Heil and Dean Yingling slipped out in silence as
others stayed to talk with Charlotte or with each other.

I don't recall a lot of discussion about that session, but in the following
months there were signs that change was coming and the nursing faculty would
have to be ready. I believe that the 1964 Civil Rights Act helped the faculty see
the need to change their behavior. By the time the new black students entered
I was in graduate school at the University of Kentucky, but Gloria assured me
that they were doing well and that some faculty believed that our session had
set the tone for this success.

Gloria managed to get the tapes of the session and from them wrote an article on how to desegregate a southern nursing school for a prominent nursing
journal. But before she was allowed to publish it, she had to clear it with Dean
Yingling. At first, both Dean Yingling and President Smith said no way. But
after some censorship of the contents, they relented and she published it. They
insisted, though, that MCV not be identified in the article. Gloria's article provided many answers for other nursing schools facing imminent desegregation,
but her institution forbade itself from receiving credit for its own pioneering
effort.

IT WAS ACTIVITIES LIKE THIS that created a love-hate relationship between Dean Yingling and me. I don't think that she personally objected to
progress for black and poor people—after all she was a nurse, and many nurses
are deeply committed to helping people in crisis. Moreover, nurses with clinical experience in teaching hospitals knew that many blacks and poor people
were in a chronic state of distress. Her problem was like that of many educated
people at the time with institutional decision-making responsibilities. They
suffered from a "'fraidy cat syndrome" that made them terrified of what might
befall them and their organizations if they were linked to any controversy. In
Virginia at that time, equal rights for African Americans was the ultimate
controversy.

So we clashed, often. Twice, Dean Yingling left notes on my desk that in
effect told me I was fired. I was on a twelve-month contract, not on a tenure

track, so she was free to do whatever she wished. I'll never forget those two nights spent grappling with the idea that I suddenly had no job. I was terrified. As an instructor I grossed only $7,000 a year, and my family was already living paycheck to paycheck.

But both of these episodes ended the same way. The next day, when I came in to pack up my belongings, there was another note dismissing the note left the day before. In a roundabout way she'd say that she never really intended to fire me. After some experience with such blow ups, I learned that each one followed a nasty letter or phone call from a parent or from President Smith's office, leveling some kind of charge that she was harboring a Communist fellow traveler who was indoctrinating people's daughters with subversive ideas, which would inevitably result in race-mixing with black men. You had to grow up in the South in the Jim Crow era to truly know the power that this message had to create panic even in good people.

MCV WAS NOT THE ONLY place my teaching led to trouble. When I took the job at MCV I also got a part-time gig teaching introductory sociology at my alma mater, the Richmond Professional Institute. RPI was only about a mile and a half west of MCV, and my family needed the extra $250 for a semester's work. While RPI had a reputation for being less conservative than other Virginia campuses, the prevailing opinion was still pro-segregation. My students at RPI were of mixed convictions. Some were outspoken white supremacists; others kept it to themselves. Thankfully, there were two or three forthright opponents of segregation.

When we got to the section in the course on race relations I brought in a friend, Rev. Miles Jones. Reverend Jones's life was the epitome of the tribulations segregation imposed on black southerners. Yet he somehow triumphed over those challenges to become the beloved pastor of Providence Park Baptist Church on the north side of Richmond. He was over six feet tall, trim, and always impeccably dressed in a conservative dark suit. He spoke eloquently and with conviction in a deep baritone voice; when he shifted into homiletic mode he could mesmerize you. He recounted to the class his version of the classic story of black southerners: what it was like personally to find no opportunity in his segregated home state and to have to leave family to seek a future in the North. As he spoke, the white students realized how unfairly different was their own path to opportunity. He had a tremendous impact. Many students later reflected to me how that hour had changed their assumptions about race. I could see that this kind of personal encounter could rock the racist beliefs that gripped our community.

One might have expected this to be seen as laudable for an introductory course in sociology, but not so. Some days after Reverend Jones's visit the chairwoman of the sociology and social work program at RPI called me in. She told me that she had received complaints about his appearance and that I should not invite any more blacks to speak in my class. It was very disappointing to hear this from a social worker who had been one of my instructors a few years earlier. Later my request to teach in the spring semester was coldly denied with no explanation. Ironically, years later the offending visitor became the chairman of the Richmond school board and had an elementary school named for him.

Actions of this kind by otherwise very decent people like my chair were common then. Often individuals who accepted at least some vague idea of future desegregation thought activists were in too much of a hurry. They never tired of intoning: "This takes time. The Negroes are not yet ready for the privileges that white people have. They have to earn their rights. They are not yet as civilized as us. You need to be more patient and realistic." Every time I heard that sermon I thought, how much longer than three and a half centuries will be needed?

IT WAS A MILD late afternoon on November 22, 1963, when I dismissed my RPI class and strolled out onto Shafer Street. An acquaintance ran up to me and breathlessly spit out, "The president has been shot!" Unable to believe him, I raced home to the radio. It was true: John Kennedy was dead. While still in shock, I thought, "I know John Kennedy was disliked by the majority of white Virginians, especially in southern Virginia, but surely there will be great grieving across the state. After all, he was our president."

But "disliked" was hardly the word to describe the attitudes of many whites toward Kennedy. Within the hour an arch-conservative associate of mine, who liked to think of me as a friend because it proved he was open-minded, called me. Elated, he asked, "Did you hear that Kennedy was shot?"

"Yes," I replied.

"Isn't this great, now we are rid of that wild-eyed liberal?"

I was stunned: this cultured man was celebrating the murder of the president of the United States. He continued by telling me that he had just come from Miller and Rhoads downtown, one of our upscale department stores, where after the announcement of the president's assassination on the public address system, triumphant cheers erupted throughout the store. Clearly, that was not the call I wanted that day.

WHILE AT MCV, I engaged in a variety of activist projects on my own time. By 1962 Jean Fairfax, the director of southern programs for the AFSC and the genius behind its civil rights efforts in Prince Edward and across the South, had pulled me into several AFSC initiatives. Typically I gathered racially sensitive intelligence used in these civil rights projects—which is to say, white people would talk to me in ways that provided vital information.

While the AFSC had a deep ongoing commitment in Prince Edward, we worked elsewhere in Virginia as well. One such effort was with Bill Bagwell and Charles Davis and the Southside Virginia School Desegregation Project, based out of the AFSC southeastern regional office in High Point, North Carolina. Bill had been a key individual in setting up the initial AFSC program in Prince Edward. I visited several Southside counties to uncover information that would aid in our desegregation efforts there.

One of them was Amelia County, the same rural county about thirty-five miles southwest of Richmond where my nursing students were assailed by gun-toting white men. "Rat" Glenn, the back-channel kingpin in the Prince Edward school closing, also had a big political presence in Amelia, where he owned vast acres of timberland. On one visit I interviewed the white county school superintendent. He misrecognized my surname as part of the Brunswick County family who owned the Peebles department store chain. As others had done in Prince Edward and elsewhere in Southside Virginia, he therefore assumed that I could be trusted to be like him, a hard-shell segregationist, and spoke freely. With little pause, he began with the patented Virginia odium toward the NAACP, our federal government, and the threat of "race mixing," ending with a declaration of how folks in Amelia intended to deal with all these "subversive elements." Without admitting that he was personally involved, he revealed a plot afoot to murder the Amelia County NAACP president, a man he said was "dangerous."

Once out of his office, I found a pay phone and tried to get in touch with Bill or Charles in High Point, with no luck. So I called the AFSC's national office in Philadelphia and spoke to Eleanor Eaton, a long-time veteran of AFSC justice-seeking work. Due to my mistrust of the local sheriff and the state police, she gave me some numbers to contact the FBI. I told an agent the story. He dismissed any possible danger, saying that they "got these rumors all the time." He went on to further "explain" to me that the FBI had no jurisdiction in Amelia, saying that the FBI was only "an information-gathering organization." He then told me to contact the county sheriff.

In so many words, he was saying that the FBI had no intention of protecting black civil rights leaders in Southside Virginia. Not having phone numbers for the Amelia NAACP officials, I returned to Richmond and called Happy Lee, head of the VCHR, and passed on to him what I had learned. He said that he would contact Lester Banks or Sam Tucker at the state NAACP. The Amelia County NAACP president was never assassinated. But I have often wondered if the AFSC had not sent me there and all those civil rights folks I reported to had not been in place, would there have been a different outcome? It was that same old conundrum that haunted me in my later career in public health: how do you enumerate the casualties you prevent from happening?

DURING THIS PERIOD of dramatic change in race relations, I continued to struggle with my parents over race. One episode with my father was particularly distressing. Dr. J. Rupert Picott, the executive director of the Virginia Teachers Association, Virginia's black teachers' professional organization, invited me to write an article with him on the Prince Edward issue for a national education journal. I was honored. This was to be my first publication. But more importantly, he was a nationally known educator, a distinguished civil rights leader, and a man of impressive intellect. We began a series of meetings to divide up the labor and then edit the manuscript.

For one of these last meetings, I invited Dr. Picott to come to my house on Kensington Avenue. On the night of our meeting, however, my father unexpectedly showed up and, as was his habit, took a seat on the sofa in the living room to watch my family's comings and goings in silence. Shortly thereafter, Dr. Picott arrived. An incomparable snappy dresser, he appeared with his usual dignity and style. I invited him in and started to introduce him to my father who, I was surprised to see, did not get up to greet Dr. Picott. In fact, he did not even acknowledge the man's gracious overture. He just sat tight as if Dr. Picott were not even there. It was an unmistakable snubbing of this gentleman, done clearly to show disrespect for Dr. Picott as a black man. I was stunned and capable of only one response—anger. Dr. Picott rescued me and seized the initiative by simply asking, "Where will we be working?" I pointed to the dining room table. Dr. Picott went over to the table, sat down with his back to my father, opened his brief case, and laid out his materials alongside mine.

I glared at my father and cursed him under my breath. He sat silent and motionless as I walked over to join Dr. Picott. I tried to think of a way to apologize, but he interrupted my thoughts by beginning to discuss what we should do next on the article. When we were done with our work, Dr. Picott got up and gave my totally unresponsive father a polite nod goodbye. I saw Dr. Picott out the door and, when he was out of earshot, stormed over to my father. The rage I had held onto for the last hour exploded. I began yelling, "Who do you think you are?" I screamed, "You aren't fit to shine this distinguished man's shoes. That kind of disrespect for people will never again happen in my house." I told him to leave. He rose from the sofa and without a word walked out my front door. In fury I slammed the door behind him. We neither spoke nor saw each other for four years.

* 15 *

Communists, Sex Fiends, and Half-Breeds
Take the Struggle to Appalachia

MY TWO YEARS of teaching at MCV proved to be a turning point in what heretofore had been a happenstance career path. The exposure to the inner workings of a big teaching hospital; the education of physicians, dentists, pharmacists, nurses, and all the other health professionals; and the challenges faced by the patients in their quest for healing all fascinated me. When I learned that there were programs for the study of how the social and behavioral sciences contribute to these processes, I knew that I had to be a part of that.

The University of Kentucky had one of the most prominent and pioneering medical behavioral science programs in the country. Two more of my patron saints—Dr. Fred Spencer, whom I had worked with at MCV, and Dr. Bob Straus, chair of the Department of Behavioral Science at the UK Medical Center —helped get me admitted for a doctorate in sociology with a concentration in medical behavioral science. They also helped me obtain a fellowship from the National Institute of Mental Health. An early interdisciplinary program, MBS required students first to satisfy all the requirements for a PhD in sociology, anthropology, psychology, or one of the life science disciplines like physiology. Then one did a second round of study with the behavioral science faculty in the Colleges of Medicine and Dentistry and conducted a major health-related study for the dissertation. My dissertation was a meta-analysis (before there was such a term) of a decade of epidemiological study on the relationship between socioeconomic status and the major chronic and infectious diseases of the day. I moved with my family to Lexington and plunged into my PhD studies in 1965.

That winter, I got a call from Doug Kelley, the executive director of the Encampment for Citizenship, asking me to be the director of the first Encampment ever held in the South. Doug had long wanted to place the summer program somewhere in Southern Appalachia. He had found what he thought was the perfect site: Union College, a small United Methodist Church–affiliated school in the Knox County town of Barbourville. Barbourville was located in the southeastern Kentucky coal field, less than forty miles from Cumberland Gap, where Kentucky, Virginia, and Tennessee all meet.

Doug Kelley had a long and distinguished record in youth community service and citizenship education. In the early fifties, as a senior at Berea College, Doug organized a group that founded the International Development Placement Association, dedicated to placing young volunteers in community work in Third World countries. The IDPA was one of the models used by Senator Hubert Humphrey in his Peace Corps proposal, and after the corps was implemented, Sargent Shriver appointed Doug as the organization's first community relations director.

I had a long history with the Encampment. I had been a "camper" (i.e., a student) and had served as a recruiter of campers across the South, on advisory and fund-raising committees, and as a guest speaker on several occasions. At one point in the early sixties there had even been some talk with Al Black, the founder, about putting my name in the hat for the executive director's job. But I had never been the chief honcho at one of the six-week summer programs.

In 1966 there were four Encampment programs; ours was the Southern Appalachian Center for Education in Democracy. It was co-sponsored by the Council of the Southern Mountains, headquartered in Berea, and the Southern Regional Council, both longtime champions of social justice and progressive development in the South. Our site was chosen to meet the goals and funding requirements of the U.S. Office of Economic Opportunity's Community Action Program, aimed at encouraging American youth to get more involved in poverty issues and volunteerism. The Encampment's traditional mission of preparing youth to become well-informed democratic leaders in public affairs was a perfect fit for the grassroots side of the War on Poverty.

One of the reasons the Encampment chose me as the director was my familiarity with the Appalachian South. For years I had traveled, conducted interviews, collected traditional music, and photographed signs of socioeconomic problems in the mountain counties of Virginia, Kentucky, Tennessee, and North Carolina. I was also studying with highly regarded experts on Appalachia at UK. My understanding of and connection with the region had been deepened by meeting folks like the activist poet Wendell Berry; the writer Harry Caudill, author of *Night Comes to the Cumberlands;* and the Louisville civil rights pioneers Carl and Anne Braden; as well as by attending a gathering at the Highlander Folk School with Myles Horton and Guy Carawan. I was also acquainted with the less publicized vein of white supremacy that ran through the mountains, as expressed to me on a visit to Corbin, Kentucky—"I'm warnin' ya, any nigga' had better be out of Corbin by sundown."

EVEN BEFORE MY spring semester ended, Doug and I began to plan the program and recruit the staff. Immediately after exams, our family moved from Lexington into a tiny ground-floor apartment in the Lakeside dormitory at Union College's Barbourville campus.

I had about three days to work with the staff before the arrival of the campers. We drew the staff from the ranks of the Peace Corps, Operation Crossroads Africa, Teachers for East Africa, and a variety of other rich experiences. They were a marvelous idealistic bunch—a rich mix of black and white, urbane New Yorkers and native southerners, academic eggheads and earthy community activists. The majority of the staff at the time was living in Kentucky; a few were natives of nearby mountain areas of the eastern part of the state. We thought that this would provide some reassuring local credibility.

There were 84 campers—49 white, 28 black, and the remaining 7 including Native, Puerto Rican, and Mexican Americans. They came from twenty-three states, the District of Columbia, Canada, and England. Most were Protestants, but Catholics, Jews, and secularists were well-represented. About a third came from rural or small town areas; just under half came from southern or border states. Almost three-fourths of the campers were on partial or full scholarships. You can imagine the cultural distances our conversations had to bridge. But as in all the Encampments, it was just a matter of time before they did.

A typical weekday program began in the morning with an outside speaker such as Frank Smith, Tennessee Valley Authority director and a former Mississippi congressman; Ed King, a Mississippi Freedom Democratic Party congressional candidate; John Y. Brown, former Kentucky congressman, state legislator, and Democratic candidate for the U.S. Senate; and Galen Martin, director of the Kentucky Human Rights Commission. Others, whose names I've lost, came to tell us of the work of the Poor People's Movement, the Southern Regional Council, the Council of the Southern Mountains, the Appalachian Regional Commission, and the Knox County Economic Opportunity Council, the local agency of the Office of Economic Opportunity. We also had a visit and talk given by my Richmond friend and civil rights collaborator Ruby Clayton.

After each lecture there was a lengthy Q and A, and then campers and staff broke out into small discussion groups. After lunch there were usually workshop meetings. Later in the afternoon we'd have leisure time or recreational opportunities. In the evening there might be a meeting of the camper self-government, a film, a panel of campers on a topic of their interest, another speaker, or perhaps just entertainment. Sometimes we took group field trips. Weekends, less structured, still included some planned educational and leisure activities.

Each of the campers spent at least one afternoon each week in community volunteer work linked to their workshop. Our workshops dealt with civil rights, economic and community development, political action, tutoring, creating a community newsletter, recreation as a tool in community organizing, and the building of community cooperatives. For one full week, campers lived in the homes of local families, usually near rural centers operated by the OEO program in neighborhoods with names like Pumpkin Run, Possum Hollow, Bimble, Salt Gum, Flat Lick, and Stinking Creek.

Weeks before our starting date Doug and I sought to prepare the little coal mining community to understand our organization. We wrote letters, made phone calls, and visited community leaders in Knox County. These contacts led us to believe that the leaders of this county would work with us on any problems that came up, including those involving issues of race. Kentucky, while once a slave state, had a small black population, and the state's leaders were giving the nation the impression that they intended to move, albeit slowly, into a new era of racial democracy.

The road to racial harmony in Knox County in 1966, however, proved rockier than anyone anticipated. Very few in the county, including well-meaning local whites, suspected the virulent white supremacy that lay just below the surface of Barbourville life. The arrival of a multiracial Encampment for Citizenship unleashed this poison, which hijacked the public dialogue from much of our original mission.

IN THE FIRST DAYS OF the Encampment a couple of our boys tested the strict ban we had on visits to opposite-sex dormitory floors. In their defense, it was the early sixties, when many college activists were challenging what were called parietal rules, so it was only natural for the kind of kids we recruited to want to flout what they saw as old-fashioned prohibitions. But we knew that this was how rumors of interracial sex—the third rail of race relations in the South of those days—got started, and so we had provided plenty of common space on the first floor where campers could assemble, even in relative privacy. Once the campers understood all of this, challenges to the rule stopped. I like to think that my patented and often repeated sermon to the campers about setting priorities in order "to change the face of America" sunk in.

Nevertheless, the word of these few early visits to the girls' floor made its way from some of the campers to the Union College students and then to individuals in the community, getting embellished as it traveled. Some in town were looking for anything with which to discredit the Encampment, and here it was—the vision of sex between black boys and white girls! It was the perfect stuff for the overheated imaginations of the white supremacists, obsessed with the sexual activity of everyone except their own people.

As the rumors grew in mythological mass, many in the county began to say that the Encampment was promoting sexual debauchery, race mixing, and Communism. Some even said it was part of a federal government plan to resettle northern urban blacks in their county. Some also spread rumors that our campers had committed vandalism at the college and in the community. As these tales circulated, relations with the community chilled. The hearsay set off a cascade of slurs and acts of harassment, intimidation, and assault. Campers and staff members who went downtown got icy stares. Merchants and public officials became guarded, sometimes openly hostile. Some residents hurled racial epithets and obscenities at us: "Go home, nigger!" and "We don't want no nigger-lovers here!" Most absurd were the whites who expressed outrage at what they called "interracial ice-cream licking." Ironically, the bulk of the rancor originated not in the rural districts where we worked most but in the town of Barbourville itself.

The rumors got back to us in a variety of ways. First were the anonymous phone calls with preposterous claims. Then were the calls and visits from self-proclaimed "friends" of the Encampment who delighted in passing on stories they had heard. Each rumor incorporated one or more of the typical ploys that spiteful white southerners used against those who sought justice for blacks. Some of these people actually believed the rumors, but many others cared not one wit about their veracity. They simply deployed them in cynical attempts to disgrace civil rights advocates and stir up the small violence-prone minority of the white population.

The rumors in the county were not just shared verbally from person to person, but were also reported as facts on the local AM radio station, in weekly newspaper columns, and occasionally as crude handbills, graffiti, and make-shift signs around town. In the latter weeks of our stay, signs created with stencils began to appear in our Lakeside dormitory. Like the other hate garbage cast our way, they incorporated the three principal white supremacist buga-boos we confronted all summer long: Race! Sex! Communism! I managed to save just two of them. One read, "U.C. Students Demand Removal of Half Breed Communist Scum"; the other, "Needed Bad: Birth Control Pills for Communists at Lakeside."

Town officials made plain to me their attitudes. The conduct of Encampment participants was a "slap in the face to the high moral standards" held by the people of Barbourville, they resented being "invaded by subversives," and they were "not going to stand for it." I took them at their word, especially after one of them told me that because of us he had joined the run on firearms and ammunition at the local hardware store.

THE RUMORS BEGAN in our first week; the abuse began with fury in the second week. The first ugly incidents occurred at the bowling alley. It was next door to our dormitory and was frequented by the campers, who went not only for the tenpins but also to buy snacks and sometimes just to hang out. Dozens of local young white males also had the habit of spending much of their spare time there, especially in the evenings and on weekends. They did very little bowling. At first their principal interest appeared to be the local girls. But after a while they became fixed on our campers. Before long they made a habit of sauntering up to a camper—black or white, it didn't matter—so as to obstruct the camper's movement. With the camper trapped in a circle of hostile locals, one of them would get up in the captive's face with taunts like, "No niggers are allowed in here!," "We don't like nigger lovers!," or, "Wait 'til we catch you outside." The hounding was often punctuated with a jabbing finger, shoving, or an explicit provocation for fisticuffs.

In one instance in July, two of our male white campers were trapped in one of these agonizing encounters just outside the bowling alley. In an obvious attempt to frighten the campers, one of the local boys said, "Any niggers and whites walking together will be shot at. I lynched a negra on Route 25 last week." Afterwards the camper told me the boy had threatened to beat him up and lynch him for telling the bowling alley manager about an earlier assault. There had not been any reports of murders in Knox County the week before, but what was a young frightened stranger to the county to believe?

I knew from years of personal experience how these confrontations played out. Often there were boys present on the scene who, even though they may have held the same basic racist attitudes as the ringleader, were uneasy about what was happening. But feeling intimidated, they succumbed to the mob momentum and shrunk from aiding the victim, dreading that they might be cast into "nigger lover" hell, a place from which one rarely escaped.

So to evade this fate and resolve the prickly moral dissonance, they would search for a reason to say that the victim somehow "brought it on himself." Such dynamics persuaded everyone, white and black alike, that support for harassing black people and their white sympathizers was ubiquitous and so it was best to just keep quiet. Cowardice in those days among most white southerners was viewed not so much as a moral failing but as a practical act of survival. It goes without saying that blacks had no chance for an exit from situations like this that was at once dignified and safe. Most chose wisdom over valor.

The bowling alley manager was friendly; he welcomed our business and didn't discriminate against us, but neither did he ever help protect us from these bullies. He was likely intimidated but also driven by the profit motive: he did not want to alienate his local customers. After all, the folks from the Encampment would leave in a few weeks.

IN THE BEGINNING, we encouraged the campers and staff to use at least some of their free time to explore the county. One of the closest attractions to us, a little over four miles from the college, was the Dr. Thomas Walker State Historical Site and Park. One day about ten of the campers joined Saundra Alexander, the Encampment nurse, for a hike to the park. They were gone for about an hour when I got a frantic telephone call from Saundra. Her voice trembled as she blurted out what had just happened. Calling from a house on the road to the park, she related how they were walking along when someone began shooting at them. I told her to stay with the campers at the house until I could call the sheriff's department, and then I would come right away in the van to get them out of there.

By now I knew the sheriff's department number by heart. As soon as the dispatcher answered, I told him the details of the incident. I urged him to send somebody right away before there was a gunshot casualty. While I had no proof, I got the impression from his pokey response that he was trying to stall. I began to wonder if he already knew about the shootings and was protecting someone involved. So I all but shouted the location of the shootings once more and slammed down the phone in fury. I jumped into the van and took off, knowing that the only weapon on board was a heavy duty tire iron under the driver's seat.

More than ten minutes must have passed before I caught up with Saundra and the campers. They were running toward Barbourville in the ditch along-side the road. Three or four of them were crying, but I heard no gunfire and saw no one about in the fields or around a nearby farmhouse. I pulled the van up on the side of the road, and the frightened youth and their nurse jumped into the vehicle, some wailing, some cursing, and a couple trying to spill out a disjointed account of what had happened. I whirled that vehicle around and took off with the pedal to the floor and didn't lift up on the accelerator until I got up to sixty-five. At that point, I heard a chorus of heavy sighs and a couple of the boys began to laugh and create their whopper versions of what just took place—as good a way as any to deal with their close call.

DESPITE THE INTIMIDATION, threats, and assaults, I thought we were doing pretty darn good. Working out of the rural OEO centers, campers were making lots of local friends because of the work they were doing: creating activities for the elderly, tutoring and reading to young children, leading games, repairing houses and sheds, clearing silt and rubbish from creek beds, visiting and running errands for shut-ins, helping in the garden and cutting firewood for families, fundraising for community projects, and organizing a neighborhood newsletter and activities associated with promoting greater citizen activism.

The harassment nevertheless continued, concentrated mostly in Barbourville. But at least no one had been seriously hurt at the Encampment. And the trouble taught everybody some ugly truths about race in America: the campers, our staff, folks at the college, the well-meaning people of Knox County, and the local and state authorities. After a whole lifetime in the South, I, too, had some learning to do. Sure, I feared a catastrophe, and so I did everything anyone suggested that might help to ensure our safety. But deep down, I thought that we would be okay and that an indelible lesson available nowhere else was being embedded in us and in this community. That's why I did not want to let this opportunity be aborted.

Yet, frightening reports about our problems were going in daily to the Encampment board. While I knew nothing of the board's deliberations, I surmised that they had become increasingly alarmed about the safety of the campers and the staff, and perhaps were also concerned about the Encampment's reputation and even liability issues if there was a tragedy. They must have wondered if I had lost control and whether they ought to send someone else down to take over the reins. After all, Doug Kelley and Al Black were the only ones up there in New York who really knew me, and Al had not seen me in several years. So they must have thought they needed to get a closer look at the first Encampment venture in a southern state.

On one of our routine calls, Doug Kelley told me that the board was sending down Allard Lowenstein from New York, an alum of the 1947 Encampment and one of the board's leading members—the next day! I had met Lowenstein briefly a couple of times at Encampment gatherings and knew a bit about his national reputation as an activist in the liberal wing of the Democratic Party. But I really did not know what to expect under these circumstances, and I was feeling a bit defensive about someone coming down to "check on me." I was also a little bit intimidated by the prominence of the guy. I feared that Lowenstein was coming to give me a pink slip, and I felt rotten as I tried unsuccessfully to get to sleep that night.

The next day, as our campers and staff played softball, the Encampment van pulled up and out stepped Lowenstein. I was startled by the burst of energy he showed at the moment he hit the ground. We exchanged hasty greetings, and I assumed that we would head over to the dorm to talk. Instead, the giant images of his eyes, magnified by the thickest glasses I had ever seen, turned to survey what was happening on the ball field. Before I knew what was happening, he was up at bat.

From some little mischievous corner of my brain where old stereotypes still resided came the thought that because Al was a hard-driving New York Jewish intellectual with thick eyeglasses, he wouldn't be much of a ball player. Lowenstein blasted my lingering prejudice about New Yorkers with a soaring fly ball that almost hit me where I stood watching in deep center field. That ball must have flown 230 feet from the plate, a phenomenal drive for softball. With this Al Lowenstein also hit a home run with me. I relaxed about his visit because he took all of the threat I had anticipated out of our discussions. I actually enjoyed seeing his amazing mind take in our predicament in Barbourville. He seemed to gain confidence in me, and he agreed that the experience for the campers, despite all its risks, was priceless. When he departed he conveyed to me his approval.* For the remainder of the Encampment, there were no further omens of closing the Barbourville site or any sense that anyone up in New York had doubts about their Kentucky director.

DESPITE ALL that had happened, the Encampment family was determined that our tormentors would not deter us. So in the fourth week, as planned, all the campers moved into the homes of twenty-five different families across the county for a week of field work. Each placement was near the site of the camper's workshop project. The match-up exceeded everyone's hopes. The campers adored their families, and the families raved about the young volunteers and the work they were doing in the community. By the end of the week the camp-

---

*For a biography of Lowenstein, including much about his involvement in the Encampment for Citizenship, see William H. Chafe, *Never Stop Running: Allard Lowenstein and the Struggle to Save American Liberalism* (Princeton: Princeton University Press, 1998).

ers were rhapsodizing about the experience. Race was never a question—except in one case where some neighboring white men repeatedly threatened a host family with violence if the black Encampment youth remained in their home. This family was so terrified and the sheriff so unresponsive that the family reluctantly asked me to bring the camper back to our dorm.

That wasn't the only incident. One evening at twilight a black camper was on his way back to his host family's house on a remote back road after a long day working at the OEO Community Center. Suddenly, about a half dozen white youths appeared and began chasing him and throwing sticks and stones at him. He finally made it to his hosts' house, at which point the boys all disappeared into the darkness. The camper sustained some troublesome but not lasting injuries. But I could see in our later debriefing that the episode made a deep and hurtful mark on him, part of which was a rising cynicism about the potential of white people to embrace an honest democracy. Tales of this episode also affected other campers. Some turned to sardonic humor to cover their fright and mistrust of Knox County whites. One such quip they created played off the sixties drug culture. When they left the safe harbor of the dorm for activities in the community, you would hear them chant, "Let's go get stoned!"

BY OUR FOURTH WEEK in Barbourville the rumor mill was running 24-7, and the phone threats, acts of harassment, and attempted assaults were now occurring almost daily. With each incident I would phone the Knox County sheriff or the town police and ask for an investigation. But all of the law enforcement officers had become evasive and passive aggressive. From all appearances they had allied with our hell makers. The town police just did not respond at all to my pleas for help. The locally assigned Kentucky state trooper was by now also keeping his distance, claiming he "couldn't be everywhere at once."

I was on the phone almost daily with Doug Kelley and with Galen Martin at the Kentucky Human Rights Commission looking for additional ideas on how to deal with this barrage of hate. The conversations offered some comfort, but Doug was in New York and had responsibility for three other Encampment sites and Galen, our only Kentucky lifeline, was some 140 miles away in Louisville. So I was alone on the ground to make the daily decisions regarding the safety of my family, the staff, and nearly a hundred young people. That reality hung heavy over me.

Doug, Galen, and I agreed that perhaps I should make another effort to reach out to community leaders and persuade them to apply some pressure to local law enforcement. So once again I called or visited the county judge, the Barbourville mayor, the radio station manager, the newspaper editor, businessmen, and others I thought might make a difference. Few of them would even speak with me, so little came of it. Mostly what I heard from those who did talk to me was either an earful of that practiced evasion so common in politicians or a big dose of straight-out acrimony.

My family and I were also sometimes targets of harassment and threats. On two different occasions I received phone calls that appeared to be from the same person. A male voice, with a regional accent and using my name, said, "We know where your children sleep, and we have a bomb just for them if you and your commie sex-fiend friends don't get out of here." I moved all the family's beds together against the inner wall of the room where we slept. And then it finally dawned on me that some of these incidents might be within the purview of the FBI. But a call to them was not encouraging. In fact, I got essentially the same response this time as I had two years earlier, when I reported the plot to murder the president of the local NAACP chapter in Amelia County, Virginia. The agent on the phone listened quietly to my complaints and then said: "I am sorry, we can't help you. We are only an information gathering organization." He sounded like he was about to hang up. But before he did, I retorted, "Well then why don't you come down here and gather a little information about what the Civil Rights Act calls 'a conspiracy to deny civil rights.'" His voice turned sullen. "This is not in our jurisdiction. Sorry." He hung up. Once again, lawmen were anything but our protectors.

The abuses persisted and law enforcement officials continued to forsake us. So by the last weeks of the Encampment, I decided that we had to impose a nightfall curfew on the campers for their safety. Despite the fact that many of our campers were pretty savvy about how racism works as a system, they still were personally wounded by the abuse. So when all the staff and campers assembled together, such as on camper government night or at call meetings, we spent a lot of time processing events of the day. Many of the northern campers were shocked that these things "could happen in America." Even some of the southerners were surprised. But it was reassuring to see how this experience advanced and intensified one of the principal aims of the Encampment program: the breakdown of psychological barriers and the building of trust between campers of different social origins. It transformed an unbound aggregate of young people who society would have assumed were fundamentally dissimilar into a truly integrated community, in which each one of them could now see past that society's haze deep into the souls of the others where we are all connected. It was my job to keep safe and nurture this fragile little experiment in democracy regardless of what outrages came our way.

I felt another special responsibility that summer too. I was a firm believer in the Encampment's mission to flood the country with young people on the way to becoming informed and dedicated democratic leaders. What I and my staff chose to do at this tender juncture in the lives of these youngsters would likely affect their future commitment to the struggles for justice. I feared that the troubles might be enough to turn campers away from hope and idealism and toward fatalism about the potential for genuine reform. I was so consumed with the adequacy of my responses to these challenges that restful sleep, peaceful meals with my wife, and relaxed play with my two babies became elusive luxuries.

ON AUGUST 13, 1966, the campers and staff all gathered out in front of the Lakeside dorm, their home for a tumultuous six weeks of perhaps the most intense emotional experience any of them had ever had or would likely ever have again. Two giant tour buses sat on the gravel driveway poised to take them home. Everywhere, happy tears trickled down cheeks and lips struggled to smile. My eyes, too, filled. The love that arises from sharing tribulation and deep emotional discovery had changed people who were strangers only six weeks earlier into beloved friends unable to say goodbye. They had "been to the mountaintop," seeing up close the noble beauty of racially egalitarian democracy and how each of them could be a nurturing part of it. These young people had witnessed a visionary prospect that few back in their hometowns would understand. They also knew that they had become the special bearers of this message and inescapably part of a world communion of witnesses to what can be.

Most of the campers climbed aboard the buses, and the doors slammed shut.

The few stragglers got into automobiles with their family members or friends and drove away, leaving the staff and me standing silent in the driveway and struggling to end this extraordinary summer in our minds. I was reminded of the words that a camper named Missy Greer, a white girl from Rome, Georgia, had written the day before when asked to submit an evaluation of her Encampment experience: "How can you ask me to 'evaluate' such an experience? . . . I don't want this experience to end tomorrow. I won't let it, I won't let these things happen. Why? Because it has meant so much to me, it's helped me to find my own cause for living, my purpose for life. Of course I already had one, but now I realize what it is."

Suddenly my thoughts were interrupted. Mary Montle, a staff member and a New York public school teacher, reminded me of yet another one of the acts of malice we had endured this summer. A few days earlier, two of the tires on her convertible had been slashed while it was parked in the bowling alley parking lot. We were certain some of the local young men who hung out there had done it, no doubt because they knew the car belonged to Mary, who was black. But we had no way to prove it. So she informed me that she and Ron Krupp, whom we all called "Killiecrankie," were going downtown to a gas station that sold retread tires. No more than twenty minutes after they left, the phone rang. It was Mary. She was hysterical, but at the same time she was trying to suppress her voice because she was being overheard by several white men in the gas station office. I could hear the men laughing and apparently enjoying themselves.

Petrified, she whispered, "They are beating him up! They are beating Killiecrankie! They are going to kill him! I am here alone with these white men!" Horrified, I responded, "I'm coming down there right now. Get out of the gas station and away from there." I hung up and immediately called the sheriff's office and gave the guy on the phone the details, despite his obvious disinterest. At the gas station, I pulled in and stopped near the front door, getting a quick glance at Mary who stood alone on the doorstep trembling and in tears. I also got a glimpse through the big window of a few guys standing inside the gas station with broad grins on their faces. Outside three men were hovering over Ron, who was down on the concrete. He was rolled up into a fetal position as they kicked him and reached down to slug him in the face. His body bounced about on the pavement with each successive blow.

I grabbed the tire iron from under the seat and raced, blinded with rage, toward Ron's assailants. As I stormed toward them, the tire iron raised over my head ready to strike, my fury could hardly be in doubt. Before I got within ten feet of them, the three attackers scampered into their nearby convertible and gunned it out of the gas station parking lot. I turned back and saw Killie-crankie lying there, hardly moving, in a pool of his own blood. Mary raced over to me and we embraced for a split second, as if to say, "We are safe now, but what of poor Ron?" We both kneeled down at his side wondering what to do first. Ron provided the answer: he began to get up. We were so relieved.

At this moment, the deputy sheriff rolled slowly into the gas station, taking his own good time to get out of his car. I hastily gave him the essentials about the assault and told him that the three assailants had just made their getaway to the left. Without a word, he backed his vehicle up and slowly pulled out onto the street—to the right. I yelled at him about his "mistake," all the while point-ing to the left. It was then I realized: I had once again been taken. The sheriff's department had never had any intention of protecting the Encampment "in-vaders." As I turned back to Mary and Ron, my eyes fell upon the three men inside the gas station, now consumed with belly laughs at our expense.

We got Mary's car and everyone back safely to the Union College campus. Our staff nurse, Saundra, took Ron to see a physician from whom we received good news—miraculously, he had no permanent injuries. After things settled down, Ron and Mary told me how the frightening experience began. They were walking from Ron's car to the gas station to pick up Mary's car, the re-treads having been installed. Suddenly out of nowhere came an old-model convertible with the three white men in it, roaring onto the sidewalk with the obvious intention of crushing them against the brick building behind them. Amazingly, they both were able to dodge the oncoming vehicle. Having failed to hit the couple, the car stopped and the three men jumped out and headed for them. Mary raced into the station and called me. They caught Ron, knocked him down, and began to kick and verbally torment him. They held him captive until I showed up.

This beating of Ron Krupp was the last straw for me. The next morning, we filed an assault and battery charge with the sheriff's office, and in the afternoon we finished up our cleaning and packing and gladly left Barbourville. In September of 1966 the three assailants were located and arrested. We were called back to Barbourville in the late fall for a grand jury hearing. While several of our staff testified, I recall only the irony of Mary Montle's appearance before the grand jury. She was asked nothing about what she witnessed at the gas station. The only question the grand jury had for her was, "What business would a Negro woman such as yourself be having in Knox County, Kentucky?" The grand jury never returned an indictment.

FOLLOWING THE racial turmoil we experienced in Knox County, two things amazed me. The first was the outpouring of gratitude from so many of the folks in the county for what the Encampment had attempted to do there; the second was the sympathy the same folks had for the abuse we suffered. Of course, such comments were almost always hush-hush so the speaker could avoid retaliation. That fear of retribution was what had always held Jim Crow together and led to the mistaken conclusion that white southerners were all of one cold mind. A minority of ardent racists protected by indifferent local leaders had besmirched Knox County's good name and belied its fair-minded white folks. Months after I had returned to Lexington, I continued receiving letters from campers and some of the Knox County placement families with stirring testimonials about the friends made, the fun had, and the lessons learned. We had done something right.

* 16 *

Confronting the Racism of the "Baron" of Kentucky Basketball

OVER THE YEARS I learned a lot of different ways to stick it to segregation and white supremacy. One unique opportunity came after I returned to the University of Kentucky from Barbourville and resumed my PhD studies. The work was intense and spare time short. But I managed to find time to play with my young daughters and, of course, to follow the basketball fortunes of the UK Wildcats. For many decades Kentucky had been one of the preeminent college basketball programs in the country under the legendary coach Adolph Rupp. His rule over the college game was such that he was known as the "Baron" of basketball. Since I had played high school, college, military, and some semi-pro basketball, I was thrilled to be in a hotbed of college hoops. In those years, Rupp's teams included great future professional performers such as Pat Riley, Louie Dampier, Dan Issel, and many others—but his squads were all-white. Some white schools in the South had already begun to recruit blacks, including Vanderbilt in Kentucky's own Southeastern Conference. But Rupp, UK's coach since 1930, apparently never planned to coach young black men.

One day early in my first basketball season at UK, I ran into Mr. Rupp at a gas station, and we began to chat about the Wildcats as he was inclined to do with fans all across Kentucky. We commiserated about the untimely injury sustained by one of his key starters. And then it occurred to me that I would never again have a chance to speak with Kentucky's most revered celebrity, who outranked the state's governor and its U.S. senators in the eyes of most

Kentuckians. So I sucked up some wind and nervously asked him, "When are you going to recruit black players, Mr. Rupp? Everybody else is." Whew! It was like I had thrown scalding dishwater on him. A scowl washed over his craggy face, and he fired back, "I'll recruit who I damn well please." With that he turned his back and disappeared into the gas station office. So much for the direct approach to assailing the color barrier of Rupp's basketball dynasty.

The University of Kentucky was an excellent and challenging academic institution. After spending hours in class and studying from early morning to late at night, my fellow graduate students and I, some of us former athletes, sorely needed exercise and diversion. But there were virtually no gyms available for graduate and professional students. Most of the facilities were controlled by the Athletic Department and reserved for intercollegiate sports teams, principally football and basketball. After some persistent requests, we finally obtained the use of some handball courts at the noon hour. We gratefully accepted these crumbs and I learned a new game.

One day during the football off-season our pack of noontime jocks arrived at the handball courts anxious to play, only to learn that we were barred from using the courts for the foreseeable future. On the bulletin board was a memo from the football coaching staff instructing the players to immediately assemble for a series of official practice sessions in this facility. David Hall, one of my graduate student colleagues, pointed out that since these off-season practices were an infraction of NCAA rules, they might provide a bargaining chip for obtaining our own facility for our noon workouts. So someone raced out for a camera and a copy of the front page of the day's *Louisville Courier-Journal* as evidence of the date and snapped pictures showing the practice announcement. Back at our study carrels with documentation of the violation, we began to plot how we would use this to obtain a permanent recreational venue. But as the discussion developed, we realized that this evidence could get much more than access to some smelly, cracker-box gym a half dozen hours a week. Someone asked, why not demand that Adolph Rupp be made to recruit one or more blacks for the basketball team? It was unanimous: "Let's desegregate the Kentucky Wildcats!"

Then arose the question of who would present the photos and our demands to the president of the university—a delegation or all of us? After some debate, we concluded that it might be more effective if it were only one person, and as luck would have it, they picked me. I called the president's office and conveyed something of the gravity of our concern without giving it all away. I was told to take our case to Dr. Robert L. Johnson, the vice president for student affairs.

On the day of the appointment it finally hit me how daunting was the task for which my so-called friends had drafted me. My stomach churned with fear that this little face-off with the administration might derail my doctorate and academic career—and still not achieve our demands.

Dr. Johnson was standing when I was ushered into his office. He was a tall and angular man in a short-sleeve shirt; his stern look did nothing to comfort me. He shook my hand and we sat down at a table. The door was shut and we were the only two in the room. Dr. Johnson was polite, but I could sense he was annoyed. "Okay, what's on your mind?" he asked, as if he knew nothing of the purpose of our meeting. But he already knew about the quid pro quo we had in mind from my earlier phone call to the president's office.

I pulled out our photo collection and showed him one of the images documenting the NCAA football practice infraction. I told him that I represented a significant number of graduate and professional students on the UK campus. Quietly studying the photos, he finally broke the silence by asking why we would resort to "blackmail" when there were many more responsible ways to make our desires known to the University.

I responded by recounting the many ways we had tried to act "responsibly," none of which had received any material response from his subordinates. I thought—but didn't say—that maintaining a segregated basketball team at a tax-supported institution in a country that claimed to be democratic was hardly "responsible" behavior. I laid it out: "We essentially want two things. First, we want consistent access to recreational facilities on the campus, and second, we want Coach Rupp to add at least one or two black players to next year's Wildcats. If these two things are done, we will destroy all of the prints and the negatives and forget the whole thing. But if they are not, then there are members of our group who want to send the photographs to the *Louisville Courier-Journal* and to the NCAA in Kansas City."

Johnson was dead silent for a moment. He seemed stunned by our audacity. Obviously disgusted, he declared, "Nobody tells Mr. Rupp what to do! Nobody!"

"Well," I said, "I don't know how you can get him to do it, but that is what our group wants done."

He clearly was in a bind, perhaps as frustrated with Rupp's stubborn white supremacy as he was with this upstart, no-name graduate student presenting an ultimatum. He seemed to be a decent guy, trapped between what was right and the antiquated behavior of a demigod whom even the president of the University feared to challenge. For a moment or two I felt sorry for him, but I thought better of it when I reminded myself that he had chosen this job and its responsibility. I also felt a hint of nausea, as I was not at all comfortable negotiating blackmail. I hated putting people who were mostly honorable in the jaws of a moral vise. But sometimes on the question of race, there just didn't seem to be an alternative. Today I still wonder if what we did was legal. I feel unclean about it, but pursuing racial equality in that day was more often than not a game of hardball.

Finally, with a deep sigh, Dr. Johnson conceded, "Okay, I will go out and recruit someone myself. I already have a candidate in mind. I can't promise you that he will be on the court in '66–67. Also, we will get a gym opened up for your group." He never asked me for the prints or the negatives. As soon as I left his office, I panicked and prepared for the retribution I was sure would come. But after a few weeks, when no one came to take me to the gallows, the uneasiness lifted.

We enjoyed using the old gym, and in a month or so I got a phone call from the vice president's office saying that our plan was "being pursued." But when we discovered that there would be no black players on the team in the 1966–67 season, I made several calls to Dr. Johnson to see why. He never made himself available to speak with me; each time a secretary would rebuff me with something like, "The vice president says to tell you we are working on it." In '67–68 it was the same. The scuttlebutt was that Rupp's racial rehabilitation program, conducted by the UK administration, was not going smoothly. We well understood that overruling Adolph Rupp would be tough. But we hoped that our confrontation with the administration would join other pressures and put an end to the all-white line-ups in Kentucky basketball.

In the end, the most devastating blow to Rupp's reign of bigotry came two months after my meeting with Johnson: the all-black starters of the Texas Western University basketball team beat the all-white Wildcats 72–65 in the NCAA finals to snatch the 1966 national title out of Rupp's hands. Then, finally, in June of 1969, the university recruited its first African American player, Tom Payne, a highly sought-after prospect from Louisville.

By then I was teaching at Virginia Commonwealth University, so occasionally at night I would make the five-hundred-mile trip across the airwaves to
WHAS-AM radio in Louisville to hear the Wildcat games. On the post-game
interview show I sometimes heard Rupp denigrate Payne in the worst way. His
veiled racist allusions made me heartsick. Those nights finally made it obvious
to others that the time was up for coaches like him. By 1972 Rupp was gone, a
relic of a time when too many coaches were blinded by racial myths and unable
to see where basketball and America were headed.

PART FOUR

Combating Old Injustices
in New Finery

✳ 17 ✳

An Activist Professor in a New University
in the Old Capital of the Confederacy

HEN I LEFT MCV for graduate school in Lexington, Fred Spencer
and I both assumed that I would likely return to take a position in
his Department of Preventive Medicine. At that time Virginia Commonwealth University was little more than a glimmer in the eyes of those who
wished to see Virginia get serious about higher education. But in July 1968 the
Medical College of Virginia merged with the Richmond Professional Institute
to form VCU, and the administration was frantically looking for faculty and
staff to launch this new institution. So they were glad to get a guy like me: an
alum known by many old RPI faculty; a veteran of teaching at MCV; a PhD
candidate with good references in a field in which they needed people; someone with credentials that could be recognized in the Medical School; and a
guy with a gung-ho, "Where do you want me to start?" attitude. So the job
was low-hanging fruit. I showed up with my family a month after the merger.

It was a year of pivotal events around the world At home, Lyndon Johnson withdrew from the presidential campaign in the wake of massive protests
against the war in Vietnam. A month later Martin Luther King Jr. was assassinated in Memphis and riots broke out across America. Abroad, student
protests in Paris and strikes by some ten million French workers nearly brought
the de Gaulle government to its knees; Alexander Dubček's reform efforts,
which came to be known as the "Prague Spring," ended with the invasion of
Czechoslovakia by the Soviets; free speech movements erupted among students and workers in communist-controlled Poland and Yugoslavia; and open

revolts against Francisco Franco's despotic policies were ratcheting up in Spain. I was in Yugoslavia at a Quaker-sponsored meeting of international activists that summer, never suspecting how my own life would be touched by such developments.

The merger of RPI and MCV by the Virginia General Assembly and the upgrading of other colleges and universities had resulted from a veritable revolution in higher education in the state. A new generation of assembly members saw that Virginia needed reform to prosper. Events like the Prince Edward County school closures embarrassed many state leaders in their efforts to bring new business to the commonwealth. Due to miserly funding for education, we had severe shortages of skilled and educated workers. We placed near the bottom in national rankings of commitment to higher education. Education advocates in the state frequently lamented, "Thank God for Mississippi."

Yet the merger of the two institutions did not happen easily, because many of the MCV faculty and alumni had little regard for RPI. Since its beginning at the end of WWI, RPI had offered opportunity to Virginia's working class, military veterans, older students, artists, and others not usually welcome at the state's elite schools. MCV was a more prestigious institution because it had a medical school and a distinguished century-plus history, including pioneering work in heart transplant surgery that earned it a worldwide reputation. MCV partisans were embarrassed to be affiliated with RPI, because they imagined it as filled with the kids of the proletariat, late bloomers, and artsy-fartsy Bohemians. In their view, the whole school was like our crowd at the Village.

In those first few years, I may have been the only faculty member appointed to both campuses. I held positions in the Department of Preventive Medicine at the School of Medicine at MCV and in the Department of Sociology and Anthropology at the former RPI campus. As a consequence, I took a lot of heat on the Medical Center campus for defending RPI and the merger. But I welcomed the challenge because of my unique experiences on both campuses and made strong arguments about how both would benefit from the change.

VCU came into being during the demise of Jim Crow, which made the moment exciting. Senator Harry F. Byrd's political machine had begun to rust away. Putting civil rights reforms to work, black Virginians were stepping up their pursuit of opportunities that before were reserved for whites. And some whites, especially young people, were now enjoying association with blacks.

The worst expressions of white supremacy were being forced underground, as the old segregation laws gave way to less obvious patterns of discrimination. Open racist comments were becoming unacceptable in polite company. Those who were intent on defending their prior state-sponsored racial privileges had to update their ideology and tactics in the wake of the era's egalitarian juggernaut.

At the same time, the relatively unified civil rights movement of the fifties and early sixties was splintering into a variety of caucuses pursuing their own agendas. Many of the white civil rights activists I had known rejoined the mainstream lifestyle, thinking their mission was accomplished. The civil rights movement had indeed won some landmark reforms, such as equal access to public accommodations, voting rights, and the right to employment on equal terms with whites, but that still left much to be done in making white-dominated institutions like business, government, education, and the professions truly fair and inclusive. The media largely stopped recording the struggle when it moved off the streets and into these institutions, but I can attest that the struggle never stopped in the way one might conclude from the news of the time.

BEGINNING IN THE summer of 1968, a little army of pioneers set about the grunt work of building a new university largely from the foundation up. There was no manual for doing this, so we just plunged into it trusting our collective experience and best instincts. We dreamed big and worked hard. We created new programs and departments, ordered thousands of books and journals for our libraries, prepared the way for the computer age, recruited hundreds of new faculty and staff, established new courses, won the faculty old-timers over to the new mission, rehabilitated old spaces, built new buildings, stumped the region for new students, and reached out to local and national TV to tell the exciting story of the birth of a new genus of higher education in the Old Dominion.

Prior to the merger, the proportion of blacks in the student bodies at both institutions was dramatically below that in the general population of Richmond, which was half African American. Many of us took the urban service mandate laid out in VCU's founding document to mean, among other things, that the new state university must become a trustworthy home for African

American students. We put recruitment of black faculty, staff, and students high on our priority list. We learned, too, that we needed to work with the whites on campus who were resisting the new day now upon us.

One of the students I recruited was James Elam, whom I met at the NAACP Youth Council when he was twenty years old. Elam had grown up in a tough Richmond public housing project. He was a survivor of a white sniper's gunfire that killed several other black victims. A bullet struck him in the spine, and thereafter he could walk only with a cane. Seeing something special in this young man, I spent time with him, encouraging his civil rights activism and inviting him on family outings. My friend Hilda Warden and I also got him involved in the Encampment for Citizenship. At VCU Elam did well academically and was elected the first black president of the Academic Campus student government. He was a living advertisement for the benefits of aggressively seeking out heretofore neglected talent among Virginia's black citizens.

I also devoted much energy to recruiting faculty for our emerging sociology department, networking in ways that yielded candidates for openings in other departments and administrative positions as well. Many individuals I spoke with were captivated by the prospect of building a new university with a mandate for urban service. Among those I recruited were two very dear friends, whom I call my brothers: Bob Young and Vincent Wright.

I met them at two different summer sessions of the Encampment for Citizenship. Bob, from Philadelphia, was at the first Encampment I attended in the Bronx during the summer of 1957. Bob and I shared many deep convictions about justice—and a love for basketball. When Bob received his doctorate in social work from the University of Pennsylvania in 1969, I encouraged the dean of the VCU School of Social Work to bring him to Richmond. To my delight Bob, his wife, Emily, and their three children joined us.

I met Vincent at the Louisville Encampment in 1969. Born in Harlem, Vincent was a gifted saxophone player who after his discharge from the army received an invitation to study with the world-renowned music teacher Nadia Boulanger at Fontainebleau in France. Later he also mastered photography, with his own artistic flair. When Vincent married a white woman and bought a house in East Meadow, Long Island, their home became the target of a racially motivated bombing. They narrowly escaped being killed. I was drawn to Vincent, like Bob, by our shared obsession with justice-seeking.

I believed that Vincent would be a good fit for our university's mission, and so I recommended him to the dean of students. The dean was anxious to recruit blacks to his student affairs operation and immediately hired Vincent as an assistant dean of students. The School of the Arts was also pleased to have him to teach photography and saxophone.

Unfortunately, the city of Richmond was not quite ready for the new era. When Vincent arrived in Richmond he could not find a place to live. Housing discrimination was still pandemic. Wherever he went he got the classic "sorry, that apartment was rented only this morning" routine. After several disappointments he found and visited what looked like an ideal place, the Franklin Towers apartments. Vincent was shown an efficiency apartment by Betty Nixon, the receptionist. It fit his budget and was close to his VCU office, so he said he would take it and offered her a deposit. She refused it, saying that as a receptionist she was not allowed to consummate rentals and that Vincent would have to phone Linwood Emory, the apartment building manager, the next day. He did so and was told that the apartment had been rented, though, Emory said, he would "love" to have Vincent as a tenant.

This made Vincent suspect that Ms. Nixon had told her boss that he was an African American. So Vincent phoned to see if I would join him in confronting the man. I called Emory and learned that the apartment Vincent saw was still available. I told him I would like to bring a friend to check it out. He agreed. When we arrived, I walked in first and told Emory that my friend would be along as soon as he parked the car. Emory again assured me that the apartment was available. Moments later, as planned, Vincent walked in. A startled Emory rattled off a garbled explanation of how the apartment had just been committed to someone else. A big grin spread across my face at his racist somersaults. Emory, now in a rage, shouted at Vincent there was "no apartment for rent for *you*!" Suddenly realizing what he had just done, he picked up the phone and pretended to tell the person at the other end that the apartment they had discussed was no longer available. It was obvious that no one was on that telephone line with him. When he hung up, Vincent filled out the paperwork, wrote a check for the deposit, and later moved in. We had desegregated Franklin Towers, it seemed.

But real integration in Richmond proved elusive, and Linwood Emory was a slow learner. A few years later, Henry Marsh, a distinguished Virginia civil

rights lawyer and later Richmond's first black mayor, asked me to be an expert witness in his antidiscrimination suit against Emory. I eagerly applied
my knowledge about the damaging health effects of his client's experience of
discrimination, drawn from the vast store of scientific findings in medical behavioral science. This, together with the threat of a civil suit, proved to be
enough to get his client into an apartment at Franklin Towers.

Emory's foot-dragging was just a small-scale example of the housing problems facing blacks in the seventies. In those days the first challenging test
given to new black VCU students was not administered by a professor. It was
the test of fortitude needed to obtain a place to live. Now on the job in the
dean's office, Vincent asked me to help check out some rental properties where
students complained of discrimination. We sought to document housing discrimination many more times with the same ruse we used at Franklin Towers,
sometimes with success and other times with nothing more for our efforts than
being chased out with angry curses and racial slurs. Our win-loss record may
not have been impressive, but those recalcitrant landlords learned that practicing racial discrimination was no longer going to be a slam dunk.

MY TEACHING TOOK many forms and served many different kinds of
learners. For my first four years at VCU I taught several standard sociology
and African American studies courses on what was then referred to as the
Academic Campus. But at the Medical Center, for my entire career, I team-
taught or complemented what other professors or students were doing with
my unique medical behavioral science material. I lectured in a variety of jointly
taught courses (on public health, psychiatry, family medicine, dentistry, phar-
macy, nursing, physical therapy, occupational therapy, and many other subjects). Many fourth-year medical students signed up for my elective, Behavioral
Factors in Medicine, in each of the twenty-six years it was offered. I served
on dissertation and master's thesis committees and consulted on hundreds of
clinical, basic science, social and behavioral science, and community studies. In
the nineties I was the first University Honors Scholar in Residence. When we
created a master's in public health degree at the Medical Center, I taught two
of the core courses and chaired the curriculum committee for the program.
I answered every call for help I could from anyone who was trying to bridge

gulfs between disciplines, the two campuses, or the university and the community. I was the quintessential utility infielder. I wasn't a star but I could play every position.

WE TRIED TO MAKE the university more responsive to African American students and the black communities of central Virginia by creating what was then called the Afro-American Studies Program. In 1969 interested faculty members and students asked the administration to authorize a budget and a committee to set up the program. The provost and some older professors fought the proposal. But after relentless insistence from student advocates, both black and white, and supportive academic arguments from us, the provost came around. It helped that similar programs were developing around the country. Academic "leaders" don't like to be left behind.

Within a year we offered such courses as Introduction to Afro-American Studies, Afro-American Art, Survey of Afro-American Music, Black History, Issues in Black Psychology, Survey of Social Science Contributions to Black Studies, and Sociology of Racism, among others. The courses became very popular among both white and black students, and soon the program had its first director, Rutledge Dennis, a young sociologist who went on to distinguish himself in the African American studies field.

Selling the program to some of the staid and tradition-bound administrators and faculty was not always easy. They dominated the university curriculum committee, which meant we had to commit lots of time and energy to get courses approved. I organized three of these courses myself. In the first, Introduction to Afro-American Studies, I invited faculty from each academic discipline to give lectures to whet students' appetites for more. The second, Survey of Social Science Contributions to Black Studies, was an overview of selected social and behavioral science findings and research methodologies that addressed racial, ethnic, and social-class issues. One class project in this course involved a community survey done by the students on the social stratification of "ethnic" names in our metro area. The students were stunned to learn how a largely unseen system of racial and ethnic prejudice could be made visible through imaginative sociological research. The third course, Sociology of Racism, was a joint effort with Vincent Wright. Both black and white students flocked to it. I was stunned by the number of students who said that seeing the two of us work together was the first time they had witnessed an egalitarian racial relationship.

IN ADDITION TO my desire to contribute to the academic future of VCU, I had a yearning to share with my fellow southerners the vision of egalitarianism I had experienced elsewhere. Were I a believer, I might have proclaimed, "I am here to do the Lord's work." And that work could only be at VCU, because it had been the site of my own transformation as a student. With ultimately more than sixty years within its fold, I became someone who could speak of the contents of its soul. My story was but a version of its own.

Of course, I knew that such evangelism would not always be appreciated, because so many still resisted letting go of old ways. That meant the university must not only generate knowledge and technology but also new forms of human relations, those of an egalitarian modernity. I sought to use my podium as a professor to help solve problems in the community. Whenever I saw a social problem or a pattern of injustice that could be addressed by my training and that no one else seemed to care about, I jumped on it. I used the freedom and authority of my faculty position to conduct nontraditional applied research, create solutions, and publicly advocate for reforms that I thought might make a difference.

A case in point was the VCU Violence Prevention Project. In the late eighties and early nineties assaults and homicides hit an all-time high in Richmond. While the white community was aghast at the ignominy this brought the city, the black community was terror-stricken for the lives of their youth. A grant opportunity came my way through which I organized a computer-based violent incident tracking system. I hired a community organizer to assist me, and together, applying our database along with lessons from the vast scientific literature on the causes and prevention of violence, we were able to seed a number of new violence prevention programs and reinvigorate some existing ones. The project became recognized as a contributor to the dramatic reduction in the number of murders and assaults in Richmond in just a few years. But funding ended with the election of Governor George Allen, and the new silver bullet for preventing violence became a media campaign extolling the "miracle" of fatherhood.

In this and all of the projects I worked on in those years, I tried to bring empirical evidence to bear on public policy choices, because I saw that the fields in which I worked—applied social psychology, sociology, anthropology, and medical behavioral science—brimmed over with findings and research methods that could shed light on so many vital issues.

I TOOK THE PRIVILEGE of being a teacher as a noble and solemn responsibility. I was very careful to keep partisan politics and ideology out of my formal teaching. But in the courses I taught—on subjects like race and ethnic relations, medical sociology, American social problems, behavioral epidemiology, preventive medicine, and public health—the data alone were quite enough to raise questions about inequality and the uneven distribution of justice with no prompting needed. Teaching was immensely gratifying. Each fall at the start of the new academic year, I felt an incomparable sensation of renewal and excitement. In the first moments of each class, seeing the anticipation in each of the students, I knew that we were going to have a rewarding learning adventure together.

From the very beginning at VCU the content of my courses and the research that I and my students did were inextricably linked to my contacts and activism. Because of my close ties to the community for so many years, it became my laboratory. As a result, I received countless invitations through the years to become involved in projects related to employment discrimination, maternal and child health, violence prevention, environmental protection, prison reform, and more. Unable to resist a call for help, I often over-extended myself, especially in issues facing African American communities. While my home base in the university provided me with a good a bit of freedom and some basic staples, I had to be mindful not to exploit the university's material resources or shortchange it on my academic duties.

✳ 18 ✳

If the Hurricane Don't Blow You Away, the Government Will

I N AUGUST OF 1969, a year after our return to Richmond, I got a call from the American Friends Service Committee in Philadelphia asking me to lead a research team to the hurricane-devastated Mississippi Gulf Coast. They wanted us to document the response of the federal, state, and local government and the private disaster relief agencies to the needs of minority and poor victims of Hurricane Camille. The hurricane had hit very nearly the same area that was hammered by Katrina thirty-six years later. In their work in Mississippi, Alabama, and Louisiana, two AFSC associates had witnessed some of the racial and class-based discrimination and bureaucratic neglect, but my team's job was to research and document the full story. I arranged for my classes and other duties to be covered, took with me two of my VCU students, and by September 16 we reached the Gulf Coast, where Ed Nakawatase from the AFSC national office joined our field team.

The category 5 storm, landing late in the evening of August 17, was one of the most calamitous to ever hit the U.S. mainland. More than 144 people died in Mississippi and Louisiana, and tens of thousands in the area lost everything—their homes, their personal effects, their means of transportation, their employment, and for many also their psychological well-being. The brunt of the hurricane was concentrated in eight counties in southern Mississippi, with its greatest damage along the coast. But heavy effects were also felt in the Mobile area of Alabama and two parishes in southern Louisiana. Shortly after the crushing hit on the Gulf Coast, strangely enough, the storm's fury set down again in Nelson County, Virginia, where 112 more lives were taken. The aftermath even reached Richmond, where portions of East Main Street were under eight to ten feet of water.

Our research was a joint venture of the AFSC and the Southern Regional Council, a liberal interracial organization headquartered in Atlanta. Our team interviewed people every day for over three weeks, taking off only one day to see what impact Camille might have had on New Orleans. We ultimately interviewed more than three hundred individuals from widely varied backgrounds and generated nearly four hundred pages of findings.

The two young men who came along to help were among my best students at VCU. Both were native Virginians enrolled in a tutorial with me, and the Gulf Coast was to be the laboratory setting for their field work. David Henley was a white southerner originally from the Appalachian region of the state. Charles McLeod, known to all as Mac, was an African American from Petersburg. Both were civil rights activists and unapologetic idealists, and neither had ever been to Mississippi.

Their relentless focus on the necessity for immediate change would sometimes collide with our goal of documenting the little-publicized injustices so long practiced in American disaster relief efforts. I, therefore, spent many long hours late into the night—when we should have been getting some sleep—wrestling with their indictments of social science inquiry as a more or less irrelevant enterprise. The irony was that the particular social science endeavor they were engaged in ultimately contributed to reforming the way the U.S. conducted disaster relief. Their skepticism notwithstanding, Dave and Mac proved to be steadfast and productive contributors. Our fourth team member, Ed Nakawatase, was a young Japanese American on the national AFSC staff. Thoughtful, deeply dedicated to justice, and good company, he added perspective and a welcome calming effect on the turmoil of our daily life there.

Because there was so much devastation, we lived and ate wherever we were fortunate enough to find accommodations. One of our "homes" was a severely damaged motel room with a roof that had yet to be repaired. Whenever it rained, water poured down on our belongings. The most comfortable housing we had was a trailer parked in Gulfport where all four of us squeezed in together.

Once we were settled, it did not take long to identify key informants and good sites to locate other interview respondents. I had undertaken this kind of opportunistic sampling many times before. I used a methodology that evolved from my time as a gang worker in South Philadelphia, as a researcher of the school closing issue in Prince Edward County, and in other field studies. In but a few days, all four of us were returning to the trailer in the evening with countless tales of how one disaster, Hurricane Camille, was creating a second: the disastrous "relief effort."

By the end of the first week we uncovered much about how Mississippi governor John Bell Williams's state disaster agencies, President Nixon's Office of Emergency Preparedness, the American Red Cross, and the federal bureaucracies, including HUD and the Small Business Administration, were largely ignoring the needs of African Americans, the poor, and working-class families and individuals—the people who had sustained the greatest relative losses. As an example, one respondent, who ran a small beauty shop, recounted to me in tears how Camille had not only devastated the building she rented but had washed away all the equipment, supplies, uniforms, and other investments that were vital for her work. She spoke of applying for a replacement loan to the Small Business Administration and a grant from the American Red Cross. Both agencies turned her down, claiming that as used items the property had no value that they were obliged to replace.

As our interviews continued the overall picture became clear: a systematic pattern of racial, class-based, and gender discrimination in the whole relief effort, including in supplying government trailers; replacing lost clothing, tools, and equipment; providing transportation to work; and other things working-class people needed for their livelihoods. The agencies involved had virtually no minorities and very few local people familiar with the area on their staffs, which compounded the discrimination. Even where personnel were not overtly racist, the agency culture, history, and the directives in operational manuals assured neglect or inferior service for the minority and poor communities. One of the more frequent complaints we heard was that, even when relief agencies did agree to offer help, they parceled it out according to prior socioeconomic status. This rendered lower-income individuals the least likely to be able to rebuild their homes, resume working, or continue their educations. Among many heretofore self-sufficient working and middle-class families, Hurricane Camille brought poverty where little existed before.

In contrast, we found agencies opening wide their doors and resources to the requests of the already wealthy real estate interests, hotel and tourism industries, big corporations, and prominent wealthy white families, notably businessmen and politicians, many of whom stood to make big financial gains from the recovery resources they received. The Small Business Administration, HUD, the Mississippi state government, the commercial lending institutions, and other funding sources offered these elites a bonanza of generous loans with very favorable terms and no-strings-attached grants for ostensibly "rebuilding" the Coast. Blacks and poor whites referred to these handouts to the wealthy as the "disaster pork barrel."

A few years later I saw just what we feared in the glittering results of this boondoggle: a panoply of resort hotels, casinos, golf courses, malls, boutiques, restaurants, yacht marinas, big name entertainment venues, and other tourist attractions along mile after mile of the Gulf Coast. But the glitter fades as one travels north through the poor neighborhoods where the thousands of low-wage service workers in the resort industry eke out their living.

In order to expedite the use of the information we were discovering daily on the Gulf Coast, the AFSC and the SRC set up a lawyer, Barney Sellers, to disseminate our findings in Washington, DC. Using our information, he made the rounds of government agencies and influential individuals on Capitol Hill and elsewhere each day, forcefully advocating on behalf of the victims of discrimination and neglect.

At the same time, he pushed for long-term disaster relief reform. Nearly every day we uncovered specific instances in which the Red Cross or some local, state, or federal agency unjustifiably denied applications for assistance, or diverted food, water, and other survival supplies away from a minority neighborhood, or was a party to harassment and abuse of the disadvantaged. I would pass them on by phone to Barney in Washington or to Eleanor Eaton, our project coordinator at AFSC in Philadelphia. In addition, we sought to identify local spokespersons from among the minority, poor, and working-class communities who would agree to testify publicly or go on camera for the media. As the evidence built up, more and more of the national press began to cover our findings, the stories of these local people, and Barney's experience in Washington. Before long, the litany of problems on the Gulf Coast reached the national nightly news.

Yet the visibility of our work on the coast proved to be a double-edged sword. With the publicity came increasing awareness of our team's unwanted snooping into activities that many in Mississippi and some in Washington did not want publicized. In the second week I began to see evidence that we were being watched. We started to get refusals for interviews from officials and others. Many in the community confirmed that we were under surveillance by the authorities. I was subjected to a series of curious run-arounds from state government officials in Jackson, especially those responsible for economic development on the Gulf Coast and in Governor Williams's office. Before long, all of us faced resistance when we sought interviews or inquired about sensitive topics.

I was nevertheless feeling pretty carefree late one evening during the second week, because Ed and I had completed what we thought was a very successful day. We had spoken with several dozen informative respondents around Biloxi. We were also feeling content from a leisurely late supper and were now driving back to our trailer. I was exhausted after sweltering all day in the relentless humidity, and I was dreaming of a cool shower before hitting the sack. Back in Gulfport, I turned west onto a street we frequently used to reach our trailer. This took us through a poor white neighborhood and then along a stretch of more isolated road. Absorbed in chat, Ed and I were oblivious to events around us.

But before we reached our turn at U.S. 49, we were interrupted by the shrill sound of a siren, a flashing light, and the sudden appearance of a local police cruiser. I pulled slowly over to the side of the road, and the cruiser drove up parallel to us. It was pitch dark, but I could make out a burly, heavy-set figure with a wide-brimmed hat and a white shirt striding toward our car. I felt a wave of anxiety as the figure shined a flashlight directly into my eyes. When the policeman got closer I caught sight of the barrel of a revolver sticking out from the curtain of light, aimed right at my face. I was seized with dread. But thinking I had better appear compliant and nonthreatening, I decided to break the silence. All I could muster was the well-worn cliche, "What seems to be the trouble, officer?" "Thas 'zackly what I wanna know," he barked back from out of the darkness.

The policeman then pushed the gun further toward my face. He asked for my driver's license and noted that it was from Virginia. "Where'd ja git this car?" he demanded. I showed him my rental car invoice from Alabama. He shined his light quickly in and about our car. He then paused for a moment.

We waited anxiously to see what he was going to do next. And then from be-hind the impenetrable sheet of light, in a deep Mississippi drawl he made a bewildering accusation: "Who do you think you are that you can come down here, harassin' our women? Our married women!"

"What women?" I asked.

"You know damn well what women I'm talkin' 'bout," he growled. He was referring to the neighborhood through which we had passed earlier. He accused us of shouting sexual overtures and threatening to sexually assault women who were sitting on their porches. "My god," I thought, "this is pre-cisely the routine that southern cops use when they try to provoke blacks to turn and run from them, to justify their use of deadly force!"

He continued: "And they are gonna press charges against you."

Groping for words I said, "That wasn't us. We have been over in Biloxi all day, and we just passed by down there on our way home. We didn't stop. It wasn't us."

"Hey boy, it ain't no doubt about who it was who was harassing them girls. It was you two a-right." With that he leaned closer to my window and shined the light over at Ed. For a few seconds I could see his plump, red, leathery face. As his light caught Ed's features, I saw a hint of surprise at discovering an Asian American in the car. I assumed this was the first time he had realized Ed was not black. His silence suggested that this changed his mind as to what to do next. With his weapon still aimed in my direction, he turned and spoke with the other officer. We could hear only murmurs of their conversation. Shortly, he returned to my car window and without any warning stuck the barrel of his pistol in my left ear and said, "Get outta here. Go back to Alabama or wher-ever you come from. We don't want your kind here, and if you come back, I'm gonna fill your ass with lead!" He backed away and dropped his light. I ner-vously tried starting up the car, which, naturally on such an occasion, stalled. Finally, we pulled away slowly, very slowly.

We took a circuitous route home because the police car followed us for a while. I did not want to lead them to our trailer, which was not much over a mile away.

"Wonder why they didn't ask where we were staying?" I asked rhetorically.

Ed replied, "Maybe they already knew." When we finally walked into the trailer my legs were still trembling.

I dragged myself out of bed the next morning and left the trailer with Mac as my partner for the day. My thoughts were still about the night before until we became absorbed with the first interview. He was a lean, elderly black man, and we were in his small, severely damaged home in Bay Saint Louis. This old gentleman was angry and anxious to talk. He shared a vivid account of how the food and water supply trucks continuously bypassed his community every day in the first few weeks after the storm. He told us that the army trucks would roar past the turn-off that led to his community on their way to make deliveries in a nearby white middle-class neighborhood, the kind of routine we found all over the Gulf Coast. The practice stopped only after Sister James, a Catholic nun and principal of the St. Rose de Lima School, ran out into the middle of U.S. 90, blocking the passage of a National Guard truck, and commanded the men to bring their load into the black community. The old man told us, "If it hadn't been for Sister James, we might've all starved." In subsequent interviews with us the Red Cross explained, "We had no way of knowing that those people were back there." How could they not know? Every black person along this part of the coast knew of this community—but all of the relief workers were white and from other places. In Mississippi the casual institutionalized discrimination was no less devastating than the acts of conscious racists.

A couple of weeks later, I had seven minutes to tell Hugh Downs and seventeen million viewers of NBC's *Today Show* the grievous story of the second disaster following Hurricane Camille. My legs quivered at my first experience on national television. Afterwards on the bus back to the Newark airport to go home, I was miserable, tortured by the worry that I had failed to make real to the TV audience the inexcusable wrongs done to hundreds of thousands of black and poor victims on the Gulf Coast.

The ultimate result of our reporting was the U.S. Disaster Relief Act of 1970, which contained measures to prevent such racial and class-based discrimination in future relief efforts. It also refocused recovery efforts from a sole preoccupation with material losses to some of the critical psychological, social, and human aspects of disasters. As another consequence of the publicity, I continued to receive telephone calls and written requests for help from individuals and agencies involved in disaster recovery in communities all across the country for another year or so. Since then I have come to think of the reforms that resulted from our efforts on the Gulf Coast as perhaps the greatest accomplishment of my professional life. But the heaviest lifting came in the months after I submitted my final report, in the campaign for reform waged by Ed Nakawatase, Barney Sellers, and others from the AFSC and the SRC in the halls of Congress.*

Back at the VCU campus and around town dozens of people stopped me on the street or called to commend my TV appearance. Bill Edwards, the VCU director of university relations, was one of the first to phone. He said that I represented the university and the story of the Gulf Coast well. He and everyone in the president's office had watched the broadcast together. I hesitantly asked him about VCU president Warren Brandt's reaction. He responded, "Well, Ed, you have to understand how Dr. Brandt's mind works." Brandt's only comment was, "That guy needs diction lessons." I thought to myself, "What can you expect from the last man alive who still has a crew cut?"

*For a comprehensive account of the impact of Hurricane Camille and analysis of problems with government and NGO response, see Ernest Zebrowski and Judith A. Howard, *Category 5: The Story of Camille, Lessons Unlearned from America's Most Violent Hurricane* (Ann Arbor: University of Michigan Press, 2005).

✳ 19 ✳

Guilty of Pushing Racial Justice Too Fast

N THE MONTHS after my return from Mississippi, there was much to please me. The student responses in my classes were better than I could have ever hoped for. The university was making significant progress in its facilities, faculty recruitment, curriculum, and reputation. And my good friends Bob and Vincent were excited about their work. But January 28, 1970, brought the most joy—the birth of my third daughter, Cecily Jane Peeples. So by 1971, our home was filled with the joyful rumpus of three lively girls: a nine-year-old, a six-year-old, and a toddler. Little did we suspect then how all of them would become justice seekers in their own rights. Their stories still await the telling.

Many young people at VCU were for the first time thinking critically about and protesting the Vietnam War, as well as a variety of domestic issues. Our cluster of progressive faculty tried hard to support them, seeing them as the next generation of activists.

But all the planets were not yet aligned. The administration was nervous about its first test runs of racial equality, fearing threats to our funding. Vincent became the first casualty of their apprehension. His appointment as assistant dean was seen by the black students and their white allies as a significant test of whether the university's deeds would match its promises. Vincent leaped into the job. He worked hard to build trust between the undergraduates and the dean of students' office. He joined the students for meals in the cafeteria and sought to learn what was going on in their world. His door was always open to any student with a problem. Combined with his teaching of the saxophone and photography in the School of the Arts and his visibility in the Afro-American Studies Program, this made him a student favorite. The student government named him faculty member of the year for 1969–70. He often received invitations to speak around town and across the state, frequently appeared in student and local newspaper articles, made radio and TV appearances, and was even appointed to the Richmond Human Relations Commission. Students, black and white, grew to count on him, especially the activist African American students and their white comrades. He earned the respect and affection of many at VCU and in the community.

At first Vincent's sensitivity toward student needs and his contribution to the mission of the dean's office were much appreciated—until he began to differ with ranking members of the administration on some student issues. Then this admiration seemed to devolve into envy. When the current dean of students left VCU for unrelated reasons, many students expected their beloved assistant dean to move up into his slot. When that didn't happen they were angry and confronted Dick Wilson, the vice president for student affairs, about his decision. Wilson's explanation to Vincent for why he was not promoted was, "Richmond, Virginia, is not ready for a black dean." In a few months Wilson quietly and without publicly adducing reasons showed Vincent the door. Hoping to minimize embarrassing protests over Vincent's being sacked, the administration waited to announce it until after the undergraduates left campus for summer vacation. As a result, few were aware of his dismissal or saw the notice of his upcoming appeal session on May 21.

I was the only advocate for Vincent allowed at the appeal hearing, and I could see from the outset that it was a sham. The adjudicating body consisted solely of administrators or their minions who were already declared as Vincent's detractors. The panel discounted what I had to say, and the chairman cut off my testimony in mid-sentence. So with the campus barren of those who prized his work the most, Vincent Wright was sent packing.

He was allowed the courtesy of working a couple more months while searching for another job. In September the students returned and found him gone. Enraged, they set off an avalanche of letters, phone calls, and demonstrations to demand his reinstatement. Stories about Vincent's termination appeared in the local daily. Someone even set fire to the President's House. Fortunately no permanent damage was done to this beautiful century-old mansion. The arsonist was never discovered, and a link to Vincent's firing was never established. But it did raise suspicions that hurt the cause.

Some members of the city's black and white progressive communities also entered the fray. One gathering supporting Vincent on the grounds of the administration building attracted close to a hundred angry protesters. Bob Young and I and several others offered some plainspoken words of support for Vincent and criticism of the administration's actions. While it was never made explicit by the administration, Bob's and my participation at the rally became a watershed event for our status at VCU. Bob was already thought of as radical for his forthright views on racial justice and criticism of the Vietnam War. So a few months after Vincent's departure, Bob was also cut loose by the administration.

In an attempt to calm the ruckus over Vincent's ousting, President Brandt told the *Richmond Times-Dispatch* that Vincent was terminated because of "inadequate performance of assigned duties." Given the distrust many blacks had for white-dominated institutions in those days, and because of Vincent's well-known accomplishments at VCU, few could believe that his contract was withdrawn for this reason. I turned to some friends who worked in key places in the administration to see what was going on behind closed doors. All of them said that whatever the avowed reasons for Vincent's dismissal, the real cause was his disregard for the traditional rules of race in Richmond.

Finally, Dick Wilson admitted to me his two reasons. First was that "Vincent failed to keep his records straight," which I concluded was a cover for the second reason: "Vincent did something unforgivable." It took some doing to finally squeeze out of Wilson what was so "unforgivable": Vincent Wright, a divorced black man, sometimes dated white women. Wilson did concede that Vincent's "unforgivable" liaisons were with single adult women on the faculty and from the community, not students. So we could only conclude that the principal motive for the dismissal was that Vincent challenged the old ways, which made the administration nervous because they believed it would threaten institutional support from the conservative state legislature and donors.

As the seventies opened, Vincent Wright's appointment to that high-profile position had represented the expectations of a whole new generation of idealistic students at VCU, both black and white. They had believed that finally racial injustice was to be eradicated once and for all, even here in the heart of the old Confederacy. But with Vincent's expulsion the students felt that VCU had betrayed them.

Senior administrative officials were surprised by the level of outrage among the students and the Richmond black community. They were mostly northerners and grievously naive about our local culture and the changing state of race relations in Virginia. In the view of many they were unduly influenced by stereotypes of white southerners—fearful of monsters they themselves had conjured. In fact, they underestimated how ready most whites at this juncture of history were to adapt to desegregation in public spaces, which they had now begun to see as inevitable. I didn't believe the administration fired Vincent because of racial prejudice. I thought that they mistakenly assumed that there would be perilous blowback from white Virginians who feared blacks were "taking over" a "white institution." Blind to the new moment in Virginia history, they drummed out a good man who could have served their other goals well.

There was no shortage of irony in this. Dick Wilson, a northern Jew and former Peace Corps leader professing to be a liberal, gave the ax to Vincent, a black man, at a southern university that was finally attempting to do right by black students—all for the presumed "unforgivable" sacrilege of dating a white woman. I thought to myself, "It's no wonder that so many black activists don't trust white liberals!"

Fortunately, Bob and Vincent landed on their feet. Bob started a rewarding career on the faculty of the newly formed Eastern Virginia Medical School in Norfolk. Vincent for a few months worked on a project for Virginia Union University, then moved on to a marvelous music education and community outreach position at Lincoln Center in New York.

BY EARLY 1972 much of the hard work of getting the university off the ground was done, and memory of my contributions had faded. But pesky racial conflicts continued to figure in the daily operations of VCU, as in so many organizational settings in those days. Greater demands for faculty productivity—as calculated by publications—arose from the administration. My unconventional academic record combined with my activism put me on the top of the renegades list kept by J. Edwin Whitesell, the prickly and hidebound old dean of arts and sciences. Seizing upon the fact that VCU's tenure review procedures had yet to be clarified or finalized, he summarily decided it was time to initiate an early tenure review for me. He appointed four members to my review committee: two students and two professors, only one of whom was a sociologist and a peer. They did a hasty review of portions of my record, ignoring the half of my work done at the Medical Center and the input of my chair there, Dr. Frederick Spencer. Only three of the nineteen members of the Sociology Department took part, and they opposed my tenure. In a matter of days, three of the four committee members voted to deny me tenure, and the mostly impassive chair of sociology, John McGrath, concurred. The motives of my three Sociology Department detractors appeared to be personal and different from those of Dean Whitesell and the administration, but they converged to serve the same end.

When I questioned the dean, he cited three reasons for my dismissal. Contrary to specifications in VCU's charter, he said that there was "no need for medical sociologists or joint appointments with the medical campus." He also told me that I was "too controversial" and that my "race agitating" was a problem. While he did not say so explicitly, he made it obvious that the third reason was the last straw: my public criticism of the administration at the protest against the firing of Vincent Wright. He may have been a Harvard PhD, but he was also a native of Southside Virginia, the "Deep South" region of our state. It was unmistakable: he was twisting the facts of the situation to get rid of me. I already knew that the ranking members in the administration feared that pushing racial progress "too fast" might hurt our funding prospects. But none of them held the classic southern white supremacist attitudes that were so plain in this man. I was actually surprised that Whitesell never mentioned the long delay in completing my dissertation, which should have been the prime negative in my tenure case. But his standard for judging this faculty member was not scholarship, teaching, service, or academic credentials; it was where I stood on preserving white privilege.

I also spoke with McGrath after the tenure decision. He admitted that he was stunned by the outpouring of letters and phone calls from students, administrators, faculty from both campuses, and people in the community questioning the tenure denial. He said if he had only known that I enjoyed such support, he would not have signed onto to the committee's vote. Sixteen of my colleagues in McGrath's own department sent ex post facto letters of support for me, several of which said that they had been systematically denied the opportunity to share their views with the committee. One example of those letters came from a senior professor with whom I'd had little personal contact,

Dr. Albert Francis. Dr. Francis wrote: "I appreciate in Professor Peeples what C. W. Mills called the 'sociological imagination.' Like all people with creative potential, I would say that he is an individualist in his sociological approach; this independence of mind might be taken as a disadvantage in some circles, but I should be very alarmed if the sociological profession was lacking in people like Professor Peeples."

Especially touching were the letters sent on my behalf from students, such as one white student, Nancy Day, who said, "Dr. Peeples is one of the very few instructors I have had as a student that did not spoon feed me and treat me like I was still in grade school." A black student, Preddy Ray, who ultimately became a leader in the Richmond community, wrote:

At a time when I was in desperate need for inspiration to continue in this university Dr. Peeples provided that inspiration. Conferences that I had with Dr. Peeples about my problems with school helped give me direction as to what to do and where to go. He extended his position as an instructor beyond the formal structure that his position predicts. I must point out the high regard and respect that Dr. Peeples has gained with his students.

Another black student, Warren Neal Holmes, who went on to pursue a PhD and an academic career, wrote of the denial of tenure:

The news of these actions has aroused my indignation and saddened me. I am indignant because a man of Dr. Peeples's academic stature, especially in the area of medical sociology, can be considered dispensable to this university. I am saddened because Dr. Peeples has injected much of his life-blood into the university. As a student, and later as a professor here, Dr. Peeples has devoted much of his time, talent, and energy to the establishment and maintenance of VCU's unique and innovative position as an urban university. Dr. Peeples inspired me to become a student, a true student. During a period of disgust with and total rejection of whites, Dr. Peeples steered me toward a course of moderation working with others for mutual goals.

I appealed the tenure decision and won a review by the senior vice presidents from each campus. They found that the initial tenure review was prematurely convened, the review committee's composition illegitimate, the evidence of my work at the Medical Center improperly excluded, and many of the charges against me ad hominem attacks irrelevant to an academic evaluation. The two vice presidents rescinded the decision and informed me that the proper date for my tenure review would be the following year. Despite the victory, the conflict had poisoned my working relationships with Whitesell, McGrath, and my three critics in the Sociology Department. So I took up Fred Spencer's offer to shift full-time to the Medical Center and with much sorrow left the Sociology Department behind. I carried with me some painful regrets about no longer teaching students in sociology and Afro-American studies, as well as about leaving behind the rich and varied intellectual fare provided by my faculty colleagues on the West Campus.

In hindsight, I suppose that I could have been a bit more politic in those first four years at VCU. But it was an era of transformation, and I saw that this was the university's once-in-a-lifetime formative phase. I doubted that the chance for real and deep change would ever come again in the same way, so I was determined to do my part to make the place comply with its own charter and the promise of equality of opportunity for all.

New Human Rights Struggles
in the Era of Stealth Racism

I N THE EARLY seventies the civil rights movement we once knew in Richmond evolved into something different. It had to because, where previously the targets had been clear and bald-faced segregation laws and customs and those who exercised and protected them, in the seventies white supremacy began to go underground—what I called "stealth racism." Drawing a veil over racism in Mississippi may have been a difficult job, but white Virginians already had a formula for putting the best face on their strategies to maintain dominance: what Douglas Southall Freeman, the Robert E. Lee biographer and longtime editor of the *Richmond News Leader,* had dubbed the "Virginia Way." Nonviolent, polite, even genteel, it still kept whites on top. The Civil Rights and Voting Rights Acts and new court decisions outlawed many of the old ways of keeping blacks down, like the poll tax and the ban on interracial marriage. But this still left many subtle racist practices and institutional habits untouched. That posed a challenge to civil rights activists: how to expose the polite sophistry as a sham for undercover white supremacist schemes calculated to preserve all the racial discrimination they could still get away with.

Taking advantage of the widespread sense that the social movements of the sixties were over, the old segregationists turned for help to the emerging conservative think tanks and right-wing talk radio to invent a new vocabulary for racist ideology and new ways to circumvent genuine integration. Abandonment of the city's public schools by the middle classes, explosive white opposition to busing, increasing white flight to the suburbs, and covert schemes to prevent significant black involvement in community planning and governance all had the effect of resurrecting racial barriers we had fought so hard to end. Those successes gave the unrepentant, open segregationists a second wind; threats, intimidation, reprisals, and occasional acts of violence once again reared their ugly heads. For example, the federal district judge Robert Merhige Jr. had to be protected around the clock by U.S. Marshals after he ordered the desegregation of area public schools through interjurisdictional busing. Merhige's son, sometimes my lunch partner, shared with me the terrifying conditions under which the Merhige family had to live.

While I jumped headlong into teaching, research, and consulting in my new position in the School of Medicine at the VCU Medical Center, thoughts of all this were never far from my mind. Again opportunities came my way to work on health and social problems that at their core arose from injustice. In the process, my earlier focus on civil rights expanded to issues on the wider spectrum of human rights. Much of this post–civil rights activism took the form of long-term projects. Many were conducted under the auspices of the university, and the administration was not always happy about that, since some of them were viewed as controversial at the time. But no matter how edgy my projects were, my immediate boss and department chair, Dr. Fred Spencer, always stuck by me.

Some of these projects were conducted within the purview of the Medical Center or the hospital. Others came from my close relationship with the Virginia State Department of Health, and still others involved the community at large. All benefited from the freedom and status I enjoyed as a professor. Having for years worked at jobs where a boss watched my every move, I appreciated how privileged I was to be a professor in a publicly supported urban university, in effect a servant of the people of my community.

AMONG THE COUNTLESS initiatives on which I worked closely with physicians and other clinicians in the Medical Center and hospital, and one that deeply engaged my do-gooder drive, was the Cancer Rehabilitation and Continuing Care Program. For years I had watched how often medicine and society in general appeared to give up on and marginalize the elderly ill and other people with severe, complicated, late-stage, and terminal medical conditions. The grim prognoses in these cases appeared to trigger in health professionals and laypeople alike a process long known in social psychological research: when we come to feel that we can't help a victim we tend to reject them. It reminded me of how some early societies directed their elderly and infirm to march out into the forest and die alone. In my experience, this pattern of forsaking hope was more common when the patients were poor or black, including advanced and terminal cancer patients and their struggling loved ones.

But, true to their essential idealism, a number of health professionals at the Medical Center also saw the discrimination against these patients as totally contrary to the pledge we all took to the noble work of the healing professions. So in the early seventies I became part of a team headed by the cancer care pioneer Dr. Susan Mellette. We received one of the first grants in the country from the National Cancer Institute for multidisciplinary team care for patients with advanced and terminal disease.

I was responsible for the research to determine whether a team approach, with a designated case manager and regular team case conferences, achieved a better outcome than the conventional treatment, which was based on the attending physician making unsystematic, chance referrals to other health professionals. I found some thrilling results in comparing our patients with those who did not have our holistic treatment. I say thrilling results because I was able to document comparatively better outcomes for our patients: nurses cared for the whole patient, not just the disease; speech pathologists helped head and neck patients learn to communicate again; physical therapists brought back movement that was presumed lost for good; occupational therapists made it possible for patients to live at home; prosthetists created more normal appearances using artificial substitutes for tissue lost to surgery; social workers found services in the community that made life easier; psychologists gave a sure hand to patients and their families as they were being tossed about on an emotional roller coaster; and the hospital clergy offered larger answers to the questions "Why me?" and "Why us?" from patients and their loved ones.

All of this activity was consolingly overseen by a compassionate medical oncologist who knew that the combined effect of all these acts of caring gave patients the gift of dignity and comforting resolution in their last months or years. To me, the affirmation of human dignity was the driving force of the civil rights struggle, so this felt like a natural extension of that commitment.

I came to understand at the deepest level how important this approach to late-stage cancer care was when I came in to work one morning and discovered a VCU faculty member on our roster as a hospice at-home patient. Having some acquaintance with him, I decided to join the nurse on her routine home visit. We found that, although he was still able to engage in some housebound activity with his family, he was suffering from severe physical and gastrointestinal issues and depression. His family was deeply distressed about him and struggling with the challenges his circumstances imposed on them. Both for research reasons and out of personal concern for a colleague, I decided to follow closely the course of his condition. So I visited him one to two times a week for around four months. With time his condition worsened, but I saw how each of the multidisciplinary staff visits little by little began both to mitigate his physical pain and discomfort and to offer him a measure of psychological relief. I also witnessed how the staff led his wife and their children slowly toward a more peaceful resolution of their own suffering in the face of their pending loss and the burden of their care for him. When he died I saw a family made as ready as any I had ever seen for the trial of grieving the loss of a loved one. This and other experiences over thirteen years with the project convinced me that as a justice seeker I must also steel myself for fights with the unfairness of nature.

IN THE MID- TO LATE seventies, the tools of applied social science were gaining recognition as useful in partnership with clinical medicine, and their application in public health was also accelerating. Having participated in the education of countless health professionals in the local and state health departments, I was deeply involved in dozens of projects with the Virginia Department of Health. It was like a second job—another sphere to address the failings of distributive justice in my community.

One of the most satisfying of these public health projects was Project Warmth, conducted by the Richmond City Health Department in the mid-eighties. Ostensibly, it aimed to reduce the outrageous number of infant deaths suffered by poor, unmarried, very high risk African American mothers in their early and middle teens. Lynda Bird Johnson Robb, the wife of Governor Chuck Robb and daughter of President Lyndon Johnson, led a campaign to prevent such deaths and managed to secure enough funds from her husband's budget to support two infant mortality reduction demonstration grants. I teamed up with a public health pediatrician and friend, Dr. Laura Funkhouser, and we won one of the grants. But Dr. Funkhouser and I thought that simply reducing infant mortality rates was too narrow an aim for the project. So we also built in methods to promote safe and healthy pregnancies, prevent further unplanned pregnancies, encourage the young mothers to stay in school, favorably influence the sisters and friends of our teens, and get the young fathers involved in the care and support of their babies.

The backbone of the program was a corps of mature women from the teenagers' own African American neighborhoods. We called them Resource Mothers, and their job was to follow the pregnancies of the girls through to delivery and mentor them in the early months with their new babies. My job was to find and train the Resource Mothers along the lines of the Chinese barefoot doctor tradition, in which indigenous laypeople are prepared to become frontline health workers in underserved communities. I persuaded the local community college to recognize participation in the training program as a year-long internship, provide federal Pell grants for our Resource Mothers, and at the end of the year award them certificates of satisfactory completion of the program at their own graduation ceremony. Dr. Funkhouser supervised the work of the Resource Mothers and monitored the medical progress of the teens.

Over the several years I worked with the project, our teen mothers never had a single infant death or second teenage pregnancy, and they suffered very few childbirth complications. The success refuted the stealth-racist critics of the project who had insisted that teen pregnancy, high infant death rates, and unhealthy babies were the results of intractable character or cultural disorders among African Americans. But the most gratifying aspect of the work for me was that, through our contacts, a half-dozen of the young mothers were enrolled in the Single Parent Support System program at the historically black St. Paul's College in Lawrenceville, Virginia. I learned later that, through the combination of their own hard work and the school's supportive environment, some of them went on to receive their college degrees.

Clearly, our project demonstrated what could be done to save the wasted potential of young black women. The Resource Mothers program still exists today under another name. But the slashing of health and human service program budgets brought on by the conservative revolution has rendered it a mere shadow of its former self.

ANOTHER MAJOR THREAT to health in black communities that some of us in public health took up was environmental racism. Dr. Edmund Ackell, a retired president of VCU still on the university payroll in the early nineties, used his position to launch a for-profit medical waste incinerator company. I overheard in a conversation, confirmed by individuals privy to details about the deal, that he was close to making the university's nine-hundred-bed hospital his first and largest customer. He had also rolled over some city officials for permission to place the facility in a densely populated, mostly residential, poor black neighborhood in south Richmond. Rev. Gwendolyn Hedgepeth, the black city council member representing the targeted neighborhood, asked me to help mount a scientific case against the plan. Enlisting my many good medical, scientific, and public health connections and the relevant literature, I assembled a strong report on the health hazards for citizens in the neighborhood.

The struggle against Ackell raged on the streets, in public meetings, in the city council, and in the newspapers. For some time it looked like he and his shadowy circle of investors would get their incinerator in a location where the distance from hospitals would be convenient, the land was cheap, and disrespected residents would lack the power to challenge its smokestack emissions or ash disposal practices. The prospects for big trouble-free profits looked bright.

But they underestimated Reverend Hedgepeth. Combining our scientific position paper with the public demonstrations and her tough backchannel negotiations, she finally got some damaging publicity out about the potentially toxic and cancer-causing agents in the facility's emissions and the other probable health risks from soil and water contamination. And she won. To my knowledge, Ackell never again tried to place such a project anywhere.

The victory affirmed for me how important it is that scholars and researchers come together with community activists to halt this kind of exploitation of poor and minority citizens by corporations and other self-interested powerbrokers. This entrepreneur may not have set out intentionally to victimize African Americans, but he knew that putting his operation in a poor black neighborhood would mean less risk of a fight than placing it in a prosperous white one. What he didn't reckon on was a strong city council member with many community allies. That blew up his calculations—and saved a neighborhood.

INHUMANE PRISON CONDITIONS, long a core expression of white supremacy in Virginia, carried on into the new era of stealth racism. With the War on
Drugs and the decline of good working-class jobs, the proportion of African
Americans in prison burgeoned. This made for even greater challenges to black
families who had male members incarcerated. I was frequently reminded of the
fate of these men and their families when I passed the two-hundred-year-old
Virginia State Penitentiary a few blocks down the street from VCU.

In 1975, I had an opportunity to join a group of Black Muslim inmates there
to create, despite an obstinate warden, a Family Life Program inside the penitentiary. Our aim was to keep families together during the men's incarceration
by encouraging visitation, education, and self-development among the inmates
in preparation for returning to their families and society, and by pushing the
Corrections Department to provide essential activities and social services to
inmates and their families.

I also tried to be personally supportive of a number of the talented and conscientious African American inmates, several of whom made good their lives
after release. One of those inmates with whom I teamed to start the Family
Life Program, Hasib Mugsit, after getting out and reuniting with his wife,
Emma, has served the Richmond community well as the administrator of the
Old Dominion Home, an adult care center that provides for the pressing needs
of many poor elderly and disabled people. Another good friend from those
days, Evans Hopkins, went on to write a powerful and poignant memoir, *Life
after Life: A Story of Rage and Redemption.*

A few times in the late seventies and early eighties, civil rights lawyers asked
me to join them in confronting another cruel injustice—the pandemic of sexual assault against inmates in our nation's so-called correctional facilities. They
wanted to know what might be done to document the consequences of male-
on-male jail and prison rape. Combing the academic literature on sexual assault, traumatic stress, and related issues, I developed a comprehensive method
for evaluating the social, psychological, economic, and health consequences for
individuals who experienced sexual assault in jails and prisons, which I called
the Stress Impact Study Technique. The methodology involved gathering data
that went far beyond the customary testimony collected by psychiatrists and
psychologists. We used that data in a string of federal civil cases and won mon-
etary awards for the plaintiffs and some institutional policy reforms.

The most notorious case involved inmates at Michigan's mammoth state prison in Jackson. A boyish-looking white youth from a small central Michigan town was forced to become the "bitch" for a pack of older black "wolves." ("Bitch" and "wolf" are examples of slang terms for the victim and the sexual assailant, respectively, in penal institutions; the fact that they are common to far-flung institutions suggests how routine prison rape was and is.) One or more of these "wolves" had their way almost daily with this boy. The victim repeatedly reported the assaults to the prison staff, but, as in prisons and jails all across the country in those days, the authorities did nothing to stop it. They saw prison rape as a means to keep the more aggressive inmates happy, which in turn made management of the prison easier for them.

The boy's mother finally discovered a local small-time lawyer by the name of William H. Van Duzer, who was outraged at the boy's plight and decided to pursue a civil suit against the prison and the state of Michigan in federal court. He somehow heard of my prior successes in court and asked me to come up to Michigan and help. Van Duzer in my mind was a saint. He was a deeply caring, religious man who put on the case out of his own pocket. I could not resist helping him.

I took one of my fourth-year students to help in the medical evaluation, and we conducted a detailed study of the impact of these rapes on the boy. When I later appeared in the federal district court in Detroit as the key expert witness for the plaintiff, I was stunned at how unprepared the assistant attorney general of Michigan was when he cross-examined me. My study of the victim had been so thorough that the cross examination was actually fun for me. The federal judge decided in the plaintiff's favor and awarded him $130,000 in damages, an unprecedented decision for a prison rape case at the time. He also ordered the prison to clean up its act under pain of contempt of court.

The fact that the victim in this case was white and the rapists black probably played a part in the victory, as it has in many others. It has long been true that white victims have tended to arouse more ire, irrespective of the race of their assailants. But the precedent set in cases like this did put prisons and jails on notice for a while that there was a cost for failing to protect inmates of all races from such atrocities.

Unfortunately for victims, though, this kind of litigation is slow, labor-intensive, and expensive, and with the rise of "law-and-order conservatism"

and the concomitant surge in prison construction and privatization of corrections, it became an unaffordable method for reform. Our efforts in the seventies and early eighties could only touch the surface of this barbarity. But I still
saw a dire need to document the devastating and lasting impact that rape leaves
on its victims, male as well as female, and the discipline of medical behavioral
science in which I worked had much more to contribute than the traditional
evaluations made by psychiatrists and psychologists. So I wrote a chapter for a
book called *Male Rape* to further the dialogue about the unspoken portion of
the sentence a judge issues when he or she sends a young vulnerable individual
to a "correctional" institution.*

BY THE SEVENTIES the successes of the civil rights movement had emboldened other Americans who experienced inequities to step up their efforts for
equal treatment: Latinos, women, gays and lesbians, and the disabled, among
others. Richmond was abuzz with efforts inspired by emerging national movements of these groups, but none involved big numbers, and those involved were
a bit flummoxed about how to make headway in the face of surging conservatism and stealth prejudice. It occurred to me that we might regain some of the
impact we once had in the civil rights movement by uniting these groups in
a forum through which human rights organizations with divergent agendas
could act en masse on specific issues whenever they could find consensus. I
hoped that such a broad human rights coalition would boost grassroots activism in our community.

At the December 1974 meeting of the board of the Richmond Council on
Human Relations, with which I had long been involved, we discussed the city's
pending official master plan. This scheme ran roughshod over minorities and
the poor. Generous funding was proposed for projects and development opportunities that benefited white businesses and prosperous neighborhoods,
while black and impoverished sections of the city were written out. Everyone
agreed that we had to push back this stealth racism now repackaged as "conser-

*For more detail, see Edward H. Peeples and Anthony M. Scacco Jr., "The Stress-Impact
Study Technique: A Method for Evaluating the Consequences of Male-On-Male Sexual
Assaults in Jails, Prisons, and Selected Other Single-Sex Institutions," in Anthony M.
Scacco Jr., ed., *Male Rape: A Casebook of Sexual Aggressions* (New York: AMS Press, 1982),
241–78. See also my introduction to the same book, xix–xxi.

vative" city planning. At our next meeting, in January of 1975 at Richmond's favorite meeting place for radicals, the Main Street Grill, I led a brainstorming session with the progressive patriots Ora Lomax, William Crump, Bruce Smith, Majorie Brown, Leola Good, Wally Bless, Rev. Joe Fleming, Curtis Holt, Barbara Johnson, and Carol Mayo. Out of this came a commitment by the board to launch the Richmond Human Rights Coalition and some of its working principles.

We sent out letters inviting 160 key human rights organizations and individuals in the Richmond area to join us at our inaugural meeting on Thursday, April 17, 1975, at St. Paul's Episcopal Church in downtown Richmond, where, ironically, General Robert E. Lee had once been a member. Forty-one individuals representing twenty-two different organizations attended. Some responded cautiously, arguing that affiliation with the more "radical" causes might jeopardize support of their own programs. Others were unqualified in their enthusiasm. But all agreed—we must recognize the common ground in our varying struggles and find new ways to collaborate, even if on occasion we might have differences. We left St. Paul's that night with a fledgling human rights coalition.

By late September we were working on several issues with our six founding organizations: Gay Awareness in Perspective, the Neighborhood Legal Aid Society, the Richmond branch of the NAACP, the Richmond Council on Human Relations, United Campus Ministry, and the Women's International League for Peace and Freedom. A number of others, unable to formally join due to limitations in their charters, became informal partners. Over time, nine more groups joined.

From then on when a concern emerged, a committee of the Coalition would conduct a quick turn-around study of the issue and then write a position statement. That position would then be considered by each of the autonomous member organizations. Those who could not endorse the statement, or some modification of it, could choose not to sign on. Meanwhile, the organizations who approved joined together in speaking out for the Coalition before city council or other targets of our remonstrations.

Over its twenty-year lifetime the Coalition labored on a variety of local, state, national, and even international issues, led by our dedicated convener Wayne Young. He replaced me after the first year. Among other campaigns

we pushed the city to establish a Women, Infants, and Children Supplemental
Nutritional Program (WIC), opposed the sometime use of dum dum bullets
by the police on human rights demonstrators and crime suspects, fought employment discrimination in city government and retail stores, pressed for the
city to divest from apartheid in South Africa, and contested our country's military intervention in Central America. We studied issues, wrote reports and
proposals, educated, networked, demonstrated on the streets, shared anger,
shed tears, and provided support for anyone who did the same.

Because our conservative local media were reluctant to give attention to
the issues we thought were crucial, many of us harbored doubts about our ef-
fectiveness. But we convinced ourselves that witnessing on behalf of justice
seeking was more important than the magnitude of public response. Despite
our modest impact we provided a small beacon of political morality, hope, and
sustenance to many activists who otherwise might have lost heart. Our well-
attended banquets each December were a testimony to this effect. Had the
Richmond Human Rights Coalition accomplished nothing else in its twenty
years of life, its diligence sustained our small but committed progressive community through a stifling conservative period.

HAVING BEEN SEEN in the fifties and sixties as akin to an outlaw, I was surprised in the eighties to find myself a city official. My friend, Councilmember
Willie Dell, had the city council appoint me to the Commission on Human
Relations. This agency was a minuscule crumb thrown by the white business
establishment, Richmond's shadow government, to a hungry civil rights community at a time when racial chauvinism was finally becoming unacceptable
in the public square. But my attitude was pragmatic: a crumb is still food, so
make of it what you can. Our state and city antidiscrimination codes may have
been toothless, but we exerted a measure of influence over organizations that
practiced racial and other forms of discrimination because our proceedings got
press coverage and perpetrators wanted to avoid bad publicity.

Thus we had a stick, however small, to use with transgressors, but we didn't
have a carrot to reward folks for exemplary behavior. As I pondered the possible effect of having, alongside tools for reproach, a means for reinforcing positive racial interactions, I came up with the idea of creating public activities to
model and bolster desirable behaviors. We could show and tell our citizens,

especially impressionable youth, that good human relations were the expected norm in this community. I knew that some would consider this hokey and doubt its impact, but I wasn't discouraged. I proposed to the commission chair, my dear friend Dr. John Moeser, and our fellow commissioners that we create a full week of events to highlight people transcending racial barriers. I argued that it would demonstrate the "normal" way in which blacks and whites should interact in Richmond. Given the city's history, they were ready to support anything that might accentuate the positive.

So we organized what we called Good News!, trading on the central message of our southern Christian tradition to showcase secular good works. We flooded the media and the city with promotional materials, and on May 7, 1983, we opened the week with a live stage performance of *Mr. Rogers' Neighborhood*, with its heartwarming and racially inclusive message to children. Dozens of multiracial and interfaith events followed. At public venues around town we put on dialogues, musical performances, celebrity appearances, and a children's musical commissioned for the occasion, all expressing the "Good News!" theme. One evening at the city's Arthur Ashe Athletic Center was dedicated to noncompetitive games. We even created a phone line on which school children could be heard reading their original poems about intergroup harmony. The week closed with a message-laden variety show featuring local talent and a cast member from the hit national TV show *Fame*.

J. Stewart Bryan III, publisher and principal owner of the *Richmond Times-Dispatch* and *News Leader* at the time, rejected my invitation to join us. His newspapers had a long racist history, including having been prime agitators for massive resistance, which his editors euphemistically defended as advocacy of "conservatism." After I spoke to him about our plans, he organized and paid for his own rival event, a super-patriotic spectacle deliberately scheduled in competition with Good News!, complete with U.S. military–sponsored fighter jet flyovers at Byrd Park. Nevertheless, about ten thousand people attended or participated in the various Good News! week activities. In the years to follow, we saw that programs reminiscent of parts of ours became ever more common around town.

But the commission was not only about good news. We also received much bad news about our community in the form of complaints from minority citizens about discrimination and other mistreatment. While often our staff could win some relief for the victims through negotiation, the statutes were so feeble that some offenders committed the same outrage over and over again. Early on I saw that our greatest leverage with habitual culprits was to gather detailed information and then put the wrongdoers on trial in the press. So when we saw a substantial pattern I asked the commissioners to authorize me to conduct a serious study of the issue.

They approved and we published two such major studies during my tenure. The one that produced the most backlash was a survey of assault and abuse against gays and lesbians in Richmond that I designed and supervised, getting a lot of good help from commission staff and many volunteers. We interviewed over five hundred Richmond-area gay and lesbian respondents about their encounters with abuse, discrimination, and hate crimes. It proved to be the largest known sample of mistreatment against gays and lesbians in the United States at the time.

The number of malevolent acts shocked even some gay activists. The findings provided clear community-wide evidence of the outrages that the local gay and lesbian movement had been condemning since its public ascendency in the late seventies. After the study's publication I was invited to be the keynote speaker at the annual meeting of the Virginia Gay Alliance, where I learned how the report had further emboldened many in the struggle to obtain legal protections. Regrettably, we didn't get an antidiscrimination provision out of it, but I saw signs that the revelations did convince a lot of heretofore unconcerned straights of the need for change.

My colleagues elected me chair of the commission in 1983, which made me privy to the inner workings of local government. What I saw was uglier than even my worst suspicions. The city was officially governed by a nine-member city council with a city manager as the principal administrator. The council was composed of four conservative whites, four liberal-leaning blacks, and a black conservative named Roy West. By lining up with the whites and voting for himself, he became the mayor by a vote of 5–4. This arrangement preserved the age-old sweetheart relationship between the council and Main Street, the home court for the city's most powerful white lawyers, bankers, and brokers. I had long known they were influential but never realized how complete was their grip over local government. While their stand-in councilpersons had always been white in the past, an occasional black conservative like Roy West had begun to appear. The four black liberal council members typically put up a good fight, but as the minority voting block it sometimes was hopeless. I never saw a single instance in which the council ever furthered a justice-seeking measure in the city without approval from Main Street.

Our local kingpins apparently had an unspoken standing order for anyone in my position that held that any "controversial" action must be cleared with the city manager, the first level of the Main Street chain of command. At first I thought, if this was the only way we could act on unequal treatment of city employees and citizens, I'd try to work with these people. My early contacts with the manager were pleasant enough. The first time I took an issue to him for an in-house administrative remedy, he reassured me, "I'll take care of it, don't worry. Trust me." He told me of his participation in civil rights demonstrations in Baltimore in the seventies, and since he was an African American, I counted him among our allies.

But as my reports to him of problems in city government increased, he began to pull back. It became more difficult to get appointments. He rarely answered my phone calls and memos to him; when he did, the response was usually a convoluted effort to sidestep the issue. It soon became clear that he was unwilling to ruffle the feathers of the powerbrokers who had little interest in rectifying the city's two centuries of racial injustice.

When I reported to the manager a scandalous epidemic of discrimination in pay, work assignments, and promotions in the city Department of Public Works and asked him to fix it, he became sullen and mumbled his well-worn bromide, "I'll take care of it." Follow-up efforts produced nothing. Meanwhile, the black employee complaints mounted and nothing happened. So I sought from the commission a censure resolution against the Public Works Department, and the media picked it up. This earned kudos from city workers and people in the community but put me on the enemies list of the city manager. Later when I greeted him in a restaurant, he angrily declared to his lunch companions and everyone else within earshot that I was "crazy."

I also had some hand-to-hand moral combat with the mayor, who had played a key role in giving away the city's controlling interest in the Richmond airport to neighboring counties, as part of a scheme no doubt cooked up on Main Street to ensure a white majority on its governing board. He was furious because I was about to disclose some serious shenanigans at the airport that might blow up the deal. The commission had been inundated with complaints from black airport workers about systematic discrimination, including incidents of abusive racist language used by whites over the walkie-talkies and the public address system in the airport terminal. Also, no blacks were allowed to work on the skilled, higher-paid maintenance crew, even when their qualifications were superior to those of the white workers. Blacks were confined to outdoor landscaping and trash removal. Meanwhile, witnesses reported Airport Commission executives tapping the airport's gasoline stock for personal use and conducting other practices that, if not illegal, certainly exploited taxpayers and airline passengers.

The mayor demanded that I keep the story quiet, but I defied him and shared our findings with a press contact. In the end, the story never got much traction because all of the firsthand witnesses were intimidated into silence by their bosses. From that time on, the mayor and a couple of members of the city council never missed an opportunity to denigrate anything I said.

These city officials put the commission in an awkward position: the city's human rights ordinance directed us to work toward the elimination of discrimination, but doing so required us to wrangle for authority with privileged blacks fronting for the white elites pulling the strings off stage. This experience was very dispiriting, because it revealed the shallowness of the so-called civil rights revolution. It was sad also because it was a wake-up call about black conservatives. Watching handsome and polished black men in tailored three-piece suits deliberately attempt to protect the white economic oligarchy against their poorer brothers and sisters taught me to stop trusting skin color to predict who would work for racial justice. The lures offered by white powerbrokers for desertion from the struggle for equality were apparently just too enticing to hold a solid line.

At the end of my term, I delivered the customary chairperson's farewell speech. It contained a laundry list of issues that I thought sorely needed attention. They included racial discrimination in work assignments, pay, and promotions and sexual harassment in certain city agencies; favoritism in the form of handouts from the city to the business community at the expense of funds for neighborhood and human resources development; a lack of ordinary civil protections for gay men and lesbians; and a severe under-representation of women on key city boards and commissions. These departing comments were covered extensively in the local press and reverberated for a time. But when the noise died down, so did public concern. Early in the next year the conservative city council majority, carried by the tailwinds of the Reagan revolution, gutted what small powers the commission had and banished it to oblivion in the bowels of the city bureaucracy.

IN 1984 fortune once again smiled on me. I met Karen Wawrzyn, an occupational therapist and progressive spirit who was to fill my life with that enduring joy, trustful sharing, and sustaining love that we all seek in a life partner. We married in 1987. For several more years I enjoyed my duties in the university and work on initiatives like those described here; but before we reached our ten-year anniversary I gained a boon that let me play house-husband while she continued her work. In 1995 Governor George Allen sought to cut the size and cost of Virginia's state government by offering thousands of us veteran state employees early retirement. It may have created a sudden rupture of the cashbox at the Virginia Retirement System, but it was a good thing for both Allen and me. He used it to get himself elected to the U.S. Senate, and it gave me the time and freedom to reflect upon my earlier years and find new age-appropriate ways to be a justice seeker.

The best part of my retirement came in January of 1996, when Karen and I adopted Camille Thi Peeples from Vietnam at the age of five months. My fourth daughter, she was Karen's first child, and a source of joy for us and her now-grown sisters, Suzy, Kate, and Cecily. As I write, she's become an accomplished student, gifted violin player, and a master of humorous repartee, which are among the many things about her that give me much delight.

Finally a Kinsman with Whom
I Am Not a Stranger

B Y THE LATE seventies the tension between my parents and me regarding race lessened somewhat. The demise of legal segregation made me finally seem a bit more mainstream and them more the outliers. With part of the uneasiness gone, my mother and I were able to revive some of the early devotion between us, especially as our contacts involved her grandchildren. But there remained an unspoken mindfulness between us—we were of two different worlds. She continued to find other places to stay overnight when in Richmond. Yet we did much to bridge those two worlds before my beloved mother, Lula Jane Stephens Gammon, passed away from a heart attack one morning after playing nine holes of golf, on October 19, 1986, at age seventy-eight.

Ever since my return to Richmond in 1968 I pledged to myself to do what I could to reconcile with my father. But my best efforts were not enough. He was still the emotionally disassociated person of my youth, so the best we could do was to spend some occasional awkward times together at VCU basketball games or when he would come and sit wordlessly on our couch as my lively daughters and I engaged in our doings of the day. Our reunion was an uneasy truce—with an occasional breach of the peace brought on by one of his race-baiting remarks to me or my friends. It was far short of a genuine reconciliation. Still, I felt great sadness about my failure to connect with my father. Edward H. Peeples IV died alone from a heart attack in his tiny and sparse room in a cheap rooming house on January 17, 1986, four months short of his eighty-first birthday.

During the most troubling years of alienation from my parents and extended kin, I longed to discover an elder who shared a passion for justice or at least would support me in my convictions. Always in the back of my mind was the question—what if there was some family precedent for my activism? Maybe someone who fought for the Union in the Civil War? If I were to find something like this and share it with my parents, would it close the schism? Our family oral tradition gave no hint of such a prospect. So I more or less resigned myself to never being forgiven or fully welcomed back into the fold.

But when I was in my late thirties, a postcard arrived from Chalmers Gaston Davidson, the librarian at Davidson College in North Carolina. He was inquiring about a "Captain" Edward Harden Peeples, a large slaveholder in South Carolina born in 1811. Davidson was conducting research for the South Carolina Tricentennial Commission, which was eventually published in 1971 as *The Last Foray: The South Carolina Planters of 1860, A Sociological Study.* I responded saying that I knew nothing of this so-called Captain Peeples, but would like to learn more. He informed me of a privately published genealogy entitled *Peebles: Ante 1600–1962,* edited by a Virginia woman named Anne Bradbury Peebles. From it I learned that this E. H. Peeples was actually my great-great-grandfather, one of South Carolina's larger slaveholders, and was eighth in line of my eleven direct male ancestors since our family first arrived from Scotland in what was then Charles City County, Virginia, in 1649.

This genealogy also revealed that John Peeples, my great-great-great-great-grandfather and the first of my line to move from Virginia to South Carolina in the mid-1700s, officially changed the *b* to a *p* in our surname during the run-up to the American Revolution. John was an advocate of American independence and was determined to distance himself from his father, William Peebles, a loyalist to King George III.

I was stunned to learn all this. My sketchy family knowledge only went back to my father and his father, both of whom were also named Edward Harden Peeples. Driven by my need to find something to legitimize my so-called betrayal of my family, I set off on an intermittent study that shook loose countless stories from the family tree. This Peeples history was particularly intriguing because my brother and I were raised with little awareness of the legacy of privilege in my father's family. Instead we were brought up with the working-class identity of my mother and her rural family.

Finding little at first about sympathetic kin folks, I put aside the Peebles/
Peeples materials until I came upon another privately published book, a history
of the Peeples family's church, the Pipe Creek Church in Low Country, South
Carolina, where my great-great-grandfather was a deacon.* The book unfolded
many details about his life.

But the most exciting discovery in the book was my introduction to William Henry Brisbane, Edward H. Peeples's pastor from 1833 to 1835. Brisbane
was brother-in-law, cousin, and best friend to my great-great-grandfather—
and a South Carolina slaveholder who became an abolitionist! Feverishly I
began to look into the story of this kinsman, Dr. William Henry Brisbane, my
great-great-uncle by marriage and a distant blood-related cousin.

Having retired from VCU in 1995, I had the free time to devour everything I
could find about him. I went to the Wisconsin State Historical Society archives
where his essays, speeches, diary, correspondence, obituaries, and memorial accounts were assembled. I also visited his final home in Arena, Wisconsin, and
his grave at Mazomanie and took countless photographs. I collected images of
him and his friends and corresponded with those who had knowledge of him.
I embarked on an odyssey to the South Carolina Low Country to visit all the
sites in the Brisbane and Peeples stories. I even traveled to Minnesota to visit
Dr. Wallace Alcorn, Brisbane's great-great-grandson and the leading scholar on
his life.

WHO WAS THIS country preacher who had me so beguiled? William Henry
Brisbane was born in Black Swamp, St. Peters Parish, in the South Carolina
Low Country on October 12, 1806. Black Swamp, now known as Robertville,
is about four miles from the Savannah River in present-day Jasper County. In
Brisbane's day this southern region of the Savannah River watershed was home
to many large plantations kept prosperous by the coerced labor of thousands
of slaves, along with a scattering of small marginal farms tilled by poor whites
barely eking out their livings. By the time of the Civil War, slaves and the handful of free blacks found in this region constituted about 83 percent of the total
population. Aside from some river commerce and a few retail businesses in the

*Coy K. Johnston, *Two Centuries of Lawtonville Baptist, 1775–1975* (Atlanta, GA: Privately
published, 1974).

towns and at the various crossroads, slave-based agriculture totally dominated the economy.

My branch of the Peeples family lived on one of these plantations, situated at a crossroads village known as Peeplesville in the wider area often referred to as Lawtonville, in what today is Hampton County. The record suggests that the Peeples's main house was modest when compared with the grand mansions found elsewhere in the state. But the house, the vast acreage, the slaves, and the prosperity of the enterprise were objects of much envy in the neighborhood. Within but a few miles were neighboring planter families including the Lawtons, the Brisbanes, and a few dozen other related families of similar means. Given the minuscule size of the elite population, intermarriage between these families was common. Even occasional marriages between blood kin were not particularly discouraged. This was the case with Brisbane, who married his own first cousin, Anna Lawton, the sister of my great-great-grandmother. For them and for the other planters and prosperous merchant households in the area, the antebellum period provided an idyllic life, sustained by the toil of a people whose only deliverance was death and a promise of heaven.

In 1821, when Brisbane was a teenager, he inherited from his uncle the Milton Lodge Plantation on the Ashley River near Charleston, and with it several dozen slves. Brisbane sold the place in 1832, and the financial independence allowed him to become a gentleman planter and study to become both a physician and a Baptist preacher. While practicing medicine, he also pastored several small churches in the Lawtonville community.

Brisbane and Peeples were so close that Brisbane referred to my great-great-grandfather as his "brother," who reciprocated by naming his first son William Brisbane Peeples. During the years of their friendship, Brisbane was widely regarded by his peers as a brilliant defender of slavery. His articles in Baptist and other statewide publications, such as the *Charleston Mercury,* contained what many slave masters in the state considered incontrovertible arguments against the rising tide of abolitionism in the North in the early 1830s. Of his pro-slavery views, Brisbane later observed, "I reposed with much quietude on the infallibility of my own conclusions." By Low Country planter standards, Brisbane's life could not have been better. While he had a reputation for being kind to his slaves, an irritation to some of the local planters, he was still seen as a paragon of planter virtue and beloved by the white community.

But a blow of seismic proportions struck Dr. Brisbane in 1835 that forever altered his life. It was the year in which an anti-slavery pamphlet, with excerpts from *Elements of Moral Science* by Dr. Francis Wayland, president of Brown University, found its way into Brisbane's hands. The essay argued that slavery was not supported in Christian scripture. Brisbane took this thesis as a personal challenge and wrote a rebuttal to Wayland in the *Southern Baptist*. But for the next few years Wayland's argument weighed on his conscience, so heavily that Brisbane went to visit Wayland in Rhode Island. Their discussions changed his mind about slavery. He came to believe that human bondage was sinful and started preaching and speaking to his friends and family of his new-found conclusions.

As his disdain for slavery grew, Brisbane decided he must discharge his overseer for whipping the slaves. Then he sold all but three of them to my great-great-grandfather. Over the next year or so Brisbane's stature in the community collapsed. At first, he denied being an abolitionist and was bewildered by what he called the "popular excitement" provoked by his change of heart. He was taunted with threats of being tarred and feathered. Before long he lost his pulpit at Pipe Creek. Finally local leaders had him thrown into the Barnwell District Jail for his "subversive" statements. As Brisbane later recounted: "No sooner did I take this step, than I became the object of calumny and abuse. Although I had broken no law of the State; had interfered with no man's privileges; had not urged my troubles upon anyone; and was doing no more than a conscientious man was obliged to do; I was, nevertheless, so threatened and vilified, that it was a question of whether I ought not at once to have to leave the country for my personal safety."* Realizing the danger of remaining in South Carolina, in early 1838 Brisbane, Anna, their three sons, and his three remaining domestic slaves escaped to safety in Cincinnati. There Brisbane freed the three slaves, but they elected to remain with the family and work for wages.

Shortly after his arrival in Cincinnati, he began to regret having sold his other slaves to Peeples because they remained in captivity. His diary entry for October 24, 1839, said, "Proposed to Ed Peeples to sell me back the negroes I sold him & told him to let me have the opportunity to get them whenever he wishes to sell any. If I could get them back they should have their

*Brisbane, "Speech of the Rev. Wm. H. Brisbane," 5.

freedom."* Brisbane asked to buy them back at the current market price. My great-great-grandfather did finally agree to sell the nineteen slaves but demanded $200 per slave over the market price, a huge sum at the time. In 1840, Brisbane returned to Lawtonville briefly, bought back the field slaves from Peeples and aided them in making the treacherous trek to Ohio.

On another visit back to South Carolina in February of 1848, Brisbane was spending the night at a relative's home when he was awakened suddenly with a warning to leave quickly. A group of angry men were on their way to "take care of him." Knowing what this euphemism portended, he and the family hastily returned under cover of night to the sanctuary of Ohio, a free state.

During his years in southern Ohio, Brisbane came to know the abolitionists James G. Birney, Gamaliel Bailey, and Salmon P. Chase, and became a confirmed opponent of slavery. Before long, he was celebrated as a public speaker and essayist in behalf of the movement—a great asset to the struggle because he had profited from slavery yet renounced it. The speech that launched his reputation was an address on February 12, 1840, to the Ladies Anti-Slavery Society of Cincinnati. Published later that year, the address received wide circulation across the North.

In the early 1840s Brisbane began his long involvement in national antislavery politics. Among his good friends and comrades in this work were Salmon P. Chase and Rev. Moncure D. Conway, a fellow southerner born to a slaveholding Virginia family who became the minister of the First Congregational (Unitarian) Church in Cincinnati. He collaborated with Levi Coffin and Edward Harwood on the Underground Railroad in southern Ohio. Through the Liberty Party, the American Anti-Slavery Society, and later the Republican Party and other groups, Brisbane met and worked with movement leaders such as Frederick Douglass, John Greenleaf Whittier, Arthur and Lewis Tappen, Joshua R. Giddings, Theodore Dwight Weld, Horace Greeley, and the Grimké sisters.

While active in abolition efforts across the North, Brisbane became focused on how white nonslaveholding southerners could help the cause if effectively organized. This was sometimes a point of dispute, even animus, with some northern abolitionists, such as William Lloyd Garrison, who wrote off the

*Johnston, *Two Centuries of Lawtonville Baptist,* 63–65.

poor whites of the South, presuming that their racism made them untrust-
worthy allies. Brisbane disagreed.

He tried to promote abolitionism in his home state of South Carolina with
open letters and pamphlets. Massive numbers of these tracts were mailed to
white voters in the upcountry where there were fewer slaveholders. Brisbane
hoped to convince nonslaveholding southerners that since they had no vested
interest in the institution, they should help end it. These missives came to be
seen as so threatening by slaveholders that South Carolina banned them from
circulation. Brisbane's friends who distributed them were beaten and jailed. In
reaction to the suppression, he adopted the pen name Brutus, gesturing toward
the way whites who renounced their racial privileges were treated as traitors by
their families, neighbors, and former friends.

In 1853 William and Anna moved from Ohio to Arena, Wisconsin, where
he pastored a number of churches in the area. He also continued to work as a
physician and in 1856 was elected vice president of the American Medical Association. He continued his abolitionist traveling, speaking and writing throughout the North right up to the Civil War. He also helped found the Republican
Party and in 1859 attempted to secure the 1860 Republican presidential nom-
ination for his close friend Salmon P. Chase. Together with his three former
slaves and his wife, Brisbane operated a farm at Arena. Sadly Anna, while remaining with him, despised living in the North and never lost her proslavery
convictions. This household conflict had to be heart-wrenching, but in those
days a divorce for irreconcilable differences was unheard of.

When the Civil War broke out, Brisbane volunteered and served eight
months as the chaplain for the Second Wisconsin Calvary Regiment until ill
health compelled him to resign. He returned to South Carolina in late 1862
to serve in Union-occupied territory as chairman of the U.S. district tax commissioners for the Sea Islands, Beaufort District. One of his assignments was
to locate abandoned plantations in the area and redistribute them to freedmen
in what was called the Port Royal Experiment, brilliantly depicted a century
later by the historian Willie Lee Rose in her prize-winning *Rehearsal for Reconstruction: The Port Royal Experiment*. These actions earned him the moniker
of "most hated man in Beaufort District" among whites, a phrase still used by
a few old members of my South Carolina family.

Brisbane's life reached a zenith at Camp Saxton near Port Royal on the morning of New Year's Day in 1863. Colonel Thomas Wentworth Higginson, the commander of one of the Union's first forces composed of liberated slaves, the First South Carolina Volunteer Regiment, presided. Higginson writes in his memoirs how at around 10 a.m. a pro-Union crowd gathered at the military installation for a grand ceremony and announcement. Masses of local officials, black refugees, soldiers, white teachers, ministers, volunteers from up North, the band of the Eighth Maine Regiment, and countless others all converged at the giant event platform.

Five thousand souls were assembled as Dr. Brisbane took out a version, not even the final draft, of President Lincoln's Emancipation Proclamation. Most in the massive crowd were slaves who had sought liberty in the Union-held Sea Islands territory. The audience was still as Brisbane began to read:

By the President of the United States of America: A Proclamation. Whereas, on the twenty-second day of September, in the year of our Lord one thousand eight hundred and sixty-two, a proclamation was issued by the President of the United States, containing, among other things, the following, to wit: That on the first day of January, in the year of our Lord one thousand eight hundred and sixty-three, all persons held as slaves within any State or designated part of a State, the people whereof shall then be in rebellion against the United States, shall be then, thenceforward, and forever free.

Higginson described what came afterwards:

Just as I took and waved the flag, which now for the first time meant anything to these poor people, there suddenly arose, close beside the platform, a strong but rather cracked and elderly male voice, into which two women's voices immediately blended, singing as if by an impulse that can no more be quenched than the morning note of the song sparrow—the hymn—"My country 'tis of thee, Sweet land of Liberty." . . . Irrepressibly the quavering voices sang on, verse after verse; others around them joined; some on the platform sung.

"I never saw anything so electric; it made all other words cheap," Higginson recounted. "It seemed the choked voice of a race, at last unloosed." After the singing stopped, the crying began; "it was silent," he said, "tears were every-where." "Just think of it," he urged, "the first day they had ever had a country, the first flag they had ever seen which promised anything to their people."*

Upon returning home to Wisconsin, Brisbane continued working his farm, preaching, involving himself in national politics, writing, and traveling about the country speaking. He also continued his medical practice, committed him-self to the temperance crusade, and developed ties with what today we would call the holistic health movement. On April 5, 1878, at seventy-one years old, after returning from a lecture delivered in Oshkosh, William Henry Brisbane "took sick" and died in his Arena home. He left behind a vast collection of papers, now housed at the Wisconsin Historical Society in Madison.

I discovered in Brisbane's story a jarring parallel with my own experience. Knowledge of him brought clarity to the meaning of my years of human rights work. In his youth Brisbane had been immersed in the institution of slavery, as I had been in the clutches of Jim Crow. Then as young men we both found our way out, he to join the abolitionist crusade and I the civil rights movement. While he was driven by the evangelical social gospel of his time, I was ani-mated by the secular humanism of mine. In two different centuries, we each traded our former pliant complicity for years of scorn and ostracism from our birth families, early friends, and community. And yet we both finally found vindication in the change for which we gave of ourselves.

Before I learned of Brisbane I was perplexed about how to rid myself of the deep hurt left by the breach with my family. But as I became more familiar with his life, I experienced an inexplicable relief from that sense of isolation. I felt, instead, a warm welcome into a timeless communion of justice seekers. An inner voice whispered to me, "Ed, you have an honored place in your fam-ily, thanks to Brisbane." It felt like I was being encouraged by a wise uncle, commending me for continuing his work and comforting me as a comrade. Brisbane's example urged me to liberate the memories of my life much as he did through the written word. That in time yielded this book.

This imagined conversation was a bit grandiose, given the difference be-tween Brisbane's trials and contributions and my own. But it enabled me to

*The Complete Civil War Journal and Selected Letters of Thomas Wentworth Higginson, ed. Christopher Looby (Chicago: University of Chicago Press, 2000), 75–77.

come to terms with living as an apostate. It reassured me that becoming a traitor to a group that claims unfair privileges at the expense of other human beings is the noblest of acts.

It also told me that all human rights movements begin with meager trickles of good works from a multitude of springs, which only after converging with greater streams finally become the rushing waters of a mighty river of justice. Brisbane's freeing his slaves was a personal act of conscience. But added to the acts of many others, it built the movement that eventually rid our nation of chattel slavery.

Learning about him got me to thinking that perhaps my small acts in defiance of segregation did something similar. He allowed me to see more clearly that the struggle for human equality and dignity is a multi-century movement in which each of us must take up the baton of justice, carry it while we can, and then pass it on to our children. Above all, his story affirmed for me that we are never alone in this work of seeking justice. All the heroes and heroines of the ages stand with us.

Peeples's History and Virginia History

James H. Hershman Jr.

ED PEEPLES'S MEMOIR reminds us that it is human beings, not abstract concepts, that create social change. Individuals like Peeples who challenge dominant powers by standing up for justice and human rights play a crucial role. Their seemingly marginal voices and actions trigger a larger social conscience that becomes a compelling moral force in society. This story can be read as part of the universal quest for human rights, but it is also very much a Virginia story, grounded in the Old Dominion's civil and human rights struggles.

In the middle of the last century, Virginia was a forbidding terrain for anyone who questioned its social hierarchy and its traditions. Strict racial segregation governed the interactions between whites and blacks. Forming a little more than a fifth of the state's population of three million people, African Americans were legally assigned to a separate caste considered inferior to all whites. Though there were challenges to racist ideology in America outside of the South in the 1940s, the caste system within Virginia was as entrenched as ever. The belief in white supremacy was reinforced by the "scientific" racism of eugenics. Behind the walls of segregation, black Virginians built their own institutions and sustained resistance to the oppressive system, most effectively by joining the NAACP's step-by-step legal campaign. Among whites, those publicly willing to criticize the racial order were indeed few in number.

Questioning the status quo on race or just about anything in Virginia brought the dissenter into conflict with the powerful coterie of white men who governed the state. Like other states in the South, Virginia had been controlled by one party since the late nineteenth century. Power within the dominant

Democratic Party was further concentrated in a faction called the Organization, led from 1925 to 1965 by Harry F. Byrd Sr. The Byrd Organization encompassed the state and local power structures and the state's federal representatives. Its fundamental principle was holding governmental expenditures to a minimum. Low levels of taxation and of public services, loose regulation, and anti–organized labor policies favored rural landowners and the few large manufacturing, extractive, and transportation industries in the Old Dominion. The Organization's continued political control rested on two pillars: a restricted electorate and the protection of white supremacy. The poll tax and registration obstacles kept the majority of eligible voters off the rolls, including many whites in cities and suburbs and almost all African Americans. Rural whites in southern and eastern Virginia were the organization's strongest supporters and were also the most adamantly committed to a traditional society, particularly the racial caste structure.

Drawing upon broader racial views in American culture and adding their own Virginia variant, the state's leadership had fashioned a rationale for their racial practices. Their cultural narrative, put forth in newspapers, popular media, and school textbooks, asserted that Virginia had a history of genteel, paternalistic race relations. Within this narrative, slavery was depicted as a benign, social welfare–like system presided over by kindly white masters. Following the end of slavery and the misbegotten Reconstruction (with its carpetbaggers and scalawags), the restoration of white rule brought the creation of dual societies that, after 1896, purported to be "separate but equal." Moreover, according to this view, African Americans were generally content with their circumstances. Complaints arose only when they were misled by "outside agitators," who were accused of being subversives with Communist Party affiliations.

Termed the "Virginia Way" by noted Richmond editor and biographer Douglas Southall Freeman, the Old Dominion's race relations were touted as different and definitely superior to those prevailing further south. Exercising their best paternalistic instincts, Virginia gentlemen largely prevented the kinds of white populist, extra-legal violence manifested in the mass spectacles of brutal lynching. Examined more objectively, the Virginia Way was a half-truth that masked a cruel reality. There were, in fact, fewer lynchings in Virginia than in most former Confederate states. Virginia's political culture had a tacit respect for legality and a dominant elite disdainful of the white egalitarianism of the Deep South. The nativist Ku Klux Klan made a significant appearance in Virginia in the 1920s, but its volatile nature carried a threat of violence that could damage the state's business reputation. Even more threatening, it was acting as a political force outside of Byrd Organization control. Not surprisingly, the state government enacted legislation suppressing the Klan's practices. At the same time, they were tightening the state's racial integrity and segregation laws.

The message to the mass of white Virginians was clear: the established leadership, using the legal powers of the state, would police the color line and protect white supremacy. One of the most direct ways that Virginia's leaders fulfilled this commitment was through their willingness to execute black men for the alleged rape of white women. Over two days in February 1951, Virginia executed seven black men for a single rape, without the death of the victim. As for the reality of "separate but equal," a mere look at the 1950 census on occupations and housing reveals it as an utter fiction—the racial gap in every category was obvious. As for the contentment of Virginia's black residents, tens of thousands fled from the harsh conditions there to the North in the Great Migration. The steadily rising resistance of those who remained further belied paternalistic claims of contentment. The Virginia Way was actually a delusion that allowed the state's elite to represent their pattern of racial discrimination as mild.

During the 1950s, black Virginians' drive for civil rights had a major collision with white rule over the issue of public school desegregation. The precipitating event was a 1951 strike staged by black high school students in Prince Edward County to protest their grossly inadequate school facilities. The students and their supporters asked NAACP attorneys to take the case as part of the school equalization effort they had litigated since the 1930s, but the lawyers told them that the civil rights group had ended that campaign—any suit now would have to challenge segregation directly. When Prince Edward's black community agreed, the attorneys filed suit in federal court. They lost in the first round when a Virginia-born judge found that segregation was legal as a long-established state custom. The NAACP appealed the case to the U.S. Supreme Court, where it was joined with cases from three other states and the District of Columbia. Virginia's lawyers contested all aspects of the NAACP's case, including the argument that segregation was psychologically damaging to black children, but the justices found them unconvincing. In May 1954, the high court ruled that segregation in public education was inherently unequal and violated the U.S. Constitution.

The ruling stunned Virginia's white leadership; its response was uncertain for almost a year and a half, though a grudgingly minimal acceptance looked possible. Unfortunately, the court's 1955 implementation decree was vague, allowing wide latitude in enforcement. Segregationists, starting in Prince Edward County, began to organize and agitate for an all-out defense of the color barrier. The few whites publicly defending the court's decision, mostly clergymen, joined the Virginia Council on Human Relations, but their position came under harsh, relentless attack. In the closing months of 1955, the editor of the *Richmond News Leader,* James Jackson Kilpatrick, made an elaborate argument that the state could "interpose" its authority to block federal laws, a concept discredited by the Civil War. He encouraged many whites to believe that they could and should resist the Supreme Court's decision and that their opposition to desegregation was a dispute over constitutional principles, not a matter of racial prejudice.

By 1956, the turn toward aggressive defiance was complete. With the Byrd Organization in control, the state government adopted a plan of massive resistance designed to block any school desegregation and roll back the gains for civil rights. Control over assignment to schools was centralized at the state level; the governor was mandated to seize and close any schools under a federal desegregation order; NAACP attorneys were threatened with disbarment. In 1958, a state commission was created to propagate the view that the defiance was about constitutional issues, not maintenance of white supremacy. Two special investigative committees of the state legislature held hearings around the state subpoenaing NAACP officials, black plaintiffs in school cases, and white integrationists. The committees persisted into the early 1960s, generating several law suits regarding their "investigations." Though black and white activists often suffered negative economic consequences and experienced harassment in the form of threatening telephone calls and hate mail, the attempt to turn back civil rights failed.

The predictable reckoning with federal authority came in 1958, when the governor closed nine schools in three communities to prevent desegregation. Finally, a strong white opposition to massive resistance emerged under the ban-ner of saving public education, though the segregationists attacked them with great vitriol as integrationists. When the courts ordered the schools to open, the governor backed down, permitting the token enrollment of twenty-one black students. Within months, the state adopted a new plan to limit desegregation that included repealing the compulsory attendance statute and providing tuition grants to students attending private schools.

In September 1959, taking advantage of the changes in the law, the local government in Prince Edward County simply refused to appropriate funds for public schools rather than desegregate. A segregated private academy served the needs of most white students. Except for a few who obtained education elsewhere, the black children of Prince Edward were denied public education for five years until the Supreme Court ruled the closing unconstitutional in 1964. Prince Edward was the only locality in the United States to close all its public schools to avoid desegregation. While the schools were closed, individuals and groups made efforts, such as those poignantly described by Peeples, to provide some services for the unschooled black youth, but the end result of the county's action was to produce an educationally crippled generation and a lasting bitterness in the community.

Massive resistance proved a brittle shield; breaking it gave a sense of inevitability to segregation's demise. As a consequence black Virginians' demand for their rights became more urgent, and they were less willing to wait for the slow pace of law suits. In 1960, they began to attack segregation with massive direct action tactics such as sit-ins and other public demonstrations. The response of most localities, aided by the media, was to follow the Virginia Way—ignore the demonstrations as much as possible, downplay them, and by all means avoid violent confrontation. For example, when the Freedom Riders made stops in Virginia in 1961, signs segregating facilities in bus stations were quietly removed so that the press would not see them and no arrests would occur, then restored after the Riders left. With few exceptions—most notably Danville in the summer of 1963—Virginia's leadership succeeded. The impression conveyed by accounts at the time and in subsequent histories is that little civil rights activity took place in the Old Dominion. Peeples describes his participation in Richmond sit-ins that were barely reported in the press. Actually, civil rights demonstrations did take place with some frequency in cities and towns across the state from 1960 to 1964.

Landmark national legislation passed in 1964 and 1965—the Twenty-fourth Amendment to the U.S. Constitution (abolishing the poll tax), the Civil Rights Act of 1964, and the Voting Rights Act of 1965—created great potential for change in Virginia's race relations. Produced by the civil rights movement, this crescendo of legislation struck down the laws requiring segregation in all public activities and, at the same time, knocked out the political underpinning of the Byrd Organization. In 1967, the Supreme Court overturned Virginia's ban on interracial marriage, the last legal barrier of the caste system. The hospital segregation Peeples describes was ended by federal court rulings in 1963 and 1967. Progress in public school desegregation had moved at a snail's pace after 1959, but in 1968, again ruling in a Virginia case, the nation's highest court ordered the absolute end of the dual school system. Large-scale desegregation in systems all over the state followed, and, with federal prodding, even the pace in higher education increased. Hundreds of thousands of white and black voters added their names to the registration rolls. In 1969, for the first time in a century, Virginia elected a Republican governor. A. Linwood Holton came from western Virginia's "mountain Republican" faction of the GOP, with views on government noticeably different from the Byrd Organization and with the unmistakably liberal aim of ending racial discrimination. Briefly, during the late 1960s and early 1970s, a new day appeared to be dawning in the Old Dominion, carrying the promise of overcoming the state's bleak racial past.

Yet hopes for further racial progress faded as the 1970s unfolded. Problems arose from geographic segregation in schools: urban whites and blacks lived farther and farther apart from each other. Since the early 1950s, many new housing developments for whites had been built. To make desegregation work, federal judges ordered extensive cross-town busing in Richmond, Norfolk, and Newport News, provoking an ardent anti-busing backlash among whites. Suburbanization created even more complication because much of it was caused by "white flight" from the cities into the surrounding counties. In a bold, sweeping remedy, the federal judge Robert R. Merhige Jr. ordered Richmond's schools combined with two suburban counties for purposes of desegregation. On appeal, the Richmond case was overturned, and, in a similar case from Detroit, the Supreme Court held that school district boundaries were inviolable borders. Thus limited, public schools in Virginia's increasingly black and poor cities and their increasingly white suburbs resegregated on a class and race basis. Within institutions of higher education, just as Peebles experienced, the momentum toward integration stalled in the mid-1970s as the state and federal governments reached an agreement curtailing federal pressure for change.

The quiet, insidious elements of institutional racism settled in throughout public life. In politics, the Republicans rejected the path Holton wanted them to follow, choosing instead to recruit a former Democratic governor and Byrd Organization stalwart, Mills E. Godwin, as their candidate in the 1973 governor's race. A prominent advocate of massive resistance in the fifties, Godwin brought many of his old supporters into the Virginia GOP. Opposing him in the epic 1973 contest was the Norfolk liberal Henry E. Howell, who used consumer issues and strong backing from organized labor to create a formidable New Deal–style black and white coalition. Howell's razor-thin defeat marked the close of the sixties' liberal surge. Thereafter, Virginia settled into a pattern of suburban-oriented politics much in keeping with conservative national political and social trends.

The civil rights movement responded to the changes in the last decades of the twentieth century by increasing its focus on political engagement, electing African Americans at every level from the city council to the state legislature to Congress and the governorship. It also sparked a "rights revolution" among other groups that suffered discrimination—women, the disabled, and gays—who employed the movement's tactics and legal precedents to assert their claims to social justice. For example, the Richmond Human Relations Commission, on which Peeples had a significant role, helped place the protection of gay rights on the agenda of local and state government in the early eighties. While the rights revolution carried the fight for equal rights forward, it had its own limitations, especially for the black community where it originated. Its legalistic approach served well to protect individuals from current discrimination, but its lack of a proactive economic component gave it no mechanism to redress the effects of past oppression on an entire group.

Ed Peeples was a committed participant in an "unfinished revolution" that appropriately has been called the Second Reconstruction. He closes his story by finding a kindred spirit in his ancestor William Henry Brisbane, a southern slaveholder who became an abolitionist and advocate for the rights of former slaves during the first Reconstruction. Their respective revolutions, the Civil

War and the civil rights movement, overcame two great evils—slavery and legal segregation—but they could not remove the racism those evils nurtured. Hence, they were unfinished. Nonetheless, the guiding principle driving both Brisbane and Peeples—demand for the basic dignity of every person—is the enemy of racism and oppressive inequality everywhere. Those struggling for social justice in the twenty-first century will find inspiration in Peeples's life. In the years ahead, we will need more "scalawags" among us.

ACKNOWLEDGMENTS

MANY HAVE STOOD with me in what I have done with my life, and so they are all in some way coauthors of this book. But these thoughts would have never become a book had I not had the good fortune of Nancy MacLean showing up on my doorstep. Until then they were nothing but an idle stack of misshapen and disjointed vignettes. She read some of them, and before I knew what happened, she had adopted me as perhaps the oldest graduate student she ever had. Since then her generous gifts of time, talent, encouragement, advocacy, line-by-line editing, and her vast knowledge of the historical context for my stories have been boundless. But her investment in this project went far beyond creating a book; it was the first real affirmation for me of my life's work. My hope is that this revelation will persuade others who served without recognition in the civil rights and human rights movements also to record their experiences.

Treasured, too, have been the generous and substantive contributions, encouragement, and friendship of historian and fellow Virginian Jim Hershman, who has brought so much important historical sinew to this project. The rich contextual embrace of my story between MacLean's introduction and Hershman's afterword makes this book more than a mere memoir. They provide the panoramic view of the long march toward "justice for all" while I provide a close-up shot of one marcher and his comrades. Their penetrating contributions do me great honor.

For bringing me to the place where I could write this book, much praise is due to those special individuals in my higher education who opened up the world and gave me the chance to do what I have done. First were Dr. Alice Davis and the other educational missionaries at the Richmond Professional Institute, who, it should be said, saved my soul. Later were Martin P. Chworowsky at the University of Pennsylvania, Robert Straus at the University of

Kentucky, and Frederick J. Spencer, many years my department chair at Virginia Commonwealth University, each truly a patron saint.

I am also much indebted to those living and passed who mentored me, inspired me, or gave me strength along the way: Bill Bagwell, Helen Baker, Lester Banks, Algernon Black, Jean Fairfax, Rev. L. Francis Griffin, June Purcell Guild, Oliver W. Hill, Rev. Miles Jones, Henry Marsh, Joyce Miller, Barbara Moffett, J. Kenneth Morland, Gordon Moss, Ethel Overby, Rev. Eugene Pickett, Rupert Picott, Harry Roberts, Spottswood W. Robinson III, Dr. J. M. and Mrs. Ruth Tinsley, and Samuel W. Tucker, among many others.

I am grateful too for the sustenance offered so generously by many of my lifelong and latter-day friends, collaborators, and comrades, such as: Les Simpson, Bob Young, Vincent Wright, Doug Kelley, Ruby Clayton Walker, Willie Dell, Evans Hopkins, John Stokes, and Brenda Edwards, to name but a few. I am also indebted to good friends and colleagues, John Moeser, Beth O'Leary, Brian Grogan, Chris Bonastia, Brian Daugherity, John Kneebone, David Bearinger, Gregg Kimball, and Brent Tarter, for their varied and specific ways of supporting and encouraging my efforts in this project. Likewise, a great debt is owed to the Reverend Dr. Wallace Alcorn for bringing me along on his scholarly journey through the world of our heroic common ancestor, William Henry Brisbane. As for the exemplary and encouraging efforts of Dick Holway, Raennah Mitchell, Morgan Myers, and the other staff at the University of Virginia Press, all expressions of my gratitude and praise can only fall short. Much credit is also due for indispensable manuscript refinements made by my anonymous readers and by Michael Rackett, my independent editor. Thanks also go to the Wisconsin Historical Society collections and staff for their contributions to this project. Regrettably the individual who most inspired me to write this book is no longer here to see the result of his faithful support. Ted Allen, the author of the two-volume racial myth-spoiler *The Invention of the White Race,* and my dear friend since the early seventies, died in 2005. (A summary of the books can be seen at http://clogic.eserver.org/2005/editors.html.)

A very special thanks must also go to Ray Bonis, Jodie Koste, Yuki Hibben, Wesley Chenault, and the other dedicated present and past professionals at the James Branch Cabell and Tompkins-McCaw libraries at Virginia Commonwealth University. Under the visionary leadership of University Librarian John Ulmschneider, they have assembled a priceless collection of twentieth-century

Virginia civil rights and human rights materials, which have been of immense help in preparing this book and will continue to aid many others in the future.

This volume also seeks to celebrate the good works of three special organizations that have provided essential nurturance in my life: the Encampment for Citizenship, which for fifty years prepared thousands of young people, I among them, for leadership in the struggle for a genuine democratic and egalitarian America; the American Friends Service Committee; and Virginia Commonwealth University, whose lofty mission became my own.

This project also endeavors to recognize at least some of the central Virginia activists with whom I shared the struggle and whose stories also need to be told: Betsy Brinson, Ray Boone, John Coleman, Phyllis Conklin, "Rev" Linwood Corbett, Bruce Cruser, Willie Dell, Edward Meeks "Pope" Gregory, Rev. L. Francis Griffin Sr., June Purcell Guild, Dr. Edward E. Haddock, Rev. Curtis W. Harris, Marii Hasegawa, Heslip "Happy" Lee, Ruby Lee, Ora Lomax, Father John J. McMahon, Wendy Northrup, Ben Ragsdale, Jean Roland-Pender, Bruce Smith, LaVerne Byrd Smith, John Stokes, Ruby Clayton Walker, Hilda Warden, Jay Worrall Jr., Larry Yates, and Wayne Young, among many others.

But the most life-sustaining support in this long process has come from my loving immediate family. First and foremost has been the ceaseless love, forbearance, and sacrifice from my dear wife, Karen. Bountiful too has been the inspiration from my beloved daughters, Camille, Cecily, Kathryn, and Suzannah, and my nephew, Mark Peeples. The rarest form of gratitude must be saved for my brother, Stephen H. Peeples, one of the most honorable and unpretentious men I have ever known, who has never wavered in his support of me or in his own sense of justice and devotion to good works in behalf of the scorned and neglected. Finally with this work I honor the memory of our cherished mother, Lula Jane Stephens, who, even as she was deeply conflicted, gave with endless love every good thing to us that she knew how to give.

FURTHER READING ON
VIRGINIA CIVIL RIGHTS HISTORY

JIM CROW AND CIVIL RIGHTS IN VIRGINIA

Chappell, David L. *Inside Agitators: White Southerners in the Civil Rights Movement.* Baltimore: Johns Hopkins University Press, 1994.

Daugherity, Brian J., "'Keep on Keeping On': African Americans and the Implementation of *Brown v. Board of Education* in Virginia." In *With All Deliberate Speed: Implementing Brown v. Board of Education,* edited by Brian J. Daugherity and Charles C. Bolton, 41–58. Fayetteville: University of Arkansas Press, 2008.

Dierenfield, Kathleen Murphy. "One 'Desegregated Heart': Sarah Patton Boyle and the Crusade for Civil Rights in Virginia." *Virginia Magazine of History and Biography* 104, no. 2 (1996): 251–84.

Dorr, Gregory Michael. *Segregation's Science: Eugenics and Society in Virginia.* Charlottesville: University of Virginia Press, 2008.

Doyle, Mary C. "From Desegregation to Resegregation: Public Schools in Norfolk, Virginia 1954–2002." *Journal of African American History* 90, no. 1/2 (2005): 64–83.

Draper, Alan. *Conflict of Interests: Organized Labor and the Civil Rights Movement in the South, 1954–1968.* Ithaca: ILR Press, 1994.

Foster, Gerald A. *The Status of Blacks in the Commonwealth of Virginia: From Prince Edward County to the Election of 1985.* Hampton, Virginia: Hampton University, 1986.

Gates, Robbins L. *The Making of Massive Resistance: Virginia's Politics of Public School Desegregation, 1954–1956.* Chapel Hill: University of North Carolina Press, 1964.

Guild, June Purcell. *Black Laws of Virginia: A Summary of the Legislative Acts of Virginia Concerning Negroes from Earliest Times to the Present.* Richmond: Whittet & Shepperson, 1936.

Heinemann, Ronald L. *Harry Byrd of Virginia.* Charlottesville: University Press of Virginia, 1996.

Hershman, James H., Jr. "A Rumbling in the Museum: The Opponents of Virginia's Massive Resistance." PhD diss., University of Virginia, 1978.

———. "Massive Resistance." In *Encyclopedia Virginia,* edited by Brendan Wolfe. Virginia Foundation for the Humanities, 2008. http://www.encyclopediavirginia.org/Massive_Resistance.

206 Further Reading

———. "Public School Bonds and Virginia's Massive Resistance." *Journal of Negro Education* 52, no. 4 (1983): 398–409.

Holloway, Pippa. *Sexuality, Politics, and Social Control in Virginia, 1920–1945.* Chapel Hill: University of North Carolina Press, 2006.

Hustwit, William P. *James J. Kilpatrick: Salesman for Segregation.* Chapel Hill: University of North Carolina Press, 2013.

Kneebone, John Thomas. *Southern Liberal Journalists and the Issue of Race, 1920–1944.* Chapel Hill: University of North Carolina Press, 1985.

Lassiter, Matthew D. *The Silent Majority: Suburban Politics in the Sunbelt South.* Princeton: Princeton University Press, 2006.

Lassiter, Matthew D., and Andrew B. Lewis, eds. *The Moderates' Dilemma: Massive Resistance to School Desegregation in Virginia.* Charlottesville: University Press of Virginia, 1998.

Lewis, George. "Virginia's Northern Strategy: Southern Segregationists and the Route to National Conservatism." *Journal of Southern History* 72, no. 1 (2006): 111–46.

MacLean, Nancy. *Freedom Is Not Enough: The Opening of the American Workplace.* Cambridge: Harvard University Press, 2006.

Mays, David J. *Race, Reason, and Massive Resistance: The Diary of David J. Mays, 1954–1959.* Edited by James R. Sweeney. Athens: University of Georgia Press, 2008.

Muse, Benjamin. *Virginia's Massive Resistance.* Bloomington: Indiana University Press, 1961.

Pratt, Robert A. *The Color of Their Skin: Education and Race in Richmond Virginia 1954–1989.* Charlottesville: University of Virginia Press, 1993.

———. "New Directions in Virginia's Civil Rights History." *Virginia Magazine of History and Biography* 104, no. 1 (1996): 149–56.

Randolph, Lewis A., and Gayle T. Tate. *Rights for a Season: The Politics of Race, Class, and Gender in Richmond, Virginia.* Knoxville: University of Tennessee Press, 2003.

Reynolds, P. Preston. "Professional and Hospital Discrimination and the U.S. Court of Appeals Fourth Circuit 1956–1967." *American Journal of Public Health* 94, no. 5 (May 2004): 710–20.

Rozell, Mark J., and Clyde Wilcox. *Second Coming: The New Christian Right in Virginia Politics.* Baltimore: Johns Hopkins University Press, 1996.

Smith, J. Douglas. *Managing White Supremacy: Race, Politics, and Citizenship in Jim Crow Virginia.* Chapel Hill: University of North Carolina Press, 2002.

Smith, Larissa M. "A Civil Rights Vanguard: Black Attorneys and the NAACP in Virginia." In *From the Grassroots to the Supreme Court: Brown v. Board of Education and American Democracy,* edited by Peter F. Lau, 129–53. Durham, N.C.: Duke University Press, 2004.

Wallenstein, Peter. *Blue Laws and Black Codes: Conflict, Courts, and Change in Twentieth Century Virginia.* Charlottesville: University of Virginia Press, 2004.

Ward, Jason. "'A Richmond Institution': Earnest Sevier Cox, Racial Propaganda, and

White Resistance to the Civil Rights Movement." *Virginia Magazine of History and Biography*, 116, no. 3 (2008): 262–93.

Wilkinson, J. Harvie. *Harry Byrd and the Changing Face of Virginia Politics, 1945–1966.* Charlottesville: University Press of Virginia, 1968.

INFLUENTIAL RACIST TRACTS OF THE 1950S AND 1960S

Hemphill, William Edwin, Marvin Wilson Schlegel, and Sadie Ethel Engelberg. *Cavalier Commonwealth: History and Government of Virginia.* New York: McGraw-Hill Book Co., 1957.

Kilpatrick, James Jackson. *The Southern Case for School Segregation.* New York: Crowell-Collier Press, 1962.

———. *The Sovereign States: Notes of a Citizen of Virginia.* Chicago: H. Regnery Co., 1957.

Prince Edward School Foundation and Committee in Support of Prince Edward. *The Issue Presented in Prince Edward County, Virginia.* Farmville, VA: Prince Edward School Foundation, 1962.

Putnam, Carleton. *Race and Reason: A Yankee View.* Washington, DC: Public Affairs Press, 1961.

PRINCE EDWARD COUNTY SCHOOL ISSUE

Bonastia, Christopher. *Southern Stalemate: Five Years without Public Education in Prince Edward County, Virginia.* Chicago: University of Chicago Press, 2011.

Foster, Vonita W., and Gerald A. Foster. *Silent Trumpets of Justice: Integration's Failure in Prince Edward County.* Hampton, VA: U.B. & U.S. Books, 1993.

Peeples, Edward H., Prince Edward County (Va.) Public Schools Collection. Virginia Commonwealth University Digital Collections. http://go.vcu.edu/peeples.

Turner, Kara Miles. "Both Victors and Victims: Prince Edward County, Virginia, the NAACP, and *Brown.*" *Virginia Law Review* 90, no. 6 (October 2004): 1667–91.

———. "Liberating Lifescripts: Prince Edward County, Virginia, and the Roots of *Brown v. Board of Education.*" In *From the Grassroots to the Supreme Court: Brown v. Board of Education and American Democracy,* edited by Peter F. Lau, 88–104. Durham: Duke University Press, 2004.

Kluger, Richard. *Simple Justice: The History of Brown v. Board of Education and Black America's Struggle for Equality.* New York: Knopf, 1976.

Robert Russa Moton Museum. http://motonmuseum.org.

Smith, Bob. *They Closed Their Schools: Prince Edward County, Virginia, 1951–1964.* Chapel Hill: University of North Carolina Press, 1965.

Spreng, Jennifer E. "Scenes from the Southside: A Desegregation Drama in Five Acts." *University of Arkansas at Little Rock Law Journal* 19 (1997): 327–412.

Stokes, John A., with Lois Wolfe. *Students on Strike: Jim Crow, Civil Rights, Brown, and Me.* Washington, DC: National Geographic, 2008.

Titus, Jill Ogline. *Brown's Battleground: Students, Segregationists, and the Struggle for Justice in Prince Edward County, Virginia.* Chapel Hill: University of North Carolina Press, 2011.

WILLIAM HENRY BRISBANE

Ash, Stephen V. *Firebrand of Liberty: The Story of Two Black Regiments that Changed the Course of the Civil War.* New York: W. W. Norton & Co, 2008.

Brisbane, William Henry. "Speech of the Rev. Wm. H. Brisbane, Lately a Slaveholder in South Carolina; Containing an Account of the Change in His Views on the Subject of Slavery." Hartford, CT: S. S. Cowles, 1840.

———, Papers. Wisconsin Historical Society, Madison.

McNulty, Blake. "William Henry Brisbane: South Carolina Slaveholder and Abolitionist." In *The Southern Enigma: Essays on Race, Class, and Culture,* edited by Walter J. Fraser Jr. and Winfred B. Moore Jr., 119–29. Westport, CT: Greenwood Press, 1983.

Rose, Willie Lee. *Rehearsal for Reconstruction: The Port Royal Experiment.* New York: Oxford University Press, 1964.

INDEX

abolitionist movement: Peeples's ancestor's involvement in, 184–92; Virginians in, xv

Abrams, Charles, 55

Ackell, Edmund, 172

activism: among little known Virginians, xxi; in post-civil rights era, 168–82; transforming properties of, xiv

African Americans: as assault victims, 22–23; as athletes, 27–28, 136–40; educational opportunities in Virginia for, 145–46; impact of Prince Edward school closings on, 86–103; in military, 63–67; prison incarceration of, 173–75; stereotypes of, 23–25, 51

Afro-American Studies Program, 149–50

Alcorn, Wallace, 185

Alexander, Saundra, 127, 134

Allen, George, 150–51, 182

Allen, Harriet, 91

Allendale, SC, 8–9, 11

All Souls Presbyterian Church, 91

Amelia County, VA: school desegregation fight in, 117–18; volunteer efforts in, 107–9

American Anti-Slavery Society, 188

American Civil Liberties Union (ACLU), 65–66

American Ethical Union, 53–54

American Friends Service Committee (AFSC), xix–xx, 45, 88–89, 100, 102, 117, 152–59

American Red Cross, 154–55, 158

anti-communism, xix, 52, 55, 58, 73, 85, 115, 124, 125, 194

anti-Semitism, Peeples's experiences with, 16, 51–52

Appalachia: community activism in, xx–xxi; Encampment for Citizenship in, 121–22

Appalachian Regional Commission, 123

Arena, WI, 185, 189, 191

Bagwell, Bill, 117–18

Bailey, Gamaliel, 188

Bainbridge Junior High School, 19–20

Baker, Helen, 88–89, 91

Banks, Lester, 118

baptism, Peeples's memory of, 17–18

Barbourville, KY, 124–35

baseball: clubs for teenage boys, organization of, 88–90; Peeples's love of, 26–28

basketball: Peeples's coaching experiences in, 46–47, 63; Peeples's love of, 26–27, 33–35, 40, 42–43, 52; racism in, 40–41, 136–40

Berea College, 121

Berry, Wendell, 122

Best, Walter, 6

Birney, James G., 188

Black, Algernon, 54–56, 121, 128

Black Muslims, 173

black stereotypes, prevalence of, 23–25

Bless, Wally, 176

211